ELITE EDUCATION

Elite Education: International perspectives is the first book to systematically examine elite education in different parts of the world. Authors provide a historical analysis of the emergence of national elite education systems and consider how recent policy and economic developments are changing the configuration of elite trajectories and the social groups benefiting from these.

Through country-level case studies, this book offers readers an in-depth account of elite education systems in the Anglophone world, in Europe and in the emerging financial centres of Africa, Asia and Latin America. A series of commentaries highlights commonalities and differences between elite education systems, and offers insights into broader theoretical issues, with which educationalists, researchers and policymakers are engaging.

With authors including Stephen J. Ball, Donald Broady, Rubén Gaztambide-Fernández, Heinz-Hermann Krüger, Maria Alice Nogueira, Julia Resnik and Agnès van Zanten, the book offers a benchmark perspective on issues frequently glossed over in comparative education, including the processes by which powerful groups retain privilege and 'elite' status in rapidly changing societies.

Elite Education: International perspectives will appeal to policymakers and academics in the fields of education and sociology. Simultaneously, it will be of special relevance to postgraduates enrolled on courses in the sociology of education, education policy and education and international development.

Claire Maxwell is a reader in sociology of education at UCL Institute of Education, London, UK.

Peter Aggleton is Scientia Professor in Education and Health in the Centre for Social Research in Health at UNSW Australia. He is a visiting professorial fellow in education at UCL Institute of Education in London, and a visiting professor in global health in the School of Global Studies at Sussex University, UK.

ELITE EDUCATION

International perspectives

Edited by Claire Maxwell and Peter Aggleton

Routledge
Taylor & Francis Group
LONDON AND NEW YORK

First published 2016
by Routledge
2 Park Square, Milton Park, Abingdon, Oxon OX14 4RN

and by Routledge
711 Third Avenue, New York, NY 10017

Routledge is an imprint of the Taylor & Francis Group, an informa business

© 2016 Claire Maxwell and Peter Aggleton

The right of Claire Maxwell and Peter Aggleton to be identified as the authors of the editorial material, and of the authors for their individual chapters, has been asserted in accordance with sections 77 and 78 of the Copyright, Designs and Patents Act 1988.

All rights reserved. No part of this book may be reprinted or reproduced or utilised in any form or by any electronic, mechanical, or other means, now known or hereafter invented, including photocopying and recording, or in any information storage or retrieval system, without permission in writing from the publishers.

Trademark notice: Product or corporate names may be trademarks or registered trademarks, and are used only for identification and explanation without intent to infringe.

British Library Cataloguing in Publication Data
A catalogue record for this book is available from the British Library

Library of Congress Cataloging in Publication Data
A catalog record for this book has been requested

ISBN: 978-1-138-79959-2 (hbk)
ISBN: 978-1-138-79961-5 (pbk)
ISBN: 978-1-315-75598-4 (ebk)

Typeset in Bembo
by Book Now Ltd, London

Printed and bound in the United States of America by Publishers Graphics, LLC on sustainably sourced paper.

CONTENTS

Contributors ix
Acknowledgements xvii

    Introduction: elite education – international perspectives   1
    Claire Maxwell and Peter Aggleton

PART I
Developments in the Anglophone world:
England, Scotland, Australia and North America   **13**

1 The historical construction of an elite
   education in England   15
   Claire Maxwell and Peter Aggleton

2 'Independent' in Scotland: elite by education?   29
   Joan Forbes and Gaby Weiner

3 Elite education in the Australian context   42
   Sue Saltmarsh

4 'Private schools in the public system': school choice and
   the production of elite status in the USA and Canada   55
   Rubén Gaztambide-Fernández and Julie Garlen Maudlin

5 The future of elite research in education: commentary   69
   Stephen J. Ball

PART II
European perspectives: similarities and differences in Scandinavia, France and Germany — 77

6 A sound foundation? Financial elite families and egalitarian schooling in Norway — 79
Helene Aarseth

7 Elite education in Sweden: a contradiction in terms? — 92
Mikael Börjesson, Donald Broady, Tobias Dalberg and Ida Lidegran

8 Elite education in Germany? Trends, developments and challenges — 104
Ulrike Deppe and Heinz-Hermann Krüger

9 Promoting equality *and* reproducing privilege in elite educational tracks in France — 114
Agnès van Zanten

10 Elite education and class reproduction: commentary — 126
Magne Flemmen

PART III
Emerging financial powers in Latin America, Asia and Africa — 133

11 'Eliteness' in Chinese schooling: towards an ethnographic approach — 135
Peidong Yang

12 'Eliteness' and elite schooling in contemporary Nigeria — 148
Pere Ayling

13 The education of Brazilian elites in the twenty-first century: new opportunities or new forms of distinction? — 162
Maria Alice Nogueira and Maria Teresa G. Alves

14 Servicing elite interests: elite education in post-neoliberal Argentina — 173
Howard Prosser

15	Elite education systems in the emerging financial powers: commentary *Julia Resnik*	186
	Some final reflections *Claire Maxwell and Peter Aggleton*	192
Index		*197*

CONTRIBUTORS

Helene Aarseth is a researcher at Norwegian Social Research Oslo and Akershus University College of Applied Sciences. Her main research interests are family cultures, class and gender. Helene's work focuses on feminist social theory and psycho-social concepts. She is the author of two books and several articles on changing masculinities, everyday life of the late modern family and parenting and social class. Recent publications in English include 'Enriching intimacy: The role of the emotional in the "resourcing" of middle-class children' (with Kari Stefansen) in the *British Journal of Sociology of Education*, 2011, 'Conflicts in the habitus: The intergenerational emotional work of becoming modern', forthcoming in *The Sociological Review*, and 'Eros in the field? Bourdieu's double account of socialized desire', also forthcoming in *The Sociological Review*.

Peter Aggleton is Scientia Professor in Education and Health in the Centre for Social Research in Health at UNSW Australia and an associate professor in the Australian Research Centre in Sex, Health and Society at La Trobe University, Australia. He is a visiting professorial fellow in education at University College London (UCL) Institute of Education in London, and a visiting professor in global health in the School of Global Studies at Sussex University, UK. He has worked for over 30 years in the sociology of education, among other specialities, and was co-director (with Claire Maxwell) of the Economic and Social Research Council (ESRC) funded *Top Girls* project, which brought together a number of the contributors to this volume.

Maria Teresa G. Alves is Professor of Educational Assessment and Research Methodology and leader of the School Inequalities research group at the Federal University of Minas Gerais (UFMG), Brazil. She is Associate Editor of *Educação em Revista*, a Brazilian journal in the field of education. Her research areas included the sociology of education, measures of educational outcomes and school effects. Maria Teresa leads research projects supported by national (CNPq, Fapemig) and international (UNESCO) funding agencies and has published many articles in peer-reviewed journals including *Cadernos de Pesquisa*, *Educação e Pesquisa*, *Ensaio: Avaliação e Políticas Públicas em Educação* and *Estudos em Avaliação Educacional*. She is currently a board member of the Brazilian Association of Educational Assessment.

Pere Ayling is a lecturer and a researcher at the University Campus Suffolk (UCS), Ipswich, UK. She is a trained sociologist with seven years of teaching experience in higher education. Her areas of specialisation include consumption, race, elite education and class (re)production strategies. She is particularly interested in how social class, gender and race intersect to (re)produce 'privilege' and 'inequality' in education and society in general. Her recent work examines the consumption of British private schooling by elite Nigerian parents, revealing the strategies through which parents reproduce their social positioning while acquiring valuable identities for their children at the same time. Her other publications include 'Diversity, equality and rights in early years' (forthcoming in *The early years practitioner's handbook*, Routledge) and 'Embodying "Britishness": The (re)making of the contemporary Nigerian elite child' (forthcoming in *Curriculum Inquiry*).

Stephen J. Ball is the Karl Mannheim Professor of Sociology of Education at the UCL Institute of Education in London. He is a Fellow of the British Academy and managing editor of the *Journal of Education Policy*. Stephen's main areas of interest are in education policy analysis and the relationships between education, education policy and social class. He engages with tools and concepts from 'policy sociology' in his work, particularly the methods of Michel Foucault and Pierre Bourdieu. Recent books include *How schools do policy* (2012), *Global education inc.* (2012), *Networks, new governance and education* (with Carolina Junemann) (2012) and *Foucault, power and education* (Routledge, 2013). He is currently leading two research projects (funded by the British Academy and Leverhulme Foundation), which explore the spread and impact of a global education policy network, specifically in Africa and India. He is also working on an international study of philanthropy and education policy with Antonio Olmedo (University of Roehampton, London).

Mikael Börjesson is Professor of Sociology of Education at Uppsala University, Sweden and co-director of the Sociology of Education and Culture (SEC) research unit. His areas of expertise include upper secondary school and higher education, transnational strategies and the internationalisation of higher education, elites and elite education. He is directing a comparative project on higher education across the Nordic countries and a study of the internationalisation of higher education in Sweden. He has recently published, together with Andreas Melldahl, 'Charting the social space: The case of Sweden in 1990' in Philippe Coulangeon and Julien Duval (Eds.) *The Routledge companion to Bourdieu's 'Distinction'* (2014), and will contribute a chapter on the marketisation of Swedish higher education ('Oraison funèbre du modèle suédois: Trois dimensions de la marchandisation de l'enseignement supérieur') to Christophe Charle and Charles Soulié's 2015 book *L'Université à l'heure de la marchandisation des savoirs*.

Donald Broady took up a professorship at Uppsala University, Sweden in 1997 where he is now an emeritus professor at the Department of Sociology and co-director of the Sociology of Education and Culture (SEC) research unit. His areas of expertise include cultural fields, elites and education, history of science, history of education, students' trajectories, transnational educational strategies and markup languages. His non-Swedish language publications include *Les élites: formation, reconversion, internationalisation* (Ed. with Monique de Saint Martin and Mikael Palme, 1995), *Formation des élites et culture transnational* (Ed. with Natalia Chmatko and Monique de Saint Martin, 1997) and, with Mikael Börjesson and Dag Blanck, 'Étudiants et chercheurs suédois aux États-Unis et en France: Stratégies transnationales collectives et individuelles' in *Les mondes universitaires face au marché* (Eds. Michèle Leclerc-Olive, Grazia Scarfò Ghellab and Anne-Catherine Wagner, 2011).

Tobias Dalberg is a doctoral student in the sociology of education at Uppsala University, Sweden. He has assisted in research projects focusing on upper secondary schooling and higher education in Sweden, globalisation and internationalisation processes and the political views of upper secondary school pupils. Tobias has also researched the formation of sustainable development as a field of study in higher education. He is currently finalising a dissertation on differentiation processes within the fields of social sciences and humanities in higher education – documenting increases in the number of disciplines observed, the expansion of these fields and the changing nature of students and university lecturers. Together with Ylva Bergström, he has recently published 'Education, social class and politics: The political space of Swedish youth in Uppsala' in Michael Grenfell and Frédéric Lebaron (Eds.) *Bourdieu and data analysis: Methodological principles and practice* (2014).

Ulrike Deppe is a postdoctoral research fellow at the Centre for School and Educational Research at the Martin Luther University Halle-Wittenberg, Germany. She has worked with the German Research Foundation funded Mechanisms of Elite Formation in the German Education System Research Unit since 2011. Her research mainly utilises qualitative methods as part of larger data triangulation processes. Ulrike's main areas of interest include the study of childhood and youth, particularly schooling experiences and the creation of relations of social inequality. Most recently, her research has focused on processes of elite formation within the Germany education system and the impact this has on student identities and processes of hierarchicalisation within and between educational institutions.

Magne Flemmen is a post-doctoral research fellow in the Department of Sociology and Human Geography at the University of Oslo, Norway. His research interests are primarily focused on social class stratification, and especially combining insights from the work of Pierre Bourdieu with the more traditional concerns of class analysis. He is currently working on a Research Council of Norway funded project on social closure in the service class, as well as various studies of class, social space, culture and politics. Recent publications include 'The structure of the upper class: A social space approach' in *Sociology*, 2012; 'Putting Bourdieu to work for class analysis: Reflections on some recent contributions' in the *British Journal of Sociology*, 2013; and 'The politics of the service class: The homology of positions and position-takings' in *European Societies*, 2014.

Joan Forbes is a reader in education at the University of Aberdeen, Scotland. Her research interests include elite schooling, poverty and social justice. A recent book (with Cate Watson) is *The Transformation of Children's Services: Examining and Debating the Complexities of Inter/Professional Working* (2012). She currently co-leads a Scottish Universities Insight Institute funded Knowledge Exchange Programme on *Children and Young People's Experiences and Views of Poverty and Inequalities*. With Claire Maxwell and Agnès van Zanten she organized a double symposium on *Elite and Private Education – European Perspectives* at The European Educational Research Association conference, University of Oporto, Portugal, 2014. Her recent publications include 'Gender power in elite schools: methodological insights from researcher reflexive accounts' in *Research Papers in Education*, 2014 (with Gaby Weiner); and 'Assured optimism in a Scottish girls' school: habitus and the (re)production of global privilege' in *British Journal of Sociology of Education*, 2015 (with Bob Lingard).

Rubén Gaztambide-Fernández is an associate professor at the Ontario Institute for Studies in Education of the University of Toronto, Canada, where he teaches courses on curriculum theory, cultural studies and the arts in education. His book, *The best of the best: Becoming elite at an American boarding school* (2009), is based on two years' ethnographic research at an elite boarding school in the USA. He is co-editor with Adam Howard of *Educating elites: Class privilege and educational advantage* (2010). His current research focuses on the experiences of young artists attending urban arts high schools in Canada and the USA. He is the principal investigator of *Proyecto Latin@*, a participatory action research project with Latin@ youth in Toronto, where his work focuses on the relationship between creativity, decolonisation and solidarity. He is particularly interested in the pedagogical and creative possibilities that arise from the social and cultural dynamics characteristic of urban centres.

Heinz-Hermann Krüger is Professor of General Education Science at the Institute of Pedagogy in Martin Luther University Halle-Wittenberg (MLU), Germany. He was Chair of the Review Board for the Research Council for Education Science at the German Research Foundation between 2004 and 2012. He has been Chair of the Graduate School in 'Education and Social Inequality' (since 2008) and of the German Research Foundation funded research unit 'Mechanisms of Elite Formation in the German Education System' (since 2011) at MLU. His fields of expertise include theories and methods in education science, research on childhood and youth, processes of schooling and higher education trajectories.

Ida Lidegran is a senior lecturer in the sociology of education at Uppsala University, Sweden, and member of the Sociology of Education and Culture (SEC) research unit. Her research covers areas such as elite formation, elite education and educational strategies of elite families, gender differences in education and the development of new transdisciplinary areas, such as sustainable development and educational sciences. She is currently directing a research project entitled 'The emergence and consolidation of a multidisciplinary subject: sustainable development as a course of study in Swedish higher education. A study in the sociology of education', funded by the Swedish Research Council. She has recently edited a special issue of the Scandinavian journal *Praktiske Grunde* on sustainable development in Swedish higher education.

Julie Garlen Maudlin is an associate professor of education in the Department of Teaching and Learning at Georgia Southern University, USA, where she teaches courses in early childhood education, curriculum and instruction and curriculum studies. A former classroom teacher and instructional coach in rural south Georgia, she is the founder and co-chair of the Curriculum Studies Summer Collaborative, an annual academic conference sponsored by Georgia Southern University's College of Education. She has written extensively on popular culture, critical pedagogy and curriculum theory, and is currently co-editing two volumes on Disney and education. Her most recent article, 'The abandonment of hope: Curriculum theory and white moral responsibility', appeared in the *Journal of Curriculum and Pedagogy*.

Claire Maxwell is a reader in the sociology of education at UCL Institute of Education, London. Together with Peter Aggleton she has led two projects exploring the experiences of young women being privately educated in England – focusing on the possibilities for agentic practice, theorising the ways in which privilege, affect and agency are mutually constituted, and considering further what is elite about the private education sector in England today. Claire has collaborated with others to bring together colleagues working in the field of elite education at a number of different conferences since 2013, including the 'Knowledge, Status and Power. Elite Education, Training and Expertise' event held at Sciences Po, Paris in October 2014. She co-edited *Privilege, agency and affect* (with Peter Aggleton, 2013, Palgrave Macmillan), has a chapter in the *2015 World Yearbook of Education*, 'Elites, privilege and excellence', and a paper (with Agnès van Zanten) in the *British Journal of Sociology of Education* 2015 special issue on elite education.

Maria Alice Nogueira is professor of sociology of education and the coordinator of Social Observatory Family–School (OSFE) at the Federal University of Minas Gerais (UFMG), Brazil. Her research has focused on family–school relationships, elite schooling and social advantage in education. She has published many articles in Brazil and abroad in peer-reviewed journals, such as the *British Journal of Sociology of Education*, *International Studies of Sociology of Education*, *Éducation et Sociétes*, *Revue Internationale d'Éducation* and *Cahiers de la Recherche sur l'Éducation et les Savoirs*. She has co-edited two books: *Família & Escola – trajetórias de escolarização em camadas médias e populares* (2000) and *A escolarização das elites – um panorama internacional da pesquisa* (2002).

Howard Prosser researches and teaches in the Faculty of Education at Monash University, Australia. He has taught history in Australian secondary schools and universities. His research interests include pedagogy, social theory, the history of ideas and ethnography. He has recently completed a study of the shifting political culture at an elite school in Argentina. As co-editor of *In the realm of the senses: Social aesthetics and the sensory dynamics of privilege* (2015), he has helped to introduce the concept of social aesthetics to educational research on elite schooling.

Julia Resnik is a senior lecturer in sociology of education at the School of Education, Hebrew University of Jerusalem. Her main research areas are the globalisation of education policy, comparative education, multiculturalism, migrant children, international education and the third sector. She edited a special issue of *International Studies of Sociology of Education* on the sociology of international education (2012) and a special issue of the journal *Globalisation, Societies and Education* on 'The power of numbers and networks: Understanding the mechanisms of the diffusion of educational models'. Julia has authored many articles in peer-reviewed journals, such as *Comparative Education Review*, *Journal of Education Policy*, *British Journal of Sociology of Education* and *British Journal of Educational Studies*, and has published many articles in francophone journals (*Education Compare*, *Recherches en Education* and *Carrefours de L'Education*). She is currently the president of the Israel Comparative Education Society.

Sue Saltmarsh is an associate professor of educational studies at the Australian Catholic University in Sydney, Australia. She has undertaken a range of ethnographic, social semiotic and discourse analytic studies in the fields of early childhood, primary, secondary and tertiary educational settings, focusing primarily on the connections between economic discourse, cultural practices and subjectivities. Her research on elite education brings together cultural and poststructural theories of consumption, subjectivity and everyday life, to consider how institutional cultures can be implicated in the production of unequal relations of power and violence. Sue serves on a number of national and international research committees and is founding editor of the journal *Global Studies of Childhood*. Her recent publications include: 'Michel de Certeau, everyday life and education policy', in Kal Gulson, Matthew Clarke and Eva Bendix Petersen (Eds.) *Education policy and contemporary theory: Implications for research* (2015) and Sue Saltmarsh, Kerry Robinson and Cristyn Davies (Eds.) *Rethinking school violence: Theory, gender, context* (2012).

Agnès van Zanten is a senior research professor in the Observatoire sociologique du changement at Sciences Po, Paris. Her main research areas are class, elites and education, school segregation and school choice, transition to higher education, widening participation and education policies. She has published widely on these topics including her books *Choisir son école* (2009), *L'école de la périphérie* (2nd edition, 2012) and her edited volume (with Stephen Ball and Brigitte Darchy-Koechlin) *Elites, privilege and excellence: The national and global redefinition of educational advantage* (2015). She is currently directing two research projects on 'Transition to higher education: the role of institutions, markets and networks' and 'Accountability and new modes of governance of educational systems'. She is co-director of the group on educational policies at the Laboratoire interdisciplinaire d'evaluation des politiques publiques at Sciences Po, and directs the *Education et société* series of books published by Presses Universitaires de France.

Gaby Weiner has worked at various universities in the UK and Sweden and is a visiting professor in the School of Education and Social Work at Sussex University and a visiting professorial research fellow at Manchester Metropolitan University. She has written and edited many publications on gender and social justice in education. Her most recent book (with Lucy Townsend) is entitled *Deconstructing and reconstructing lives: Auto/biography in educational settings* (2011). She has taken part in several EU-funded projects including the Eurokid Antiracist website project (with Chris Gaine) and, more recently, projects mapping gender differences in education across Europe, identifying 'good practice' on gender equality. Her chapter in this collection draws on her work (with Joan Forbes and others) on independent schools in Scotland, their utilisation of social and other capitals and their gendered regimes and practices.

Peidong Yang is a postdoctoral fellow in the Division of Sociology, School of Humanities and Social Sciences (HSS), Nanyang Technological University, Singapore. He received his doctorate from the University of Oxford in 2014 for a dissertation on mainland Chinese student-migrants and Singapore's 'foreign talent' policy/programmes. Previously, Peidong undertook research in sociology at Cardiff University, under a Nippon Foundation Fellowship, studying seafarers' trade unionism in India. His current scholarly interests include migration (especially student and talent migration), education and media/internet culture in China. Parts of Peidong's doctoral work have appeared as journal articles in *SOJOURN*, *Asian Journal of Social Science* and *Frontiers of Education in China*. He has also published articles on Indian maritime trade unionism and Chinese media/internet culture in journals such as *Global Labor Journal* and *Media, Culture and Society*.

ACKNOWLEDGEMENTS

This book derives in part from an international symposium on *Private and elite education – Perspectives of young people and school* – held at the Institute of Education, University of London on 7–8 November 2012. The symposium was held as part of the dissemination and impact enhancement process associated with the *Top Girls* research project (RES-062-23-2667) funded by the UK Economic and Social Research Council (ESRC).

We would like to thank the ESRC for its support for the event, which enabled us to bring together presenters to discuss the outcomes of their research, identify areas of commonality and highlight issues requiring further examination.

We also thank colleagues within what is now the UCL Institute of Education for their support for the event – especially Chris Husbands (Director, UCL Institute of Education), Gary McCulloch (Head of the Department of Humanities and Social Sciences, UCL Institute of Education) and Anushka Leslie, who played a key role in ensuring that the symposium ran smoothly.

INTRODUCTION

Elite education – international perspectives

Claire Maxwell and Peter Aggleton

This book is concerned with 'elite education'. Specifically, it seeks to document the ways in which two key mechanisms pervasive in education today play out across various national contexts. First, many schooling systems claim to be acting as a vehicle for social mobility by 'rewarding' academic ability and ambition with the opportunity to pursue high status, sometimes accelerated, trajectories into higher education and beyond (Brown 2013). However, a second significant pressure shaping education configurations is the way in which well-resourced groups act to ensure that their demands and choices are met (van Zanten and Maxwell 2015). In many cases, a commitment to promoting social mobility through education is linked to the principle of democratisation – increasing equality of opportunity for all to receive a rigorous and relevant schooling experience (Green 2013). In contrast, elite group and elite status recruitment cuts across the openness of this process, rendering democratic outcomes less likely. It is the various ways in which this dialectic is articulated across different national contexts – how desires for democratisation work within and alongside the demands and expectations of elite groups – that shape the purpose and structure of a national elite education system. It is this problematic that we examine further through the collection of papers offered here.

Education is largely acknowledged to be a structuring mechanism through which powerful groups seek to secure and advance their social and economic position (Ball 2013, Ball and Nikita 2014). Schooling choices therefore reflect evaluations made by social groups around the particular sets of academic credentials that are believed to carry weight in different employment sectors and across various social spaces. Thus, in many local, national and even international contexts, particular types of institutions are understood as forming part of a network of 'institutional wormholes' (Nespor 2014, p. 27) that more or less guarantee progression into future dominant economic and social positions. Education is, moreover, for many members of the better-off social groups, a critical strategy of distinction

(Bourdieu 1986) – either securing and extending the resources that families already have access to, or the means through which to accumulate particular kinds of capital seen as critical to future progression. The chapters in this book examine, across different national contexts, the ways in which dominant social groups (the elites) have managed by various means to shape educational provision to meet their needs, using it as a mechanism through which to engage in boundary-maintenance work (Lamont and Molnar 2002) between their particular group and Others. Critically, however, the papers also highlight the ways in which elite education institutions themselves (and often the state) explicitly or inadvertently support the strategies of distinction encouraged by elite groups.

Unsurprisingly, the marketisation that has so effectively pervaded most schooling systems – and which includes neoliberal efforts to increase privatisation within education – has had a significant effect on national education configurations. Introducing market principles into education, with the goal of increasing choice, effectiveness and efficiency (Ball 2013), has led to processes of increasing differentiation between educational institutions. As a result, different schools aim to attract particular constituencies, shaping their offer accordingly (as the chapters on England, Scotland, Australia, Brazil and Nigeria argue). The case of Sweden highlights how particular institutions have begun to specialise in specific curricula areas in their attempts to be seen as elite and distinctive, while in Scotland and Brazil (and in some cases England), international qualifications and the acquisition of global languages is fore-fronted to appeal to particular audiences. The situation in China is interesting, where, by stealth almost, privatisation has crept into a state-funded system committed to meritocracy and a functionalist approach to training the future leaders of China. Here, only economically elite groups can afford to send their children on the relatively recent Sino-American and Sino-Canadian programmes geared towards preparing students for higher education in North America. Elite education therefore does not follow a straightforward private/public divide. In Brazil, Argentina, Australia, Canada and America, for instance, there are high-status, academically selective publically funded and run schools attracting particular social groups: usually the so-called cultural elite or, in the case of parts of Australia, a large East Asian cohort (see also Khan's 2015 description of the elite education market in New York City). In the case of Scotland and in Nigeria, for some elite fractions being educated within a national system is not the strategy of choice – an 'English' elite education is specifically sought after instead (see also Fahey 2014).

Some systems of elite education may have started out with the goal of providing opportunities for those most academically able to take up future leadership positions. This was to a large extent the case in England between the fourteenth and eighteenth centuries, and the principle behind the grammar school system in place between the 1940s and 1970s. Identifying and providing specialist training for future elites has always been the principle supporting the French education system and is still a strongly held belief today, even if evidence suggests that it is a system which largely caters for those groups which are most highly resourced economically and culturally (van Zanten 2015, van Zanten and Maxwell 2015). A commitment to meritocracy, whereby those who are most academically able are offered opportunities to succeed educationally and pursue elite tracks within the system, is also a strong feature of the Chinese, Argentine and Brazilian examples provided here, as well as being a feature of publically funded specialist programmes and/or schools in Sweden, Canada and the USA. However, attempts by government policy to increase choice and introduce market principles, as well as pressures from dominant social groups to access exclusive, excellent and globally oriented education for their children, have had the effect of diversifying the schooling infrastructure, whereby it is more often than not the elites who benefit most, as the Brazilian chapter powerfully demonstrates.

But who are the elites and what is an elite education? These are still questions academics struggle to resolve. While we and many others favour a Bourdieusian-informed approach to the question of how best to define elites (Savage and Williams 2008, Khan 2012, Maxwell 2015), our understanding of who these groups are has a direct impact on how we can best analyse what makes an educational institution, the type of niche it occupies and/or the specific trajectory followed by an 'elite'. We therefore asked all the authors in the book to engage with this particular question in their chapters. Those who have already worked on these matters in the field of elite education take an approach which examines movement into dominant positions over the life course (see the chapter on Sweden in this collection, but also Wakeling and Savage 2015), while others focus on the discursive and affective structures that shape the formation of elite identities and sensibilities, and which usually have the effect of legitimising one's advantageous social and economic position (Gaztambide-Fernández et al. 2013, Howard 2013, Maxwell and Aggleton 2014, Khan 2015). The chapters variously trace the ways in which elite status is signified within an education system, with some focusing in more depth on the kinds of practices and affective structures that powerfully reproduce, but also extend and affect, processes of distinction between social and economic fractions within and across society.

Although elite education is now a transnational business – with students, teachers and education packages in movement globally (Brooks and Waters 2011, Resnik 2012 and this volume, McCarthy and Kenway 2014, Ball this volume) – we initially sought to source chapters that focused on the national context, so that we could provide an in-depth review of the formation of elite education systems (specifically secondary schooling) and their consequences in different countries. The book is therefore comprised of 12 substantive chapters examining 13 different national contexts. The contributions outline how elite education systems have been established in different countries and how these have changed in the first decade and a half of the twenty-first century. We approached authors writing about elite education in different parts of the world, seeking to focus on the following key regions: the Anglophone world, Europe and emerging economic powers in Latin America, Asia and Africa. Together, this approach enables us to consider similarities and differences within and across regions. Such a focus on the local, the national and the regional means the book is able to offer some insight into how best to conceptualise elite education as a more global, rather than nationally bounded phenomenon.

A summary of the book

The first part of the book focuses on the Anglophone world and, in particular, on countries with a relatively long tradition of a specific form of elite education, usually within the private sector. While important contributions already exist on elite education in England, Australia and the USA , far less is known about the Scottish and Canadian contexts. Furthermore, the chapters from England, Australia and North America offer important new insights into this topic.

The chapter on England takes a historical approach, examining how the construction of an elite education has changed over time. It examines the emergence of the 'public school' movement in England in the fourteenth century, which was aimed at educating 'poor (male) scholars' for a future in the Church or legal profession, but demonstrates how, over time, those benefitting from such an education in the so-called 'Great Schools' came from a significantly narrower demographic group. The late nineteenth and early twentieth centuries witnessed the establishment of an overtly classed system of education. Despite calls for democratisation in the latter half of the twentieth century, which led to a period of comprehensivisation, the position of the private, elite schools has remained largely unchallenged. Maxwell and Aggleton argue that the historical construction of an elite education, as an academic but well-rounded education focused on the development of the 'whole person', continues, to this day, to be associated with the private sector. Illustrations of how schools differentially take up the construction of an elite education, while seeking to develop a particular niche for themselves in a local, regional and national marketplace are provided. The chapter offers a unique insight into the situation in England in that it integrates an analysis of the history of girls' elite education into the broader narrative of boys' education – examining similarities and differences between them, both historically and currently.

As the authors of the next chapter argue, despite assumptions that Scotland is simply an extension of the English case, the history and present-day configuration of the elite education in Scotland is unique. That said, important differences exist between publicly funded schools and their fee-paying elite counterparts in terms of the qualifications offered, the overall level of attainment secured and the extra-curricular provision that is expected. Unlike in England, where many elite schools are located rurally, the majority of Scottish elite institutions are based in urban areas. Forbes and Weiner offer a fascinating account of the development of the fee-paying sector in Edinburgh, which boasts a very specific history linked to the establishment of a number of so-called hospital schools from the mid-seventeenth century onwards. The chapter also offers insights into findings from an important recent programme of research, which contributed much to theorisation of the ways in which capitals are activated and accumulated in elite schooling in Scotland. Finally, the authors highlight an important tension between public support for a schooling system that pursues academic excellence and promotes the need to specifically educate the future elite, and a particularly Scottish disposition for understatement and concern for civic values, such as social solidarity, cooperation and bookishness.

Sue Saltmarsh's overview of elite education in Australia emphasises the local, regional and national specificities of different forms of provision. The chapter highlights how elite spaces exist within the three schooling sectors – public, private/independent/fee-paying and the sector run by the Catholic Church – complicating processes for capturing the meaning of an elite education in Australia today. Saltmarsh highlights how the highly selective admission processes for certain state schools or programmes mean they too compete for elite status in Australia's highly marketised environment. Critically, the author argues that despite Australia's cultural pluralism and a commitment to making the most of its location within Asia, part of the independent elite school sector continues to embrace Englishness and, by association, whiteness as a signifier of elite status. A further contribution that Saltmarsh's chapter makes is to offer an analysis of research conducted to date on elite education in Australia, identifying three different research orientations: one focused on social semiotics, discourse analysis and social history; another attending to the ways in which elite schools perpetuate and reproduce inequalities; and a third approach which qualitatively examines the production of elite subjectivities and how these inform wider social relations.

The fourth and final chapter on the Anglophone world focuses on Canada and the USA. Here Gaztambide-Fernández and Maudlin consider the 'publification of elite schooling' in the USA and Canada. Despite a policy context committed to increasing educational choice, the authors' careful analysis highlights how access to elite schools and programmes within the publically funded sector is still largely limited to those with the requisite economic and cultural capital. The chapter builds on some of Gaztambide-Fernández's earlier work on how specific practices within elite institutions shape the discursive and affective structures which make possible young people's embodiments of a sense of entitlement to their position(s) of privilege. The authors stress the need for researchers to look at the specificities of 'how elite status is produced and transferred through social and cultural mechanisms'. Gaztambide-Fernández and Maudlin highlight how, although elite programmes exist within the public sector in Canada and the USA, because the institutions in which they are based have access to fewer resources, this limits the opportunities for students to become 'excellent' at something, which means that possibilities for embedding a sense of entitlement among students remain more precarious.

Ball rounds off this part of the book by offering some thoughts, in part stimulated by his reading of the preceding chapters, concerning the key conceptual issues that the field of elite education must engage with. First, he considers what the term 'elite' means and the importance of contextuality in our understandings of who elite groups are. He emphasises the relativity of elite status and the importance role that geography plays in conceptualisations of elites, their clustering in the global cities of the world and their high degree of spatial mobility. This, Ball argues, has implications for their connectedness to localities and a sense of 'belonging' that sits outside national frames of reference. Ball considers how such an untethering affects the way elite groups connect (or do not) to the communities in which they (temporarily) reside, as well as their broader commitments to social justice efforts.

A significant set of conceptual challenges Ball highlights comprises (a) the necessity to distinguish conceptually between 'elites' and other relatively advantaged groups, (b) the changing nature of elites – and the arguably increasing importance of wealth, (c) the importance of research that attempts to identify commonalities and differences between different kinds of elite groups, and (d) the need for a more intersectional approach to the future study of elites.

The second part of the book focuses on four countries in continental Europe: one country, France, well-known for its elite education system; Germany – where the notion of elite education has only recently been actively taken up by policy, but is beginning to have a significant impact on processes of hierarchisation, especially within the higher education sector; and two Scandinavian neighbours, Norway and Sweden, where quite different policy approaches have affected the constitution of the schooling system, but not necessarily the efforts of elite families to ensure their children receive the 'best' education and are adequately prepared to take up their future positions as dominant social actors across various employment sectors.

Aarseth's chapter on Norway emphasises the strong public support for comprehensive schooling that exists in Norwegian society, where it is felt that all children should be educated together and schooling is conceived of as an equaliser. This may, in part, be because of Norway's history as a country earlier occupied by its Danish and Swedish neighbours, which means that Norway does not have a longstanding bourgeois class of its own. Drawing on findings from a recent research study, Aarseth shows how the 'increasingly marketised and radicalised competitiveness in the workplace' (Chapter 6, this volume) experienced by the financial elite in Norway, seeps into the ways in which this group engages with children's education and schooling. She demonstrates how members of this dominant social group reconfigure a societal commitment to egalitarianism as a resource which will better prepare their children for a competitive and challenging future where, through a 'sound foundation', they will be more able to rise to the top to become not only economically but also emotionally successful.

Börjesson, Broady, Dalberg and Lidegran look at the situation in Sweden, where the structure of the schooling system is quite different. Despite a strong commitment to democratisation and egalitarianism before the 1990s, Sweden has since established a schooling system that encourages competition and privatisation. Although most schooling remains publically funded, a commitment to school choice and an environment that encourages external providers to enter the education marketplace have meant an increase in the number of institutions in each phase of the education system and a growing emphasis on the development of specific 'tracks' through it. Börjesson and colleagues offer three different definitions of 'elite education' – meritocratic, social and functional. Based on their findings from examining the development of the Swedish education system over time, they conclude that as the education system expands, so the overlap between processes of meritocracy, efforts to ensure the intergenerational reproduction of social position by dominant social groups, and commitments to training future dominant agents across social fields begin to merge, with the end effect that dominant social groups largely maintain their positions. Börjesson and colleagues, using Geometric Data Analysis, map the space of secondary education in Sweden, allowing them to highlight which institutions and programmes are elite, identifying the educational strategies pursued by elite groups, and examining relations within and between different fields of education.

In the following chapter, Deppe and Krüger introduce us to key features of the German education system where, until recently, public discourse promoting egalitarianism has pervaded policy. Despite earlier differences within the system – in the late nineteenth century, for example, three types of schools existed, and only those students taking the *Arbitur* in the *Gymnasien* were able to go to university – the beginning of the twenty-first century has facilitated a more open commitment to elite education, through an emphasis on 'excellence'. Some schools now offer programmes for 'gifted' students, and private institutions within the school and higher education sectors have become more visible. The recent Federal Government *Excellence Initiative* is specifically focused on promoting particular universities and university departments as world-leaders. These changes have led to hierarchisation within the education system, and it is the effects of this and the ways social groups and institutions themselves have responded to these structural changes that the authors are researching. Deppe and Krüger outline an ambitious research programme which aims to examine four mechanisms driving the formation of elite education across the schooling and higher education sectors, and the impact this has on elite social group and educational institutional identities: family and individual strategies in relation to educational choice; recruitment and selection procedures of students and staff by institutions; processes of distinction engaged in by families and schools/universities; and the means by which collective identities are forged within different elite institutions.

Our final chapter in this section focuses on France. Here, van Zanten traces the historical origins of the French elite education system, which began with the establishment of 'special training schools', later known as *les grandes écoles*, with the aim of training men for high-level positions in the army. Over time, the number of specialist higher education elite institutions has grown, to encompass many fields of professional life – finance and management, political administration, engineering, the sciences and so forth. van Zanten argues that the competitive examination to enter these programmes – the *concours* – has been central to constructing these institutions as elite. She goes on to show that, despite many attempts in the eighteenth, nineteenth and twentieth centuries to ensure that the elite education system is more firmly based on meritocratic principles and is accessible to all, strong mechanisms of sponsorship between the most prestigious secondary schools and elite *classes préparatoires* continue to ensure that students from families with higher levels of economic or cultural capital continue to be over-represented in France's elite higher education system.

The book's focus on elite education in different European countries is brought to a conclusion through a thoughtful commentary by Flemmen. Reminding us of some of the earlier contributions of class theory, he explains how, in the present day, processes of social stratification are understood as mediated as much by schooling as by family and social class origin, an argument that draws on Bourdieu's work. Flemmen emphasises how education is used by elite families as a strategy for converting economic forms of capital into social and cultural assets, which are later traded back for economic capital in the labour market. The strategic use of schooling and higher education facilitates the resolution of a key tension for the dominant classes identified by Parkin (1979), whereby their legitimacy rests on the need to demonstrate the possibility of a degree of entry into elite status. Thus, the acquisition of high-status academic credentials signals that the maintenance of a dominant position is justified meritocratically. However, Flemmen also reminds us that reliance on the acquisition of educational credentials and status is more precarious than the inheritance of wealth and status more directly through the family, and an overreliance on the need to secure academic qualifications can invoke a range of anxiety-driven, affective responses. Given the significant effects that the development of elite tracks within education and the desires of elite groups have on the dynamics of the schooling system as a whole, Flemmen emphasises the importance of examining these circuits of relations in driving processes of inequality.

The third, and final section of the book looks at the development of elite education systems and processes in the emerging financial centres of Latin America, Asia and Africa. While many members of elite groups in these countries choose to send children abroad for their education (Brooks and Waters 2011, Fahey 2014), national education systems have also been reconfigured over time to ensure that future leaders are identified and appropriately educated locally. Furthermore, different social groups have found ways of ensuring that their children receive the kind of education they desire for them. As countries in the Global South improve their economic and political standing, elites in these countries seem more likely to look inwards to access the kinds of educational experiences needed to support them in efforts to maintain their dominant social position over time (Rizvi 2015).

Yang's ethnographic account of the emergence of a new kind of elite programme in an elite secondary school in a province of China provides an illuminating account of how a society, changing rapidly as a result of growing economic wealth, is simultaneously beginning to re-configure its education system to engage with exactly these concerns. He examines how different socio-political periods in China's history have shaped the stated purposes of education. The development of a system of 'ruthless meritocratic selection [based on] exclusivity and competitiveness' was an attempt to identify and train the future technocratic and scientific elites responsible for running the country. Yang offers a detailed account of the ways in which the hierarchisation of secondary education plays itself out in the day-to-day lives of students and teachers – focusing on institutional relationships and personal subjectivities. He suggests that the rote learning approach to pedagogy prevalent in the Chinese education system may actually reduce the effect of socio-economic status on academic attainment. He then explores how increasing affluence and the reorientation of certain groups within China towards the global, has led to the infiltration of conceptions of elite schooling from the West into the

Chinese system. He introduces us to the Sino-American programme, which exists as a separate track in some academically elite schools. Unlike the education provided by the rest of the school system – these programmes charge fees and expect their students to be able to afford the later cost of a North American college education. Students 'choosing' this track are no longer able to compete with their Chinese peers for the highly competitive recruitment process into the top Chinese universities, as they follow a different curriculum. In this way, the increased financial means available to a few families in China enables them to access these new international programmes, offered only by certain schools, and ensures that a small group of Chinese young people from economic elite groups are educated separately, for a very different kind of future.

The second chapter in this section examines experiences in Nigeria, focusing both on how particular Nigerian elite groups come to choose an English education for their children and how markers of Englishness and whiteness are utilised by private schools in Nigeria to constitute themselves as elite. Ayling examines how, historically, elite status for Nigerians was connected to having an English education (a consequence of the country's colonisation by the UK). In Nigeria today, processes of modernisation have meant that it is no longer just the privileged few who become educated. Thus, different forms of distinction through education have become necessary. Drawing on Bourdieu, Ayling argues that it is the place at which one is educated and how these institutions cultivate particular forms of embodiment that have become crucial markers of elite status. Through a qualitative investigation of Nigerian parents who have chosen to send their children to some of the most elite English boarding schools, Ayling explores how members of the traditional Nigerian cultural and economic elites work to distinguish themselves and their children from newer economic groups, through an emphasis on proper manners, style and spoken English. The chapter also describes aspects of the elite private education market within Nigeria, which largely constructs its claims to elite status through an emphasis on an English education, in schools either led by a white, English headteacher or which boast white teachers in their staff teams. Ayling's work emphasises the hold that the colonial legacy retains on the country, and calls for scholars drawing on Bourdieu to ensure they take account of how imperialism, even in the present day, continues to shape practices of social distinction.

The book then shifts its focus to Latin America. Nogueira and Alves explain that Brazil is a country with significant levels of income disparity and a relatively diverse group of elites. The authors distinguish between economic elites and cultural elite groups, and although the difference in income between these two groups is large, parents working as university professors or in other public sector institutions can still be counted as belonging to the highest earning 2 per cent of the Brazilian population. At the heart of the chapter lies an examination of whether recent Brazilian education policy, which has sought to increase access to higher education for less socially and economically advantaged groups, has had any effect on reducing the impact that family economic resources has on the academic outcomes of students. Nogueira and Alves illustrate two important trends in Brazil: first, the intensification of the use of private education and, second, a growing internationalisation of schooling trajectories – both of which undermine policies seeking to promote opportunities for children attending state schools to access higher education. An analysis of the National High School Examination data reveals that exclusive and academically selective public sector secondary schools are more likely to admit children from more well-resourced families, and that the most expensive private schools also boast the highest end-of-school exam results. This, in turn, affects who is admitted to the elite universities of Brazil.

Our final substantive chapter focuses on Argentina. Here, there exists a distinction between the use of private sector schooling by members of the economic elite classes, and public sector, academically selective schooling by cultural elite groups. Private provision of schooling has been growing since the 1960s, but the sector is comprised of a wide range of different institutions, with the majority being low-fee Catholic primary schools. Prosser's chapter focuses on the smaller group of independent schools, and in particular those originally set up to educate the children of the British colonialists. These schools tend to offer both local and international curricula, usually taught in two languages. Prosser explains that, since the late 1980s, growth in the provision of private university education has led to an entrenchment of divisions between students who are publicly and privately educated, as separate trajectories through the education system have emerged. The chapter traces the story of one elite 'English' school, which has shown itself capable of innovating in response to broader economic and societal changes. Prosser illustrates how the school is global in its ambitions and attracts a very elite clientele, while at the same time seeking to develop a programme of social-mindedness and an ethos of service to the community. The latter he sees as a direct response to the 'post neoliberal turn' in Argentine society and politics, and part of an effort to ensure its students do not become too 'out of touch' with their own communities.

The section on elite education in the emerging financial powers of Latin America, Asia and Africa is brought to a conclusion by a commentary offered by Resnik in which she considers how particular global economic and cultural processes – such as the emergence of new economic elite groups, the democratisation of education, the influence of public management and market logics and the introduction of standardised comparisons by the 'education industry' – have had an amplified impact in the nations of the Global South. Resnik argues that the private education sector provides a profit-making space for education corporations largely located in the north – offering both schooling for the poor but also international programmes of study taken up by elite schools. She emphasises that international programmes of education frequently adopt a particular pedagogical approach and curricula content which affects not only the learning experience of students on these programmes of study but also local and national curricula, by contributing to a progressive de-nationalisation of the host country's education system. Resnik goes further to suggest that the emphasis on 'international' experience within elite education in the Global South today has had the effect of embedding separatist traditions of education between the most well-resourced groups and their less advantaged peers in countries which previously boasted a tradition of more open forms of public education.

We end the book with some final thoughts on the rich contributions it contains, highlighting four ways in which it may be useful to think about 'elite education' in the future: as a trajectory experienced by individuals or groups; as a label conferred upon specific institutions; as a set of culturally and socially linked systems and practices; and as part of a broader education system, in which changes in one area have consequences for the broader system as a whole. We conclude by pointing to four priorities for future research on elite education: first, distinguishing in more nuanced ways between concepts of elite education, elite educational institutions and elite education systems; second, critically examining the links between internationalisation, globalisation and elite forms of education; third, highlighting occasions or moments when the reproduction of privilege has contradictory effects; and finally, extending the theoretical tools drawn upon and developed through such work.

References

Ball, S. (2013). *The education debate* (2nd edition). Bristol: Policy Press.
Ball, S. and Nikita, D. P. (2014). The global middle class and school choice: A cosmopolitan sociology. *Zeitschrift fuer Erziehungswissenschaft*, 17(3 Supplement), 81–93.
Bourdieu, P. (1986). *Distinction. A social critique of the judgement of taste*. London: Routledge & Kegan and Paul.
Brooks, R. and Waters, J. (2011). *Student mobilities, migration and the internationalization of higher education*. Basingstoke: Palgrave.
Brown, P. (2013). Education, opportunity and the prospects for social mobility. *British Journal of Sociology of Education*, 34(5–6), 678–700.
Fahey, J. (2014). Privileged girls: The place of femininity and femininity in place. *Globalisation, Societies and Education*, 12(2), 228–243.
Gaztambide-Fernández, R., Cairns, K. and Desai, C. (2013). The sense of entitlement. In C. Maxwell and P. Aggleton (Eds.), *Privilege, agency and affect* (pp. 32–49). Basingstoke: Palgrave Macmillan.
Green, A. (2013). *Education and state formation: Europe, East Asia and the USA*. Basingstoke: Palgrave.
Howard, A. (2013). Negotiating privilege through social justice efforts. In C. Maxwell and P. Aggleton (Eds.), *Privilege, agency and affect* (pp. 185–201). Basingstoke: Palgrave Macmillan.
Khan, S. R. (2012). The sociology of elites. *Annual Review of Sociology*, 38, 361–377.
Khan, S. R. (2015). Changes in elite education in the United States. In A. van Zanten, S. Ball and B. Darchy Koechlin (Eds.), *Elites, privilege and excellence: The national and global redefinition of educational advantage* (pp. 59–70). London: Routledge.
Lamont, M. and Molnar, V. (2002). The study of boundaries in the social sciences. *Annual Review of Sociology*, 28, 167–195.
McCarthy, C. and Kenway, J. (2014). Introduction: Understanding the rearticulations of privilege over time and space. *Globalisation, Societies and Education*, 12(2), 165–176.
Maxwell, C. (2015). Elites: Some questions for a new research agenda. In A. van Zanten, S. Ball and B. Darchy-Koechlin (Eds.), *Elites, privilege and excellence: The national and global redefinition of educational advantage* (pp. 15–28). London: Routledge.
Maxwell, C. and Aggleton, P. (2014). Agentic practice and privileging orientations among privately educated young women. *The Sociological Review*, 64(2), 800–820.

Nespor, J. (2014). Schooling for the long-term: Elite education and temporal accumulation. *Zeitschrift für Erziehungswissenschaft*, 17(3 Supplement), 27–42.

Parkin, F. (1974). *The social analysis of class structure*. London: Tavistock Press.

Resnik, J. (2012). Sociology of international education – an emerging field of research. *International Journal in Sociology of Education*, 22(4), 291–310.

Rizvi, F. (2015). The discourse of 'Asia Rising' in an elite Indian school. In A. van Zanten, S. Ball and B. Darchy-Koechlin (Eds.), *Elites, privilege and excellence: The national and global redefinition of educational advantage* (pp. 126–139). London: Routledge.

Savage, M. and Williams, K. (Eds.). (2008). *Remembering elites*. Oxford: Blackwell.

van Zanten, A. (2015). A family affair: Reproducing elite positions and preserving the ideals of meritocratic competition and youth autonomy In A. van Zanten, S. Ball and B. Darchy-Koechlin (Eds.), *Elites, privilege and excellence: The national and global redefinition of educational advantage* (pp. 29–42). London: Routledge.

van Zanten, A. and Maxwell, C. (2015). Elite education and the State in France: Durable ties and new challenges. *British Journal of Sociology of Education*, 36(1), 71–94.

Wakeling, P. and Savage, M. (2015). Elite universities, elite schooling and reproduction in Britain. In A. van Zanten, S. Ball and B. Darchy-Koechlin (Eds.), *Elites, privilege and excellence: The national and global redefinition of educational advantage* (pp. 169–184). London: Routledge.

PART I
Developments in the Anglophone world
England, Scotland, Australia and North America

1
THE HISTORICAL CONSTRUCTION OF AN ELITE EDUCATION IN ENGLAND

Claire Maxwell and Peter Aggleton

There exists a handful of schools in England which are nationally (and internationally) believed to be 'elite' institutions – because they have a long history of being positioned as such within national discourse, and because their alumni disproportionately occupy positions of power across various occupational sectors – politics, law, the media (Sutton Trust 2012).

Wakeling and Savage (2015), drawing on findings from the analysis of their large-scale data set – the BBC's *Great British Class Survey* – suggest that certain schools and universities form part of an 'elite track', whereby not only does social class origin strongly influence the probability of attending an elite school, but also it increases the likelihood of going to an elite university and becoming a member of the 'elite' social class (a newly developed multi-dimensional social class category in Savage *et al.* 2013). Such a positive correlation between 'origin–education–destination pathways' (Wakeling and Savage 2015, p. 182) is found in many countries, and is a matter that our own more qualitative research has begun to engage with: namely, how does an elite education extend family resources, shaping them into the dispositions that affect longer term outcomes? (Maxwell and Aggleton 2014a, 2014b; see also Forbes and Lingard 2015, van Zanten 2015).

In this chapter, however, we offer the beginnings of a historical analysis focusing on how the concept of an 'elite education' has been constructed over time. Our goal is to facilitate critical reflection on what an elite education might mean in England today. Of special interest are the ways in which social and economic change, as well as the broader policy context, shape the purpose of an elite education and therefore the way in which some schools become construed as being elite. In thinking about the purpose of an elite education, we will also consider the kinds of knowledges that are valued, the importance placed on schools as spaces that facilitate particular kinds of social mixing and the emphasis placed on the academic credentials that are secured through particular forms of schooling. We will conclude by considering the extent to which an 'elite education' is best understood as a meritocratic endeavour or a mechanism for maintaining social advantage and invoking social closure over time.

Before the nineteenth century

In the Middle Ages, the Church was the main provider of education in England and established a number of Grammar Schools. These schools had a vocational purpose – to prepare young men to go on to university and later take up various positions within the Church and the legal profession – the sectors largely responsible for running the country. Although 'In the Statute of Artificers of 1406, . . . it was declared that, "every man or woman, of what state or condition that he be, shall be free to set their son or daughter to take learning at any school that pleaseth them within the realm"' (Flemming Report 1944, p. 7), very few of the 'labouring' classes sent their children to school. However, for a few this possibility did exist, and the sons of landowners may have found themselves at the same school as the sons of merchants living in the same town. Among the nobility and aristocracy, both young men and women tended to be educated at home, to receive 'an education suited to the life they were expected afterwards to lead' (ibid., p. 7, also Purvis 1991). In a few cases, young noblemen might be educated in the great monasteries of the time.

The second half of the fourteenth century is identified as the time when the concept of the 'Public School' first emerged. The Bishop of Winchester established Winchester College in 1382, which for the first time offered '[a] close link with a college at one of the Universities [only Oxford and Cambridge universities existed at this time], the communal life of scholars boarding together and drawn from different parts of the country, the charitable intention to aid poor scholars and to provide recruits for the service of the Church, even . . . provision . . . for the "sons of noble and influential persons"' (Flemming Report 1944, p. 7). Thus, 70 'poor scholars' and up to ten young men from the upper classes found themselves being educated together. While the poor scholars were funded via endowments, pupils from the nobility paid for their education. Eton College was founded some 58 years later in 1440. Again, provision was made for 70 poor scholars and 20 sons of noblemen or 'special friends of the College' (ibid., p. 8).

However, Winchester and Eton were unusual as educational institutions. During the sixteenth and seventeenth centuries, industrialisation led to the growth of Grammar Schools in the form of local day schools (often wealthy men would endow or establish a local school). Over time, a small number of these schools began to achieve a certain standing in the public eye. Their reputations were enhanced when members of the upper classes identified these schools as institutions worthy of their patronage or when they began to receive public support from high-profile individuals. This led to a process of social differentiation between Grammar Schools (English 1991). The Clarendon Commission of 1861–1864 officially labelled institutions such as Winchester, Eton, Westminster, St. Paul's, Merchant Taylors' and Charterhouse as the 'Great Schools', a title which many have retained to this day. With some schools introducing provision within their statutes for 'foreigners' from the local parish to attend if they paid an appropriate fee (see Harrow for instance), and others (such as Eton) more flexibly interpreting their foundational charters and charging all students for their education in one way or another, education was in fact no longer free for all at many of these schools.

The nineteenth century

Thus, by the beginning of the nineteenth century, there was a growing awareness that particular schools were more elite than others in terms of the social groups they recruited and the public and occupational roles these pupils would take up in the future. Furthermore, debates about the purpose of education began to emphasise the advantages of a 'public', as opposed to a 'home', education for the sons of the upper classes. Such an education was believed to foster the confidence needed for an individual to take up a future public role, it encouraged competition and contributed to lasting friendships that led the way to 'worldly humour and advancement' (Bennett 1787, in Cohen 2004, p. 20). The importance of Thomas Arnold's developments during his time as Headmaster at Rugby (1828–1842) also did much to stem the kinds of criticisms that had begun to be levelled at grammar schools – poor teaching and living conditions, ill-disciplined young men – through a renewed focus on the formation of a moral (Christian) character and the importance of training the aristocracy to remember their social responsibilities towards the poor (Honey 1977). These kinds of discussions, and broader changes to the social and economic structure of English society at the time, began to embed a trend for the increasing use of 'public schools' by the aristocracy, as well as a desire from newly wealthy industrialists to send their sons to such institutions.

The mid- to late-nineteenth century was a critical period for the further development of the concept of an elite education in England. Hitherto, theoretically at least, there had been a largely Church-run provision of 'free' education for all (with a number of privately run small schools), with the specific purpose of equipping scholars to go to university and take up positions of authority within the Church and the law. Over time, individual schools emerged as the 'chosen' (Karabel 2005) institutions, sometimes because an individual Headmaster might introduce reforms to the education being offered and be seen as a particularly successful leader of the school, or because groups of high-status families might choose to send their sons to a particular school. In these schools, the sons of large landowners and, increasingly, those of wealthy industrialists were predominant (English 1991). Thus, industrialisation, urbanisation, increasing complexity of occupational structure and the instability of the Church as the body ruling the country (Simon 1987), ushered in a new era for the social organisation of schooling, one which remained largely in place until the 1960s. The new economic classes sought to buy social advantage through access to the most highly reputed schools (Fox 1985) and with their increasing political power they were able to push for the purpose and content of educational provision to be reconsidered.

The Clarendon Commission (1861–1864) was launched to examine the operation of, and the quality of educational provision at, the so-called nine Great Schools then considered to be the 'chief nurseries of our statesmen' (Public Schools Commission 1864, p. 56). Being so identified further entrenched the standing of these nine as the elite schools of England. One of the recommendations of the Commission was that the selection of scholars to enter these schools should be competitive – which had the effect of raising the academic standards, but also introduced the need for boys who hoped to gain entry to attend preparatory schools beforehand which would specifically prepare them for such an exam (a system which is still largely in place today). Second, while the Commission recommended that the curriculum include the classics, a modern language, the sciences, history and geography, it also gave the governing body of these schools the discretion to decide which subjects to focus on.

Perhaps more crucial for shaping the broader education system in England was the Taunton Commission (1864–1868), which was established to consider all other secondary education provision, except that provided by the 'Ancient Nine' (Ringer 1979, p. 208). Education for the 'labouring classes', which until then usually consisted only of elementary-level (primary) schooling, was the focus of a third commission – the Newcastle Commission (1858–1861). The Taunton Commission laid the foundations for a tripartite system of secondary school education. First grade schools were (mostly boarding) schools that combined the traditional classical curriculum (Latin and Greek) with some modern studies, and were loosely modelled on the Great Schools. These schools had a leaving age of 18 years and were tasked with getting their (male) pupils into university (Walford 2005). The Commission specified that first grade schools were for the upper middle and professional classes, those with large unearned incomes, professional and business men – including the clergy, doctors, lawyers and the 'poorer gentry' (Simon 1987, p. 100). Second and third grade schools, on the other hand, were local day schools, with a leaving age of 16 and 14 years respectively. Second grade schools were for young men preparing for a career in the army, in medicine, engineering, the law and so forth, and were for the sons of the 'mercantile and trading classes' (larger shopkeeper, rising businessmen and tenant farmers with a relatively large plot of land). Greek was not taught in these schools, which meant there was no possibility of these young men gaining entry to Oxford and Cambridge universities, but the curriculum included mathematics, science and literature. Meanwhile, third grade schools (for the sons of smaller tenant farmers and those of small tradesmen) introduced elements of Latin, basic mathematics, science, geography and a foreign language. Simon (1987) argues that third grade schools were specifically developed to bind 'the petty bourgeoisie and the upper working class firmly to their social superiors . . . so isolating them from the working class with whom in the past they had formed a sometimes powerful and threatening alliance' (p. 101). Free education was abolished and fees were introduced, proportionate to the grade of school.

These changes were supported by the growing, wealthy middle classes, seeking greater access to schooling that would confer gentlemanly status upon them and a university education. Crucially, they were also encouraged by the gentry and aristocracy who understood the urgent need for reform if they were to try to limit the occupation of these elite institutions by other social groups. In this sense, both dominant social groups and state intervention had created the impetus to put in place provision which caused a differentiation and segmentation of the education system (Simon 1987, van Zanten and Maxwell 2015). In the words of the Taunton Report (1868, p. 93), 'Education has become more varied and complex ... the different classes of society, the different occupations of life, require different teaching'. By the end of the nineteenth century, therefore, England had an overtly class-based, fee-paying education system in place, whereby social mobility was restricted and the curriculum determined by the perceived needs of each social group to take up its future position within society. As each grade of school had a different leaving age, future prospects were determined less by the academic qualifications attained at the end of secondary schooling than by the status of the school attended (McCulloch 2004). 'To be educated at a "public" school became, by the close of the century, the *sine qua non* for most leading positions in society' (Simon 1987, p. 102).

This epoch of history also ushered in the first signs of marketisation within the education system. The mid- to late-nineteenth century saw the establishment of a new group of boarding schools (Radley College, St. Edward's School in Oxford, Marlborough College), inspired by Thomas Arnold, Nathaniel Woodard and J. L. Brereton (Honey 1977) and others of the Oxford Movement (Walford 2005), which in turn opened up the possibility of a 'public school' experience for a slightly broader section of the upper and middle classes. The establishment of these new schools also gave rise to further discussion of the need to offer a more 'modern' curriculum, as not all pupils attending them could expect to live comfortably off their family's estate. As the size of the middle classes grew, so did the demand for the first grade schools they accessed to mirror the educational experience that the Great Schools were offering. Steedman (1987) therefore labelled the elite schools as 'defining institutions' highlighting the 'role and power of this group of schools to define other components of the secondary system in their own image' (p. 114).

Girls' elite education

The Taunton Commission identified the secondary schooling of girls as 'unfavourable', in terms of the very small number of schools and the 'thoroughness and foundation[s]' of the education provided (Schools Inquiry Commission 1868, Vol. 1, Chapter 6, p. 3). Those girls and young women who received an education, usually did so in the home. However, there also existed a small number of private 'fashionable' boarding schools (Purvis 1991, p. 68), mainly established in the seventeenth century, in cities such as Oxford, Manchester, London and Brighton. The focus of young women's education at the time was on the accomplishments needed to be 'ladies of leisure' (Walford 2005, p. 85) – reading, writing, religion, French, singing, dancing, needlework and household management. The curriculum for girls and young women was seen as appropriately superficial, in direct contrast to the educational provision for boys, which should be narrow but have the necessary depth (Cohen 2004).

Many schools for girls were developed alongside or following the establishment of new schools for boys. Thus, after the opening of Cheltenham College (1841) for boys, the need for a girls' school was identified, which led to the founding of Cheltenham Ladies' College (1854). Another important development shaping the provision of education for upper- and middle-class young women was the establishment of Queen's College and Bedford College, both in London, in 1848 and 1849 respectively, which aimed to train female teachers and governesses (Walford 2005). From these colleges emerged a pioneering group of women educators who went on to lead institutions such as North London Collegiate School, Camden School for Girls and Manchester High School. These women – most notably Frances Mary Buss, Dorothea Beale and Emily Davies – opened up debate about the purpose of girls' education and sought to make their schools accessible to girls from a wider range of social class positions (Purvis 1991).

Due to pressure from high-profile female educators, the Taunton Commission also reviewed the situation of girls' education and noted that, with the growing middle-classes, unmarried women needed an adequate education so as to be able to secure employment (Delamont 1978), while also arguing that women needed to be intellectual partners to their husbands:

> The most material service may be rendered to the husband, in the conduct of his business and the most serious branches of his domestic affairs, by a wife trained and habituated to a life altogether different from that of mere gentleness and amiability of which we have spoken; a life of no slight intellectual proficiency, and capacity for many functions too commonly thought to be reserved for the male sex.
> *(Schools Inquiry Commission Report 1868, Vol. 1, Chapter 6, p. 2)*

The Commission concluded, 'there is weighty evidence to the effect that the essential capacity for learning is the same, or nearly the same, in the two sexes' (ibid, p. 6). Thus, more academic forms of education became integrated into the curricula of girls' schools, while at the same time continuing to focus on 'ladylike accomplishments' (Purvis 1991, p. 127). This was necessary to ensure that the fee-paying middle- and upper-class families continued to feel the educational provision was appropriate for their daughters, as these clients were essential to maintaining the financial viability of many schools. Delamont (1978) has argued this put the pioneering headmistresses of the time in a position of 'double conformity' – a constraint that arguably shaped the educational provision of current private and elite schools, at least until the 1970s and 1980s (Purvis 1991).

Alongside the rise in prominence of high-status day schools for girls, a number of boarding schools were established towards the end of the nineteenth century (Wycombe Abbey, Roedean, Downe House), influenced by the founding of Cheltenham Ladies' College. These boarding schools 'continued the emphasis upon being exclusive, elite institutions for the daughters of gentlemen thereby differentiating themselves from the more socially heterogeneous high schools'

(Purvis 1991, p. 87). One could argue that, to some extent at least, this same differentiation exists today between girls' academically selective, private day schools and the kinds of families that choose a boarding school education. Furthermore, just as the Great Schools for boys collectively organised themselves in order to protect their interests through the establishment of the Headmasters' Conference in 1869, so too the desire for, and growth of, education provision for upper- and middle-class girls led to the formation of the Girls' Public Day School Company in 1872, and other similar associations, with the purpose of managing and funding the various leading schools at the time. So, by the beginning of the twentieth century, significant changes to the education of young men and women had taken place, especially those from the upper and middle classes, with an increasing focus on a broader and more academic curriculum.

The twentieth century

The beginning of the twentieth century heralded a commitment by the state to become actively involved in secondary education, at least for an elite minority of the age range, as outlined in the 1902 Education Act. 'Modern' schools were established alongside the more academically orientated grammar schools, where the focus of the former was on the 'practical' (Sadler 1930 in McCulloch 2002, p. 37). This system was consolidated in 1944 when a tripartite organisation of schooling was introduced, in which academic ability became the main determinant of school destination.

During the first half of the twentieth century, most, if not all, of the previously identified 'elite' boys' public schools remained outside the control of the state (McCulloch 2004) because they did not receive any direct government or local authority funding, a situation which continues to this day. Meanwhile, other grammar schools and local day schools (including many of those for girls) were at least to some extent dependent on local authority or central government funding through the issuing of grants to keep their school financially afloat. Thus, the public schools remained largely independent of state interference and continued to cater for their relatively socially exclusive clientele (McCulloch 2002). At the same time, however, debates about the purpose of education and the content of the curriculum throughout the twentieth century often focused on exploring ways in which the ideal of a 'traditional English education', as developed and practised within the Public Schools, could be integrated into the state system (ibid.).

The introduction of comprehensivisation in 1965 was perhaps the most radical attempt to 'democratise' the English education system. Although a small number of local areas retained a system that led to the differentiation of pupils at age 11 via academic selection, which in turn determined whether they attended a grammar or comprehensive school for their secondary education, across much of the country secondary schools were no longer to be differentiated by the type of curriculum offered. All young people from a local area were now to have access to a free education in the same school. Yet, despite a desire to put all schools on an equal footing, neighbourhood differences in terms of social class and ethnic background composition continued to differentiate the academic qualifications that pupils secured within and across English comprehensive schools and arguably served to fuel growing new middle-class anxieties about the education being received by their children (Reay et al. 2011). The overall effect of comprehensivisation was not, many have argued, the emergence of a strong meritocratic system. Furthermore, some governments continued to look to the public schools to provide opportunities for social mobility through the provision of scholarships (see the scheme proposed in the Flemming Report of 1944 as well as the Assisted Places Scheme between 1980 and 1997 – Whitty et al. 1998, Power et al. 2010).

Thus, not only did some governments continue to provide ideological and financial support to the public schools (Walford 2005), the size of the independent/private education sector continued to grow, to include more than the well-known public schools. With the introduction of the new tripartite system in 1944, grammar schools had to decide whether to renew their relationship with the state via direct grant or voluntary aided schemes, or become entirely financially independent. Later, in 1975, when the direct grant scheme was phased out, these schools had to decide whether to become state-maintained comprehensive schools or join the independent/private sector.

The twentieth century was a period of significant social and economic change in England, with a state-led development of the national education system. Yet, the position of the elite public schools remained unchallenged by policy enactments, and one might argue that the 1960s' commitment to comprehensivisation reinforced the division between higher and lower social classes and the education they pursued (McCulloch 2002). Meanwhile, research on the school choices made by the middle classes has emphasised that these have often been shaped by ideological factors, the provision of opportunities to take up scholarship opportunities, such as through the Assisted Places Scheme, and the increasing financial ability of certain middle-class fractions to pay for a private education (Ball and Vincent 2007, Power et al. 2010, Reay et al. 2011).

The increase in the number of fee-paying schools throughout the twentieth century, as well as the continued presence of grammar schools in certain parts of the country, together with the emergence of high-performing state schools, has driven marketisation processes whereby schools must distinguish themselves – through the social groups they attract and/or the curriculum offer they provide – in order to maintain their financial viability. Research continues to emphasise how those families who can afford it choose where to buy a home by considering where the best schools are located (Hansen 2014). Furthermore, the need to remain financially viable has meant that some of the older single-sex public schools have become co-educational (a trend that continues into the twenty-first century), and others have merged with local, fee-paying junior schools.

Elite education in England today

The end of the twentieth and beginning of the twenty-first centuries have seen 'increased privatization' (Walford 2005, p. 167) within the education sector with, among other initiatives, the introduction of Academies, Free Schools and other educational innovations, which together have contributed to the present 'fuzzy and patchy system of schools' (Ball 2013, p. 3) in England. While many of these new initiatives are still largely state-funded, but managed by non-government interests, 7 per cent of the school-age population choose to be privately educated – funded through families paying fees for their children's education in schools overseen by an independent body. Although historically boys and girls, young women and young men were educated separately, now three-quarters of all fee-paying schools admit boys and girls. Historically, the Great Schools and first grade institutions were mainly boarding schools, but over time the proportion of day schools has increased as the state demanded that previously grant-maintained schools decide whether to fully join the state-led system or become independent. Today, only 11 per cent of pupils in the fee-paying sector board full time. There is also a strong international student market for the fee-paying English education sector, constituting 5 per cent of pupils across all schools (with close to 40 per cent coming from Europe and another 40 per cent of international students coming from China, including Hong Kong) (Independent Schools Council 2014).

The education system in England today is more heavily dominated by market principles and policy discourses emphasising school choice (Ball 2013) than ever before. This, and the 'logic of capitalism' (Holmwood 2014, p. 608) more broadly, has altered the occupational structures of the country, the social fields that dominate and the constitution of the political establishment, reshaping the social organisation of class in England into a more fractured, differentiated set of social groups (Savage 2014, see also Khan 2015 for his discussion of changes in US social and economic structures). Such changes to the social, economic and political/policy context have, to some extent at least, altered the ways in which an elite education is constructed today.

In thinking about this, it is important to recognise that the legacy of the Great Schools and the 'traditional English education' (McCulloch 2004) they supposedly offered – with its strong academic focus, its commitment to extra-curricular activities as central to the development of the whole person (who is morally responsible), and its desire to promote particular forms of 'surety' (Maxwell and Aggleton 2013) – continue to shape the way in which many schools develop their curriculum. Successive governments, often of quite different political persuasions, continue to promote such an approach to education as both appropriate and necessary through efforts to incorporate the 'private' into the state system (McCulloch 2004). Moreover, due to the market pressures that the English education system now works under, the need to differentiate one's offer has become imperative. It is crucial therefore to analyse how the historical legacy of the education provided by the Ancient Nine continues to shape, albeit in carefully differentiated ways, how schools seeking to maintain or become 'elite' as dominant agents in their social fields (Bourdieu 1998), shape the curriculum and education products offered.

We aim to illustrate this claim by drawing briefly on examples from our recent four-year longitudinal study of four fee-paying schools in one area, involving interviews with 91 young women and 16 senior members of staff (Maxwell and Aggleton 2013, 2014a, 2014b).

Two of the four schools in our study had been established in the mid- to late-nineteenth century. One – formerly a boys' school but now a co-educational boarding school – was one of the schools that emerged after the Clarendon Commission as a new first grade school. It is a school with a national reputation, on the fringes of the 'elite' group of public boarding schools, and (therefore) takes tradition seriously, with a strong commitment to sport, attendance at chapel and the provision of a very full programme of extra-curricular activities. Yet, because of its position on the edge of 'the Premiership' in the market of elite schools, as one housemaster put it – they have seen their student demographic became more 'varied', largely because the social and economic composition of English society has shifted – with the financial and business sectors dominating in terms of wealth and the numbers of people employed in these social fields. This traditional co-educational boarding school now hosts a substantial minority of international students (over one-third in total at the time of the research) and many of its pupils come from 'new money' families. In interview, the deputy head teacher contrasted this with the situation that prevailed in the 1970s and 1980s, when the majority of pupils came from the professional middle class and the English landed gentry. Furthermore, partly in an effort to distinguish themselves from their competitors, but also to meet the expectations of their clientele, the school has focused on developing a 'kinder, more caring' atmosphere than might be expected in some of the most traditional (boys-only) elite public schools.

Meanwhile, the deputy head teacher at the much smaller, girls-only boarding school in our study, explained how it had maintained a stable cohort of pupils over the past decades, who all came from much more similar backgrounds – the upper classes, where wealth is most usually linked to landownership and title – as generations of women from the same family returned to the school to be educated. While the school provides sport, music, leadership and service work opportunities – a 'whole' curriculum – and many of the young women we talked to as part of our study were extremely able and ambitious, it does so in an understated way, not having the space or resources to build a '£3 million equestrian centre' as one of its regional competitors had recently done (a school known to have a more mixed demographic profile and one of the well-known nationally elite boarding schools).

Significantly, and despite their differences, senior leadership teams in both the above schools were committed to building on their school's legacy, which in part was shaped the kind of families they aimed to attract. However, concern for survival in a highly competitive education marketplace, and the changing demographic of families who can now afford to purchase a public school education, also shaped the way in which a school developed.

Significantly, the curriculum offer developed by a school is partly shaped by the social groups that a particular institution is likely to attract. A commitment to 'the academic' remains imperative in elite education – as academic attainment at the end of secondary schooling is closely monitored and regularly reported on in national and fee-paying sector 'league tables'– perceived to be an immutable metric of quality and eliteness (though not all elite schools submit their results for inclusion). Academic qualifications are also crucial in determining university entrance, an arguably more competitive endeavour nowadays than when only a small proportion of pupils were able to apply, depending on the kind of school they attended. Some private schools are less academically selective and therefore have to ensure they can provide a rigorous academic education, while also distinguishing themselves in other ways – through the relatively closed social network they provide access to (as was the case in our girls' boarding school mentioned above) or through the provision of internationally recognised qualifications, such as the International Baccalaureate (as was the case for our co-educational boarding school).

Gender, legacy and the demographic profile of students also influences the curriculum offer and the ways in which different schools construct themselves as elite. The girls-only boarding school in our study appeared to us to be caught in the bind of 'double conformity' that Delamont (1978) so eloquently described. During interviews with the all-female senior leadership team, it became clear that its members were trying to find middle ground between the expectations of the upper classes that had long sent their children to this school, and their own more emancipatory desires for the education they were seeking to provide. This was reminiscent, at least to some degree, of some of the tensions the early female education pioneers must have struggled with in the mid-nineteenth century. Meanwhile the other girls-only local day school in our study had a more varied demographic profile, where more mothers worked and family income was usually earned within the financial and business sectors. Here, the unabashed promotion of the neoliberal and successful 'top girl' (McRobbie 2009) was sought after by parents and largely reproduced in the habitus of the young women we interviewed. But even this school, which was able to promote itself as one of the most academic girls' schools in the country, was hampered by processes of double conformity – not only because some of the young women interviewed were intent on emulating their own mothers' trajectories by becoming home-makers when they had their own children, but also because of a lack of acknowledgement that an espoused 'top girl' trajectory would be hampered by the ways broader gender relations shape future economic and employment possibilities for women (Kenway *et al.* 2015).

The middle classes have always been the social group to benefit most from the increasingly marketised and privatised space of education. Not all schools in the fee-paying sector are beyond the means of professional families, just as some of the state-maintained schools, particularly those in socially economically prosperous neighbourhoods, offer an education which produces strong academic results. Certainly, some of the recent education 'innovations' offered by the Academies and Free Schools movement in England, have provided some middle-class groups with the opportunity to mould these new institutions in ways that perhaps sit more comfortably with left-leaning political positions, while still pushing for an academic and rounded curriculum. But the tension, as witnessed in debates throughout the twentieth century (McCulloch 2002), about how to create socially inclusive education institutions which also guarantee the academic qualifications and future opportunities sought by the middle classes, is as yet unresolved. As Power et al. (2010) and Reay et al. (2011) argue, initiatives aimed at providing greater opportunities for social mobility and social inclusiveness tend to benefit the middle classes most. The current context favours young people with academic credentials in the form of qualifications (national or international), a university education (preferably an elite one) and who belong to privileged social networks that have been cultivated through family ties, schooling and university trajectories (Dogan 2003, Mangset 2015, Wakeling and Savage 2015). Thus, in England today, an elite education continues to be associated with being schooled in a relatively closed social space (mainly through the mechanism of being fee-paying), which emphasises an academic education within a broad curriculum focused on cultivating 'soft' leadership skills (Brown et al. 2014) and social networks – both of which are still highly valued in the employment market. This is arguably a similar version of the 'elite' education offered by the Great Schools of the eighteenth, nineteenth, twentieth and now twenty-first centuries, but one that has become increasingly accessible to a broader demographic range of families, especially those who have accumulated the financial capital with which to purchase education.

References

Ball, S. J. (2013). *The education debate* (2nd edition). Bristol: Policy Press.
Ball, S. J. and Vincent, C. (2007). Education, class fractions and the local rules of spatial relations. *Urban Studies*, 44(7), 1175–1190.
Bourdieu, P. (1998). *The state nobility: Elite schools in the field of power*. Cambridge: Polity Press.
Brown, P., Power, S., Tholen, G. and Allouch, A. (2014). Credentials, talent and cultural capital: A comparative study of educational elites in England and France. *British Journal of Sociology of Education*, 47(2), 284–300.
Cohen, M. (2004). Gender and the private/public debate on education in the long eighteenth century. In R. Aldrich (Ed.), *Public or private education? Lessons from history* (pp. 15–35). London: Woburn Press.
Delamont, S. (1978). The contradictions in ladies' education. In S. Delamont and L. Duffin (Eds.), *The nineteenth-century woman: Her cultural and physical world* (pp. 134–163). London: Croom Helm.
Dogan, M. (2003). Introduction: Diversity of elite configurations and clusters of power. *Comparative Sociology*, 2(1), 1–15.
English, B. (1991). The education of the landed elite in England c. 1815–c. 1870. *Journal of Educational Administration and History*, 23(1), 15–32.
Flemming Report. (1944). *The public schools and the general educational system*. London: His Majesty's Stationery Office. Available at http://www.educationengland.org.uk/documents/fleming/fleming.html (accessed 2 June 2015).
Forbes, J. and Lingard, B. (2015). Assured optimism in a Scottish girls' school: Habitus and the (re)production of global privilege. *British Journal of Sociology of Education*, 36(1), 116–136.
Fox, I. (1985). *Private schools and public issues: The parents' view*. London: Macmillan.
Hansen, K. (2014). Moving house for education in the pre-school years. *British Educational Research Journal*, 40(3), 483–500.
Holmwood, J. (2014). Beyond capital? The challenge for sociology in Britain. *The British Journal of Sociology*, 65(4), 607–618.

Honey, J. R. D. S. (1977). *Tom Brown's universe: The development of the Victorian public school*. London: Millington Books.

Independent Schools Council. (2014). *ISC Census*. London: Independent Schools Council.

Karabel, J. (2005). *The chosen: The hidden history of admission and exclusion at Harvard, Yale and Princeton*. Boston: Houghton Mifflin.

Kenway, J., Langmead, D. and Epstein, D. (2015). Globalizing femininity in elite schools for girls: Some paradoxal failures of success. In A. van Zanten, S. Ball and B. Darchy-Koechlin (Eds.), *Elites, privilege and excellence: The national and global redefinition of educational advantage* (pp. 153–166). London: Routledge.

Khan, S. R. (2015). Changes in elite education in the United States. In A. van Zanten, S. Ball and B. Darchy-Koechlin (Eds.), *Elites, privilege and excellence: The national and global redefinition of educational advantage* (pp. 59–70). London: Routledge.

McCulloch, G. (2002). Secondary education. In R. Aldrich (Ed.), *A century of education* (pp. 31–53). London: RoutledgeFalmer.

McCulloch, G. (2004). From incorporation to privatisation: Public and private secondary education in twentieth-century England. In R. Aldrich (Ed.), *Public or private education? Lessons from history* (pp. 53–72). London: Woburn Press.

McRobbie, A. (2009). *The aftermath of feminism: Gender, culture and social change*. London: Sage.

Mangset, M. (2015). Contextually-bound authoritative knowledge: A comparative study of British, French and Norwegian administrative elites' merit and skills. In A. van Zanten, S. Ball and B. Darchy-Koechlin (Eds.), *Elites, privilege and excellence: The national and global redefinition of educational advantage*. London: Routledge.

Maxwell, C. and Aggleton, P. (2013). Becoming accomplished: Concerted cultivation among privately educated young women. *Pedagogy, Culture and Society*, 21(1), 75–93.

Maxwell, C. and Aggleton, P. (2014a). Agentic practice and privileging orientations among privately educated young women. *The Sociological Review*, 64(2), 800–820.

Maxwell, C. and Aggleton, P. (2014b). The reproduction of privilege: Young women, the family and private education. *International Studies in Sociology of Education*, 24(2), 189–209.

Power, S., Curtis, A., Whitty, G. and Edwards, T. (2010). Private education and disadvantage: The experiences of Assisted Place holders. *International Studies in Sociology of Education*, 20(1), 23–38.

Public Schools Commission. (1864). *The Clarendon Report*. London: Parliamentary Papers.

Purvis, J. (1991). *A history of women's education in England*. Buckingham: Open University Press.

Reay, D., Crozier, G. and James, D. (2011). *White middle class identities and urban schooling*. Basingstoke: Palgrave Macmillan.

Ringer, F. K. (1979). *Education and society in modern Europe*. London: Indiana University Press.

Savage, M. (2014). Piketty's challenge for sociology. *The British Journal of Sociology*, 65(4), 591–606.

Savage, M., Devine, F., Cunningham, N., Taylor, M., Li, Y., Hjellbrekke, J. and Miles, A. (2013). A new model of social class? Findings from the BBC's Great British Class Survey Experiment. *Sociology*, 47(2), 219–250.

Schools Inquiry Commission. (1868). *The Taunton Report*. London: His Majesty's Stationery Office.

Simon, B. (1987). Systematisation and segmentation in education: The case of England. In D. K. Mueller, F. Ringer and B. Simon (Eds.), *The rise of the modern educational system: Structural change and social reproduction 1870–1920* (pp. 88–108). Cambridge: Cambridge University Press.

Steedman, H. (1987). Defining institutions: The endowed grammar schools and the systematisation of English secondary education. In D. K. Mueller, F. Ringer and B. Simon (Eds.), *The rise of the modern educational system: Structural change and social reproduction 1870–1920* (pp. 111–134). Cambridge: Cambridge University Press.

Sutton Trust. (2012). *The educational backgrounds of the nation's leading people*. London: Sutton Trust.

van Zanten, A. (2015). A family affair: Reproducing elite positions and preserving the ideals of meritocratic competition and youth autonomy. In A. van Zanten, S. Ball and B. Darchy-Koechlin (Eds.), *Elites, privilege and excellence: The national and global redefinition of educational advantage* (pp. 29–42). London: Routledge.

van Zanten, A. and Maxwell, C. (2015). Elite education and the state in France: Durable ties and new challenges. *British Journal of Sociology of Education*, 36(1), 71–94.

Wakeling, P. and Savage, M. (2015). Elite universities, elite schooling and reproduction in Britain. In A. van Zanten, S. Ball and B. Darchy-Koechlin (Eds.), *Elites, privilege and excellence: The national and global redefinition of educational advantage* (pp. 169–184). London: Routledge.

Walford, G. (2005). *Private education: Tradition and diversity*. London: Continuum.

Whitty, G., Power, S. and Edwards, T. (1998). The assisted places scheme: Its impact and its role in privatization and marketization. *Journal of Education Policy*, 13(2), 237–250.

2
'INDEPENDENT' IN SCOTLAND
Elite by education?

Joan Forbes and Gaby Weiner

A central sociological question has been how to understand the ways in which privilege is reproduced by and through education. A key difficulty for such work has been the limited possibilities for conducting research in institutions that successfully transmit power and privilege. This chapter seeks to examine this question through a focus on private and elite schooling in Scotland, both historically and in current times. The chapter opens with an initial discussion of what it means to be 'elite' in Scottish education. This is followed by a review of the literature on Scottish private and elite schooling. The role played by the Scottish capital city of Edinburgh is highlighted since fully one-quarter of the city's pupils attend private schools. Discussion then turns to the Scottish Independent Schools Project (SISP), and its research into capitals, power, space, gender and reflexivity, in order to identify the specific practices and processes surrounding elite schooling in Scotland.

The conceptual frame

The Scottish fee-charging education sector discursively positions itself as 'independent', rather than as private or elite (see Highet 1969). This positioning promotes the perception that independent schools in Scotland value themselves (and are valued) primarily for their autonomy, 'freedom' from state management, as well as for their academic excellence. Similar to other countries (Gaztambide-Fernández 2009; van Zanten 2010) Scottish independent schools exhibit characteristics informed both by their historic foundations and by subsequent efforts to differentiate themselves from others in terms of their values and practices (Lingard *et al.* 2012).

Scottish elite schools are both economically and typologically elite, with many having historical legacies that have had a profound impact on school cultures. Geographically, most elite schools are located in large conurbations, particularly Edinburgh. While some schools educate particular privileged sections of Scottish society, in cities like Edinburgh the range of social groups educated independently is far wider. The most distinctive feature of the Scottish sector is that these schools, particularly in urban centres, are *academically* and *civically* elite – even if, in an 'understatedly' Scottish way (cf. McCrone 2005; see also Paterson 2003). In Scotland, 'elite by education' (Highet 1969, p. 288) continues to be promoted through a focus on capitals being institutionalised and credentialised by way of a selective and exclusive education system (Bourdieu 1984, 1986), that in turn produces 'people of influence' (Walford 1990, p. 39).

The independent sector is distinctive from the state sector in the structure and content of curricula, the public examinations pupils sit and examination success rates. Unlike state schools, which in general enter pupils for Scottish Qualification Authority examinations, independent schools more commonly enter students for English qualifications and the International Baccalaureate. Examination pass rates are consistently higher than in state schools. In 2013, the Higher Examination A–C pass rate for the independent sector was 93 per cent, while nationally it was 77.4 per cent (SCIS 2013). Independent schools are also distinct in having a longer school day; scheduled activities at weekends, during school holidays, before and after the formal school day; and school-organised travel for sports and cultural events within Scotland and beyond.

Research on elite schooling in Scotland

There has to date been little research into elite education in Scotland. The main reason for this, we argue, is that its existence challenges national narratives on the purpose of education. The enduring idea of a 'peculiarly Scottish form of educational democracy' (Paterson 2003, p. 3) is premised on education being about 'general academic, and therefore liberal' learning in school institutions (ibid. p. 3). Historically, the concern in Scotland has been with collectivism, 'bookish' individualism, 'respect for academic study' (ibid. p. 8), cooperation rather than competition, and civic engagement rather than market forces or *laissez faire*-ism. Thus, the purpose of Scottish education has been to reconcile individual opportunity with social solidarity characterised by equality of citizenship within a common culture and society (ibid.).

The independent sector challenges such collective notions of Scottish education by exhibiting exclusiveness in terms of offering secure and confined spaces for schooling in sought-after, affluent urban residential areas or within extensive grounds in more rural areas, separate from the local communities. Neither do they advocate social democratic values – indeed, following the ending of local and central government grant aid and the comprehensivisation of state education in Scotland in the 1970s, the schools chose 'independence' and separation over inclusiveness and social unity (Highet 1969).

A second significant point is that previous studies of Scottish fee-charging schools have generally been included in edited books on the British private sector as a whole (e.g. Walford 1984, 2003, Griggs 1985) rather than treated as a specific category. Likewise, the move towards educational ethnography within the sociology of education, from the 1970s onwards, tended to focus on 'British' private and elite independent school institutions and settings as a whole, which usually included some content on Scotland (e.g. Walford 1984, 2003).

The exceptionality of the Scottish sector only becomes visible therefore in school histories (see, for example, Shepley 1988 on St George's School for Girls, Edinburgh; and Webster 2005 on Robert Gordon's College, Aberdeen), published recollections of former pupils about their schooling, especially in Edinburgh (e.g. Roberts 2007, 2009), specific articles or chapters on the importance of the independent sector in Scotland (see Kerr 1962, Walford 1987), and descriptions of the system in various editions of the publication *Scottish Education* (see, for example, Roberts 2013).

So what studies have been undertaken on elite schools in Scotland? Sara Delamont's noted ethnographic study (1984) of an academically and socially exclusive girls' 'public' (private) school in Scotland – 'St Luke's' – examined how privileged girls endowed with cultural capital achieve academic success, albeit as 'consumers' and not 'active ... users and ... producers of knowledge' (1984, p. 84). Another study, by Walford (1990), prompted by the 1988 Education Reform Act, an English statute, explored the purchase of schooling privilege, how it drives processes of educational and social inequality and how it produces social class disconnections. However, his study did not examine differences *between* fee-charging schools in the Scottish context, or between the Scottish and English sectors, and thus failed to produce a fine-grained understanding of 'Scottish elite education' and its effects.

The most comprehensive study on Scotland's fee-paying schools before our own research was carried out by Highet (1969) some 40 years ago. At a time when the UK government was pursuing a 'comprehensive schooling' policy, Highet's goal was to explore the relevance of such a policy to provision in Scotland, given 'the lack of Scottish evidence' (p. 3) available to justify such education policy change. Using survey methodology, Highet argued that the UK government's 'comprehensive education as all-inclusivism' policy of the 1960s (p. 280) was designed to eradicate the private/state school divide in England, which had been seen to produce a 'social elite', 'social divisiveness and ... deep gulfs ... between England's social classes' (p. 289). Highet maintained that such a policy had little relevance to Scotland because, geographically, comprehensive state schools were already the norm in most of the country, with the exception of Edinburgh. Furthermore, at this time there was local and central government funding for some private schools. Highet (1969) argued that the practices of selection by such Scottish fee-paying local authority- and government grant-aided schools had produced an intellectual elite or 'elite-by-education' (p. 288) and therefore concluded that it was important that Scotland should retain its academically selective schools, whether or not they were fee-paying.

Elite or fee-paying schools in Scotland

The Scottish education system is distinct from that of other UK countries; and since the re-convening of the Scottish Parliament in Edinburgh in 1998, responsibility for education has been devolved from the Scottish Office of the UK

Government to the Scottish Government. For Scotland, as the 2014 referendum on independence testifies, 'nation' is an ideological and historical category which has political-symbolic implications for the present (McCrone 2005). Also, as already argued, the very presence of elite schooling in Scotland defies the predominant collective ideology underpinning Scottish education as a whole. So how did fee-paying schools emerge and what then is the situation currently in Scotland?

Fee-charging schools in Scotland currently cater for around 4.5 per cent of the population (SCIS 2013), but, as we shall see, their influence is far wider. For example, it was found in 1986 that in Scotland '41 per cent of a wide ranging sample of "people of influence" had a private school background' (Walford 1990, p. 39) and this influence appears to have been sustained, evident, for example, in the schools attended by current Scottish politicians, judiciary, CEOs, and Rich List members (Commission on Social Mobility and Child Poverty Commission (CSMCPC) 2014). For Walford (1990) people of influence include high court judges, first division civil servants, merchant bankers and major life-insurance company chairpersons and directors, and Members of the UK Parliament. Walford notes that the figures offer 'an indication of the long-standing relationship that exists between some private schools and positions of power and influence' (ibid., p. 39). Walford apart, there has been no major research which has explored the relationship between elite schools and take-up of influential positions in Scottish society.

It should be noted that, in terms of social structure, Scotland has a relatively small upper class in the form of land-owning aristocracy, who have largely been educated in English 'public schools' (Highet 1969). A few members of the Scottish upper middle class also choose to send their children to public schools in England. Otherwise, the private sector in Scotland caters for what might be termed the middling classes. Fee-paying schools in Scotland, such as Loretto School near Edinburgh, Fettes College in Edinburgh and Glenalmond College in Perthshire, were founded on the English 'public school' model and associated with the 'Anglicisation' of Scottish middle- and upper-class boys and their assimilation into the British upper and upper middle classes; a process termed 'cultural cloning' (Mangan 1998, p. 71; Paterson 2003). Such 'Anglo-Scottish' boarding schools mainly recruit from the 'middle-middle-class', although may include students from higher social groupings, as well as some students from lower social groupings who are supported by bursaries and scholarships (Highet 1969). Numerically and perhaps culturally more significant are the large, mainly urban fee-charging day schools such as George Heriot's School in Edinburgh; Hutchesons' Grammar School in Glasgow; and Robert Gordon's College in Aberdeen, all of which have their origins as endowed charitable 'hospitals', though these were later part-funded by central government grant aid (Highet 1969; Paterson 2003). In Edinburgh, such schools cater for a quarter of the school-age population – with considerably higher proportions in some postcode areas. These schools, it can be said, mainly cater for the 'middle-middle-class' from the city and surrounding areas (Highet 1969).

These former hospital schools are distinctive in a number of respects. For example, they like to see themselves as part of the Scottish 'national, democratic tradition'

(Paterson 2003, p. 52). In contrast to English-model 'public' schools, they 'regard[ed] themselves as serving a local middle class, augmented (however meagrely) by bursary pupils' (Paterson 2003, p. 52). The schools continue to make some provision for academically strong pupils from lower income families in the forms of means-tested bursaries, academic scholarships or free places (Anderson 1983).

In the academic year 2012–13, the number of pupils attending any kind of Scottish fee-paying school was 18,318 (secondary), 10,721(primary) and 1,682 (nursery) (SCIS 2013). Day pupil numbers (excluding nurseries and schools for children with additional needs) and boarding pupil numbers were 25,815 and 3,224 respectively. Twenty 'mainstream' independent schools (i.e. without specialist provision for additional support needs) offered boarding provision. The number of day pupils and boarding pupils from overseas was 388 and 901 respectively. Average fees were £10,173 p.a. (secondary day school) and £26,910 p.a. (secondary boarding). For comparison, the median income in Scotland at the time was £23,000 (Scottish Government 2014). In addition, individual schools itemise 'extra' charges for stationery, textbooks, lunch, uniform, English language tuition and so forth.

Some of the Scottish middle classes also send their children to 'good' state schools. For example, Edinburgh, Glasgow and its environs and Aberdeen and its environs, have several high-performing state secondary schools (age 11–18) located in middle-class catchment areas (Denholm 2013). Such academically successful state schools compete for students with nearby large independent day schools.

As noted previously, Edinburgh has the largest number of independent schools at both primary and secondary stages, followed some way behind by the cities of Aberdeen and Glasgow (SCIS 2013). Reasons for Edinburgh's distinctive positioning include the city's historical position as Scotland's capital and home of the Scottish Parliament, state church and legal system, as well as its status as a major centre for international banking and business. Highly paid people who desire the most prestigious form of education by which to extend advantage to their children thus drive this particular market.

The historically significant presence in Edinburgh of former 'hospital' schools is another factor determining the city's prominence. These were charitable educational institutions for poor boys, founded by successful Scottish merchants from the mid-seventeenth century onwards. A pivotal legal intervention by the Merchant Company of Edinburgh changed the nature of these schools. The Company petitioned for a 'permissive' clause to be added to the 1869 Endowed Hospitals (Scotland) Bill, to permit the hospital schools to continue to organise their own endowments, rather than have their endowed funding redirected to general state education or their schools absorbed into the state-funded system. As Roberts (2013, p. 122) relates, parents were quick to exploit the situation:

> prospectuses were circulated for low cost boys' and girls' day schools. By the end of September 1870, 3,300 pupils were crammed into the hospital buildings founded by Mary Erskine and George Watson . . . The city's many small private schools lost out. As one of the 300 teachers who fruitlessly petitioned

> Parliament put it …'. … £10 a year for a girl, and £6 for a boy, are sums that cannot be paid by working people'. … . Thenceforth large day schools accounted for much of the city's private education. They occupied the middle of a hierarchy linked to the level of fees.

Thus, while in England the Endowed Hospitals Bill sought to absorb schools into the new state-financed sector and thereby offer education free of charge, the 'hospital' schools in Scotland, which had hitherto offered free boarding and education for poor children, became fee-charging institutions. The year 1869 was therefore a pivotal moment in the creation of Edinburgh's 'mass-market' for middle-class private schooling, which has continued until today.

In 1969, a century later, the future of private schools across Scotland, was again at issue. In the intervening period, Scottish secondary schools had been reconfigured into four categories: wholly state-funded schools (over 3,000); wholly private schools (120), many with small pupil numbers; local authority schools (26) funded by local councils augmented by low fees; and grant-aided schools directly funded by central government (27) with higher fees scaled according to parental income and equivalent to direct-grant grammar schools in England (Highet 1969). Plans were afoot, however, to withdraw state funding from schools charging fees, thus placing the future of the two latter categories in doubt.

When grant aid finally came to an end in 1979, most schools, including the former hospital schools in Edinburgh, Aberdeen and Glasgow, opted for independence rather than join the new 'comprehensive' state system. These schools, it was argued, needed to continue to employ their selection processes in order to retain their high academic standards. Politics and policy across the rest of the UK moved swiftly towards comprehensive schooling, with academic selection in Scotland and elsewhere only possible thereafter in the newly expanded independent sector.

More recently, Scottish fee-charging schools have benefited from charitable status allowed through the Charities and Trustee Investment (Scotland) Act (2005), which affords them a variety of tax breaks. In the period 2005 to 2013, for example, the required 'public benefit' criteria of charitable status were met primarily through claims to widen access through means-tested bursaries for 'clever' pupils whose parents are unable to meet the full fees. Historically, as was the case in hospital schools, charitable foundations have offered scholarship and bursary awards, but such funding tripled after the Act from £12.5 million (2005) to £35 million (2011) following the reinforced requirement for charities to show public benefit outcomes (SCIS 2013).

What then has been the attraction of private schooling? In the case of Edinburgh, it is the 'family' school, attended by previous generations of family members. Strong links exist between particular schools (and the families attending them) and certain professions, particularly (Scots) law. As one Edinburgh mother noted: 'You can say that not merely Edinburgh law but pretty well Edinburgh itself is run by Academicals [Edinburgh Academy] and Watsonians [George Watson's College]' (Highet 1969, p. 221, parenthesis added) – thus constituting a peculiarly Scottish academic *and civic* elite.

In Highet's 1969 study, the reasons given by parents for sending their children to fee-paying schools included the 'schooling process' (Highet 1969, p. 223) – that is, an academic education which incorporates tradition, community belonging and self-discipline. For about half the parents, 'the old school tie' (that is life-long advantages accrued from the school attended) was felt to be worth paying for. Cultural and social factors aside, however, the 'universal overriding reason for sending [children to these schools] was for "the better education" parents say that fee-paying schools provide' (ibid., p. 245). Parental qualms about selective schooling focused on the insufficient number of such schools for all who wanted them rather than, as might be expected, on lack of provision for those students who failed the schools' entrance examinations.

These large independent day schools may be judged as displaying less social 'elite-ness' than other schools in the sector. However, as we have seen, the idea of 'elite' remains analytically salient to understanding both the role of the sector and differences between schools in the sector (Savage and Williams 2008). The large day schools in Edinburgh and Glasgow are traditionally 'kin', in terms of similarity of fee level, social ranking and educational standing (Highet 1969). Some 40 per cent of Edinburgh parents in Highet's (1969) study acknowledged social standing or 'snobbishness' (p. 240) as a reason for choosing private education. 'Sending [a child] to a fee-paying school is [seen to be] the done thing in Edinburgh' (ibid., p. 243) both to 'keep up' with the neighbours and/or not wishing one's children to 'feel out of it' (ibid., p. 232). Thus, for certain groups in these cities, private schooling in city day schools is constituted as normal behaviour.

Relatively few of the schools attract many students from outside Scotland. Unlike England and the USA, Scotland has only two or three preparatory boarding schools acting as guaranteed 'feeders' to elite senior schools at the age of 14. Nor does Scotland have a significant fee-charging denominational sector, such as the Roman Catholic school sector in Australia. Distinctive features of the Scottish elite market today therefore are its relative stability in pupil numbers and institutions, and its affordability for the middling social classes. The financial crisis of 2007–08 and ensuing economic recession hence caused fewer closures of private schools in Scotland than elsewhere in the UK.

In response to the 'charity test' and the need to demonstrate public benefit and confidence in the schools – and no doubt also viewed by the schools as attempts to participate in civic society – the sector has sought to be seen to work with influential partners, such as Scottish Government departments, mainstream education groups and public bodies. Sector teachers have been active, for example, in national curriculum developments and as exam assessors for the Scottish Qualifications Authority. Sector representatives have also organised national conferences open to all teachers.

The Scottish Independent Schools Project

Against this background, the Scottish Independent Schools Project (SISP) SISP set itself the task of exploring the processes of independent schooling in Scotland and, in particular, their use of social and other forms of capital and how the acquisition and extension of such capitals shape the potential futures of students. As part of the Applied Educational Research Scheme (AERS),[1] the aim was to explore the production of advantage as a means of providing insights into the reproduction of disadvantage – the primary focus of other AERS case studies.

The criteria for independent or elite schooling adopted in the study included: registration with the Scottish Government Schools Directorate; being subject to inspection by Her Majesty's Inspectorate of Education; being independent of local education authority management; providing full-time education for pupils of school age; entering students for senior secondary public examinations; charging tuition fees and/or providing scholarships and bursaries; being affiliated to professional associations, such as the Headmasters' and Headmistresses' Conference (HMC) and the Girls' School Association (GSA); and being listed as members of the Scottish Council of Independent Schools (SCIS).

The project initially focused on the identification and classification of the full range of independent schools (70+) in Scotland, as well as how each school presented itself through its website, prospectuses and related literature. This research found that each school promoted a distinctive set of characteristics linked to institutionally based values and curriculum emphasis, and a specific array of norms and values which could be linked to its particular market positioning (Forbes and Weiner 2008).

In the second phase of work, we undertook in-depth case studies of three schools: an *urban girls' school*, historically independent of government aid and in the 'Anglo-Scottish' tradition category, all age (preschool to age 18), mainly day students, with a roll of between 500 and 1,000 pupils; *an urban boys' school*, also in the historically independent and Anglo-Scottish tradition category, with primary and secondary stages, and a roll of between 400 and 500 students, mainly boarding; and an *all-age (five–18) co-educational school*, in the charitable foundation and former central government grant-aided category, located in a small town, with a pupil roll of 1,000–1,500, mainly day pupils with around 100 boarders.

The concept of *capital* informed the study, specifically the social capital theorisations offered by Bourdieu (1986). Central to social capital theory is the idea that social relations in the form of social networks, shared norms and relations of trust and confidence constitute valuable assets for individuals, groups and society, nationally and globally. It was hypothesised that independent schools were likely to be particularly successful in utilising such social networks as a means of benefitting their students. The concept of social capital was extended to include Bourdieu's notion of multiple capitals (economic, cultural and symbolic) whereby the accumulation of resources in these areas is also seen as advantageous. Theoretical insights derived from Foucault (see e.g. Gordon 1980) were also utilised as a means of understanding the flow of power and knowledge in schools and how they are accumulated, distributed and encountered.

The SISP project focused primarily on exploring how elite schools promote themselves, and also their students' acquisition and activation of social and other capitals through their practices. The research team included people with a number of areas of expertise, including research on gender and other kinds of educational in/exclusion. Thus, while the original project design did not specify gender relations as a key focus, gender emerged as an important element of the research.

Theoretical contributions provided by the SISP research studies

A number of findings and insights emerged from the research. Website and documentary analysis revealed that schools differentially invoked a range of discourses and practices relating to symbolic and reputational 'branding' in order to appeal to 'their' particular socio-economic fraction of Scottish society. For example, the 'Anglo-Scottish' girls' school sought to attract Scottish and overseas parents seeking a liberal academic and girl-focused education in which learning assuredness and agency were central, via school community and social relationships. The 'Anglo-Scottish' boys' school targeted affluent Scottish families seeking an English-model public school education alongside promoting the development of softer forms of masculinity, considered appropriate for successful participation in global business. The large co-educational school's reputation for public examination success and its full programme of sport, musical and cultural experiences aimed to appeal to parents seeking an 'academic-plus education' as a point of entry into high-status professions (Forbes and Weiner 2008, Horne *et al.* 2011, Lingard *et al.* 2012).

Questions were posed about power relations in the case-study schools, for example: whose interests and experiences were seen as central; which – and whose – aspirations and preferences took precedence; whose realities and experiences were legitimated; who decided what constituted appropriate knowledge and practices; what forms of knowledge were understood as necessary to change current ways; and who was expected and allowed to act (Forbes and Weiner 2008, and see also Bishop and Glynn 1999). In examining these questions we found that the schools had considerable stocks of social capital which were, however, 'understated', indeed omitted from promotional materials, in keeping with the deep-rooted and instinctive Scottish civic value of 'under-statement' (cf. McCrone 2005).

For example, it was striking that the schools' websites did not capitalise on the reputations of famous and influential former pupils, parents or members of their boards of governors, an omission which might be viewed as a missed marketing opportunity. However, for the schools and 'their' potential clientele, such low-key public representation of their social connectedness symbolises the traits of modesty and self-deprecation that are shared and so highly valued in Scotland. Such understated messages, alongside representations of, for example, abundant academic, cultural and international resources, was used to 'naturally' connect the schools with their perceived market (Forbes and Lingard 2013, Forbes and Weiner 2008).

It was also found that the schools encouraged distinct, strongly bonded social-spatial relationships and territorial cultures, which set them apart from the surrounding community and geographical area (Forbes and Weiner 2012, Forbes and Lingard 2013). For example, schools' distinctive spatio-temporalities, including the rhythms of extended and intensive formal and informal learning schedules, institutionally 'locked-in' their pupils to the schools' multiple capitals regimes. Furthermore, the schools' distinctive institutional architectures, heritages and traditions fostered particular practices that were exclusive, intensively demanding of staff and students and gendered in nature (Horne *et al.* 2011, Forbes and Weiner 2012).

Subsequent analysis revealed discriminatory practices operating at different levels (governance, institutional, individual). For example, markedly different gender-power regimes governed each case-study school, which interestingly also had an impact on the research process, including access, research relationships and feedback to schools (Forbes and Weiner 2013, 2014a). Unsurprisingly perhaps, SISP found that the ways in which gender and other structural categories, such as social class and economic wealth, are drawn on and interpreted within the schools are shaped by schools' historic cultural and social identifications and by the economic and social fraction from which current school students are drawn and with which they identify. Methodologically, such insights demand that theoretically informed studies should engage with these 'intersectionalities', that is, the intricate ways in which such social categories intersect and effect the interlocking identities of individuals (Crenshaw 1991; Forbes and Weiner 2014b).

Finally, the research highlighted the need for reflexivity as a means of examining the norms and expectations of researchers and researched, and for vigilance in regard to networks of power in elite spaces and, in particular, how the 'powerful researched' seek to control access, process and outcomes (Gaztambide-Fernández 2009, Forbes and Weiner 2014a). Reflexivity (see e.g. Bourdieu 2007) made it possible to acknowledge researchers' self-positionings and standpoints on power and knowledge and to illuminate and examine, rather than silence, issues of dis/continuities between individuals and institutions which cut across gender, social class, ethnicity and other intersectionalities (Crenshaw 1991, Forbes and Lingard 2013). A substantive finding was the importance of understanding the impact on the research of researchers' and participants' personal biographies (e.g. Scottish or Commonwealth country national) and characteristics such as ethnicity, age, economic status and social status (e.g. 'professorial' status and 'research institution' affiliation categories), all of which intersect in intricate ways (Forbes and Weiner 2014a, 2014b).

Researcher reflections and pointers for the future

This chapter has set out to add to the hitherto limited research on private and elite education in Scotland. It has revealed the continued influence of the fee-paying sector in Scotland – and particularly in Edinburgh – but also how this urban, predominantly local day-school provision serves a broader socio-economic group compared to other elite groups who send their children to English-style 'public' boarding schools in Scotland or elsewhere. A review of earlier research opened the way for us to identify the social and economic segments of Scottish society that have used and continue to use independent schooling and to seek to understand the dimensions of capitals and power imbricated in the spaces occupied by the schools.

We found that the schools in our study position themselves as competitive businesses, developing their particular values and practices through close attention to the market (Forbes and Weiner 2008, Lingard et al. 2012). Hence, McCrone's (2005) work on the understated nature of national Scottish cultural capital and existence of specific 'national' characteristics, such as modesty and self-deprecation, enabled us to explore school relationships and their particular clientele. Most fascinating about the Scottish fee-charging sector is that its raison d'être in the form of 'elite-by-education', remains very much at odds with central Scottish narratives of democracy and collectivism; yet the sector remains widely accepted as important for the formation of future generations of influential agents within the nation.

To understand more fully Scottish elites, research is needed on how such elite schools continue to play an important role in the production of 'persons of influence' or 'state nobility' (Bourdieu 1996); and why that role remains broadly uncontested. Thus further studies might focus, for example, on the perceptions and experiences of 'influential' former students, thereby revealing the effects of schools' different configurations of capital resources and their strategic spatio-temporal deployments. Currently naturalised, understated and inadequately understood, such educational institutions require closer examination in terms of the life-long advantaging effects they have and their social (re)production practices.

Relatedly, such schools have come to constitute an accepted and symbolic part of Scottish cultural heritage, cityscapes and landscapes – with their familiar 'iconic' historic architecture on open view within a town or cityscape coincident to their privacy and exclusivity as educational spaces. Therefore, another potential research focus might be on schools' particular configurations of capitals and how these are expressed through their physical capital resources, including their architecture and social space (Bourdieu 1984). An additional focus could also be on the effects their particular stocks of physical capital have on the essential daily rhythms of school practices, as well as the schools' position within a wider national socio-cultural imaginary.

In summary then, we need to know more about how interlinking social categories reproduce an unequal 'Elitist Scotland' (to paraphrase the title of the recent examination of schooling background and in/equality of opportunity in the 'Elitist Britain?' report, CSMCPC 2014) and the specific role of independent schooling in this process of (re)production. Accordingly, as a first step, future research, including the UK government-sponsored annual surveys on 'Elitist Britain?' (CSMCPC 2014), will be redesigned to disaggregate Scottish data, thereby producing analyses that are able to inform Scottish educational and policy decisions. Indeed, we suggest that a separate annual survey on school background and social mobility in Scotland should be undertaken by a wholly Scottish Commission.

Finally, our review of studies to date serves to highlight the need for further investigation on Elitist Scotland and how schooling drives such processes, whether in English-model independent schools in Scotland or in 'public' schools in England. Such a focus will also facilitate an examination of the processes by which the majority in Scotland is structurally disadvantaged, in part because of the schooling trajectories open to its members. A key question that remains is how, in this small avowedly equal and democratic country, a small social segment of the population is allowed to maintain, through processes of schooling, the capitals and resources which enable it to continue to dominate civic society.

Note

1 This project was funded by the Scottish Funding Council with some additional funding provided by the University of Edinburgh, Bell Chair, via the Godfrey Thomson fund.

References

Anderson, R. D. (1983). *Education and opportunity in Victorian Scotland*. Edinburgh: Edinburgh University Press.

Bishop, R. and Glynn, T. (1999). *Culture counts: Changing power relations in education*. Palmerston North, NZ: Dunmore.

Bourdieu, P. (1984). *Distinction*. London: Routledge.

Bourdieu, P. (1986). The forms of capital. In J. Richardson (Ed.), *The handbook of theory and research for the sociology of education* (pp. 241–258). Westport, CT: Greenwood.

Bourdieu, P. (1996). *The state nobility. Elite schools in the field of power*. Cambridge: Polity.

Bourdieu, P. (2007). *Sketch for a self-analysis*. Cambridge: Polity.

Commission on Social Mobility and Child Poverty Commission (2014). *Elitist Britain?* Available at https://www.gov.uk/government/uploads/system/uploads/attachment_data/file/347915/Elitist_Britain_-_Final.pdf (accessed 2 June 2015).

Crenshaw, K. (1991). Mapping the margins: Intersectionality, identity politics and violence against women of colour. *Stanford Law Review*, 43(6), 1241–1299.

Delamont, S. (1984). Debs, dollies, swots and weeds: Classroom styles at St Luke's. In G. Walford (Ed.), *British public schools policy and practice* (pp. 65–86). London: Falmer.

Denholm, A. (2013). *Revealed: Scotland's best 50 schools for Higher exam passes*. HeraldScotland newspaper. Available at http://www.heraldscotland.com/news/home-news/revealed-scotland-s-best-50-schools-for-higher-exam-passes.1387466220 (accessed 2 June 2015).

Forbes, J. and Lingard, B. (2013). Elite school capitals and girls' schooling: Understanding the (re)production of privilege through a habitus of assuredness. In C. Maxwell and P. Aggleton (Eds.), *Privilege, agency and affect. Understanding the production and effects of action* (pp. 50–68). London: Palgrave Macmillan.

Forbes, J. and Weiner, G. (2008). Understated powerhouses: Scottish independent schools, their characteristics and their capitals. *Discourse: studies in the cultural politics of education*, 29(4), 509–525.

Forbes, J. and Weiner, G. (2012). Spatial paradox: Educational and social in/exclusion at St Giles. *Pedagogy, Culture and Society*, 20(2), 273–293.

Forbes, J. and Weiner, G. (2013). Gendering/ed research spaces: Insights from a study of independent schooling. *International Journal of Qualitative Studies in Education*, 26(4), 455–469.

Forbes, J. and Weiner, G. (2014a). Gender power in elite schools: Methodological insights from researcher reflexive accounts. *Research Papers in Education*, 29(2), 172–192.

Forbes, J. and Weiner, G. (2014b). *Gender sensitive research in schools: Insights and interventions on gender, social class, economic wealth, and other intersections*. Paper given at the Scottish Universities Insight Institute Seminar Series 2013–14: Children's Rights, Social Justice and Social Identities in Scotland: Intersections in Research Policy and Practice. The Scottish Universities Insight Institute, Glasgow, 23 June 2014.

Gaztambide-Fernández, R. (2009). What is an elite boarding school? *Review of Educational Research*, 79(3), 1090–1128.

Gordon, C. (Ed.) (1980). *Michel Foucault. Power/knowledge: Selected interviews and other writings 1972–1977.* Brighton: Harvester.

Griggs, C. (1985). *Private education in Britain.* London: Falmer.

Highet, J. (1969). *A school of one's choice. A study of the fee-paying schools of Scotland.* London: Blackie.

Horne, J., Lingard, B., Weiner, G. and Forbes, J. (2011). Capitalizing on sport: Sport, physical education and multiple capitals in Scottish independent schools. *British Journal of Sociology of Education*, 32(6), 861–879.

Kerr, A. J. C. (1962). *Schools of Scotland.* Glasgow: MacLellan.

Lingard, B., Forbes, J., Weiner, G. and Horne, J. (2012). Multiple capitals and Scottish independent schools: The (re)production of advantage. In J. Allan and R. Catts (Eds.), *Social capital, children and young people. Implications for practice, policy and research* (pp. 181–198). Bristol: The Policy Press.

McCrone, D. (2005). Cultural capital in an understated nation: The case of Scotland. *British Journal of Sociology*, 56(1), 65–82.

Mangan, J. A. (1998). Braveheart betrayed: British by calculation and choice: The Scottish middle class in the age of Empire. In M. Allison, J. Horne and L. Jackson (Eds.), *Scottish Centre research papers in sport, leisure and society, Volume 3* (pp. 70–84). Edinburgh: Moray House.

Paterson, L. (2003). *Scottish education in the twentieth century.* Edinburgh: Edinburgh University Press.

Roberts, A. (2007). *Crème de la crème: Girls' schools of Edinburgh.* London: Steve Savage.

Roberts, A. (2009). *Ties that bind: Boys' schools of Edinburgh.* London: Steve Savage.

Roberts, A. (2013). The independent sector. In T. G. K. Bryce, W. M. Humes, D. Gillies and A. Kennedy (Eds.), *Scottish education. Fourth edition: Referendum* (pp. 120–128). Edinburgh: Edinburgh University Press.

Savage, M. and Williams, K. (2008). Elites: Remembered in capitalism and forgotten in social sciences. *Sociological Review Monograph*, 56 (s1), 1–24.

Scottish Council of Independent Schools (SCIS) (2013). *Facts and statistics.* Available at http://www.scis.org.uk/assets/Uploads/2013-SCIS-Pupil-Numbers-Press-Release4.pdf (accessed 2 June 2015).

Scottish Government (2014). *Poverty and income inequality in Scotland 2012/13.* Available at http://www.scotland.gov.uk/topics/statistics/browse/social-welfare/incomepoverty/publications (accessed 2 June 2015).

Shepley, N. (1988). *Women of independent mind: St George's School, Edinburgh and the Campaign for Women's Education 1888–1988.* Edinburgh: St George's School.

van Zanten, A. (2010). The sociology of elite education. In M. Apple, S. Ball and L. A. Gandin (Eds.), *The Routledge international handbook of the sociology of education* (pp. 329–339). London: Routledge.

Walford, G. (1984). *British public schools: Policy and practice.* London: Falmer.

Walford, G. (1987). How important is the independent sector in Scotland? *Scottish Educational Review*, 19(3), 108–121.

Walford, G. (1990). *Privatization and privilege in education.* London: Routledge.

Walford, G. (2003). *British private schools: Research on policy and practice.* London: Woburn Press.

Webster, J. (2005). *The Auld Hoose: The story of Robert Gordon's College.* Edinburgh: Black & White.

3
ELITE EDUCATION IN THE AUSTRALIAN CONTEXT

Sue Saltmarsh

Australian schooling is generally categorised in line with historical differences that have existed in the funding and governance structures of the sector: public, Catholic and independent. However, distinctions between and within these three groupings have altered considerably in recent decades, requiring a reconsideration of the ways in which elite schooling might be recognised and understood. This chapter identifies some key distinguishing features of Australia's different schooling sectors, and suggests that within each there are examples of what might be considered 'elite' schools. I consider how, in the Australian context, there is more to the elite status of schools than the privilege commonly associated with financial wealth, or the social and political influence of its key stakeholders over time.

While wealth and influence can and do matter to a school's elite status, and to the 'positional advantage' (Ball 2003, p. 56) afforded to its clientele, these are not the sole defining features of such schools. In particular, I am interested here in problematising why it is that the independent sector schools modelled on the English public school tradition so persistently typify what is broadly considered 'elite' schooling in Australia. The chapter argues that elite status is contingent not only on criteria such as exclusivity or the high cost of fees, but also on the success with which particular schools are 'consecrated' as elite (Saltmarsh 2007) within Australia's highly competitive and racialised educational marketplace (Gulson and Webb 2012).

As in other Anglophone nations, Australian schooling operates within a marketised landscape that is intensely competitive and highly stratified. Australian scholars have extensively documented the influence of successive neoliberal government reforms that have subjected Australian schooling to market forces in the latter part of the twentieth century, continuing to the present (Marginson 1997, Campbell et al. 2009, Proctor 2011, Campbell and Proctor 2014). Within this marketised context, the terminology used to refer to both schools and sectors is contested and varied, and meanings associated with each has changed over time, as shifts in regulatory requirements have occurred and access to government funding has altered. Historically, government funding has been directed primarily to schools in the public sector. However, policy shifts from the 1950s onwards have gradually seen schools in all three sectors being substantially supported through public funding and increasingly subject to common regulatory frameworks (Campbell and Sherington 2006, Campbell and Proctor 2014).

A history of elite schooling can be traced in all three sectors, and evidence suggests that the social segregation that exists between the public and private sectors also 'exists within each of the sectors' (Windle 2009, p. 233). This highlights the need to broaden current conceptualisations of elite schooling as consisting *primarily* of prestigious private schools in the independent school sector. In researching elite boarding schools in the USA, for example, Gaztambide-Fernández argues that there is a lack of clear criteria by which elite schools are identified, and that there has been a tendency to 'ignore distinctions between elite schools and other nonpublic schools as part of an argument for the importance of choice in the marketization of education' (2009, p. 1091). He argues that five distinct dimensions can be used to describe these schools as:

> (a) typologically elite, based on their identification as 'independent schools'; (b) scholastically elite, based on both the expansive and sophisticated curricula they offer and their particular pedagogical approaches; (c) historically elite, based on the role of elite social networks in their historical development; (d) geographically elite, based on their physical character and location; and lastly, (e) demographically elite, based on the population that attends elite boarding schools.
>
> *(ibid., p. 1093)*

While such a typology can be helpful in making epistemological, methodological and practical distinctions, it also highlights precisely the significance of local, regional and national specificities to what might be considered 'elite' within a given context.

Australia provides a case in point, in so much as there are forms of elite schooling in the public, Catholic and independent sectors. For example, while Australia's public education system serves a broad cross-section of the community, academically selective public high schools have been established in Australia since the nineteenth century. These schools are placed 'in a strong market position', particularly in states 'where a long tradition of such schools for high-flyers complicates the public/private binary' (Angus 2013, p. 9). These high-achieving schools maintain exclusivity through rigorous admissions processes, with entry gained on the basis of test scores, or in the case of selective performing arts high schools, through a highly competitive audition process. While selective schools are broadly perceived as catering to students on the basis of merit, irrespective of socioeconomic status, scholars have pointed out that diversification in the public sector has given rise to a range of schooling options that are by no means available to all (Campbell and Sherington 2006, Windle 2009, Rowe and Windle 2012, Angus, 2013).

Thus, while public sector schools do not enjoy the 'embarrassment of riches' (Windle 2009, p. 233) of high fee-paying schools whose receipt of government subsidies has 'massively increase[d] their resource levels' (ibid., p. 233), the intensification of selectivity within the public sector is nonetheless a significant feature of the Australian educational landscape. Preparing one's child for entry into a highly desirable public school is one means by which parents can either attain or maintain middle-class social positioning (Windle 2009, Angus 2013, Weis and Cipollone 2013). Whether through openly competitive processes, or 'through a complicated mix of zoning, examination-based entry into "accelerated programs", and specialized curriculum pathways' (Angus 2013, p. 10), such schools offer specialisms that render them highly 'visible as "schools of choice"' (Windle 2009, p. 233). These schools have held particular appeal among non-Anglo families, many of whom come from cultural backgrounds that greatly value academic achievement, and often invest heavily in private tutors and practice testing in order to help their children access, and excel within, these schools (Ho 2011). Such has been the appeal of selective secondary schools to these families, that most selective high schools now have student bodies where 85 per cent or more of the pupils come from non-English speaking backgrounds, with the majority being Asian (Ho 2011, Millburn 2011). In the light of successive government initiatives that seek to extend Australia's regional economic and political influence in Asia (see, for example, *Australia in the Asian Century* (Australian Government 2012) and *Australia Educating Globally* (Australian Government 2013)), the status and potential influence of these selective public schools – a number of which regularly top league tables ahead of elite private schools – should not be underestimated.

The success of these schools in the 'Asian Century' raises questions about the ways in which elite education has typically been understood as serving the purposes of socially dominant groups. The prestige of Australian selective high schools is more readily apparent among migrant families, not normally considered among society's privileged classes. However, their success in preparing an already multilingual, academically capable student population to compete and excel in Asia-literate terms is highly significant in one of the world's most culturally diverse nations (UNESCO 2009). Cultural polarisation among these 'scholastically elite' (Gaztambide-Fernández 2009) selective schools, and their particular appeal to a more culturally diverse demographic, is a stark reminder that the drift from public to private sector schooling has been most pronounced among Anglo-Australians (Ho 2011). The symbolic and material place of whiteness in securing the prestige of some independent sector schools over the highly selective public sector schools that outperform them is significant in Australia as in other parts of the world with colonial histories (Connell 2003, Saltmarsh 2008, Epstein 2014, McCarthy *et al.* 2014).

Despite the high demand for places in selective public schools (Windle 2009), recent decades have also seen a steady increase in the number of student enrolments in private schools. As Simon Marginson argues, opinion polls in the mid-1990s showed that almost two-thirds of people expressed a preference for private secondary schooling either in the Catholic or independent sectors. As Marginson put it, 'the desire for elite schooling was becoming universal, though by definition its realization could only ever be limited to a few' (1997, p. 238). Private schooling's long-established cultural appeal in Australia, driven in part by its role in the 'circuit of privilege' (ibid., p. 24) linking elite secondary schooling and university participation, was further entrenched through subsequent injections of public expenditure and the renovation and expansion of private sector schooling (Marginson 1997). By the mid-1990s, the widespread desirability of private schooling was accompanied by policy shifts that saw a decline in the number of public schools, an increase in the number of Catholic and independent schools and in the amount of government funding received by the latter. Australian Bureau of Statistics data illustrate the significance of these policy shifts, as the first decade of the new millennium saw a 21 per cent increase in private schools student numbers, and only a 1 per cent increase in students attending government schools (ABS 2010, 2011). Annual growth rates in both independent and Catholic school sectors have continued to outstrip those in public sector schooling (ABS 2013).

The strength of Australia's non-government sectors differs from other Anglophone nations (Campbell and Proctor 2014), in which elite private schools typically make up a smaller proportion of educational provision than in Australia. It is worth noting that the disparities of wealth between sectors are also reflected within them. The stratified nature of these sectors means that some independent and Catholic schools serve clientele that are not particularly affluent or influential, while the elite private schools in these non-government sectors attract millions annually in fees, donations, investments and other revenue sources in addition to the receipt of government subsidies. Schools in the Catholic system range from parochial or 'systemic' schools to independent schools not run directly by Catholic Education Offices (ibid.). Catholic systemic schools are non-selective, have moderate fee structures, cater for families in a wide range of socioeconomic categories and offer concessions to parish families in circumstances of economic hardship. However, single-sex selective schools run by wealthy and influential Catholic orders bear little resemblance to their systemic school counterparts and are counted among Australia's most prestigious and exclusive educational options.

The independent school sector is also characterised by variability. Some schools have strong religious and cultural affiliations, and a number cater for Indigenous communities, at risk students and students with disabilities. Independent sector schooling, therefore, is by no means a guarantee of elite status. However, the relatively small percentages of Indigenous students, students with disabilities, those in remote geographic locations and/or in the lowest socioeconomic quartile who attend independent schools by comparison to other sectors has invited criticism that '*disadvantaged students are not evenly spread across the independent sector and are concentrated in very small pockets*' (Kenway 2013, p. 294, italics in original). Others are similarly critical, arguing that middle-class families are most advantageously positioned within the education market, and most likely to choose – and be able to afford – private school options (Campbell *et al.* 2009, Angus 2013). This is particularly the case with independent sector high-status, high fee-paying schools typically modelled on the English public schools, and it is these schools that the research literature tends to refer to as elite private schools.

Australia has a long history of elite private sector schooling, that from its inception was modelled on the English educational tradition (Symes and Preston 1997). This tradition has shaped perceptions of what is meant by 'elite' schooling (Kenway and Fahey 2014), with much research on elite schooling focused on Anglo contexts (Koh and Kenway 2012). This methodological blind spot reflects observations made elsewhere (Saltmarsh 2005, 2007) that assumptions of whiteness – of which 'Englishness' is a signifier in the Australian context – underpin much of what is taken to be 'elite'. As scholars interested in the representational practices of such schools have argued, the everyday 'symbolic architecture' (Synott and Symes 1995, Symes and Meadmore 1996, 1999) of contemporary schooling drew its inspiration from the nineteenth-century English Public School and remains the bedrock feature of schooling's organisational culture (Symes and Meadmore 1999). Australian private schools that tacitly reproduce English heritage in the form of boarding, prefectures, 'house' systems and disciplinary regimes are able to trade on these as signifiers of superior status and worth. This, together with high fees that maintain and protect the exclusivity of such schools, caters to idealized notions about their perceived quality.

Another critique of elite schooling is the extent to which it is seen as serving the interests of what Connell (1977) referred to in the late 1970s as the ruling class in Australian society. For Connell, private education in elite Catholic and independent schools was the domain of ruling class elites, whose success in secondary and tertiary education mirrored their dominance in the social hierarchy. Such a relationship between social class, academic outcomes, future positions of power within wider society and having attended an elite non-government school has been well documented (Saltmarsh 2005, 2007, 2008, Campbell *et al.* 2009, Kenway 2013, Campbell and Proctor 2014).

Elite public sector schooling has been subject to less scholarly critique. However, selective public schools also play a role in the production of power and social privilege via academic, sporting and other areas of excellence. Indeed, a number of selective public schools actively promote their successes in this regard. As one selective public secondary school website informs readers and prospective families:

> Fort Street High School was established in 1849. As the oldest selective high school Fort Street has a unique place in history of the State of NSW [New South Wales], having educated and nurtured some of the most prominent and influential citizens in Australia.
>
> *(Fort Street High School 2014)*

This role in preparing future leaders is an often explicitly articulated goal of elite schools, such that 'the missions of elite schools have traditionally emphasized that leadership is a responsibility of the privileged and powerful and that the schools have a special role to play in preparing students for positions of social, political, and economic importance' (Cookson and Persell 2010, p. 16). While such goals are by no means confined to non-government schooling, it is nonetheless worth noting that in Australia's current political context, recent media reports observe that 78 per cent of the present government cabinet has been educated in private schools (Wade and Khaicy 2013). As recent research on the role of high-status private schools in the education of global elites underscores (Koh and Kenway 2012, Kenway *et al.* 2013, Kenway and Fahey 2014), the spheres of influence of these schools and their constituents extend well beyond the borders of the nation state. The role of elite private schools in cultivating 'transnational capitals' (Kenway and Koh 2013, p. 271) is an important means by which students are prepared to take up influential roles in political, economic and cultural fields on the global stage, and by which the branding and elite status of such schools is maintained globally.

The variations described above render any single definition of 'elite' inevitably slippery and inadequate within the Australian context. Instead, they point to the need to better understand those 'systems, practices, and policies that work to reinforce the social, political, cultural, and economic privilege of dominant groups' (Howard and Gaztambide-Fernández 2010, p. 2), irrespective of the sectors in which such privileging occurs. Variations within and between Australian schooling sectors suggest that new ways of understanding social dominance may be required. As the example of high-achieving selective public schools illustrates, the association of 'elite' education with schools closely modelled on English heritage, traditions and the whiteness they imply (Saltmarsh 2005, 2007), may no longer be adequate for understanding how patterns of social dominance are changing in response to cultural pluralism in the 'Asian Century' (Australian Government 2012).

Theory and method: researching elite schooling

Australian humanities and social sciences research concerning elite schooling has several theoretical and methodological influences. The three research orientations considered here are concerned, first, with representation, and the ways that elite schools are seen as 'institutions entrusted with the education and consecration of those who are called to enter the field of power' (Bourdieu 1996, p. 74). Drawing on the work of social semioticians, discourse analysts and social historians, I argue that elite status can be theorised through a recognition of the multiple ways that representational practices discursively 'consecrate' certain types of schools as sites of power, privilege, and educational, social and moral superiority.

The second research orientation pertains to issues of social class, and the ways sociologists of education examine how elite schooling perpetuates social inequality through a stratified system that excludes all but the wealthy from the power and privilege associated with a 'ruling class' education (Connell 1977). Such studies have included a focus on how an inequitable distribution of funding privileges independent over public sector schooling (Angus 2013, Kenway 2013). In addition, questions of social class and school choice – theorised in the Australian literature predominantly through Bourdieu's notions of social and cultural capital – come into play as researchers contemplate how consumers and middle-class parents operate and manoeuvre within the education marketplace.

The third influence in researching elite education in Australia is in qualitative research approaches to understanding elite schools as sites in the production of subjectivities and social relations. These approaches turn the analytic gaze toward sites of power and privilege, or what has been referred to as 'studying up' (Howard and Gaztambide-Fernández 2010). Australian studies of this kind have been interested in the complex processes associated with parenting and school choice, as well as in the ways that school ethos and everyday practices shape students into particular types of educational subjects (Charles 2007, 2010, Allan and Charles 2014). Others have turned their gaze both upward and outward, undertaking multinational, multi-sited ethnographic studies of elite schools and globalisation (Kenway and Fahey 2014). Again, Bourdieu features prominently as a theorist of social class, as do poststructuralist theorists when attending to gender and subjectivity.

These research orientations each share an indebtedness to historians of education whose work traces how present day systemic, institutional and popular constructs of elite schooling articulate with earlier educational configurations. This work provides a strong foundation for understanding how elite schooling traditions have developed into their current forms (see for example Campbell and Sherington 2006, Campbell *et al.* 2009, Campbell and Proctor 2014). As suggested earlier, Australian discourses of 'elite' education rest on presumptions of Englishness that derive from the earliest days of the colony and endure within the 'colonial present' of Australian cultural politics (Gulson and Parkes 2009). Thus my discussion of research approaches is framed by an understanding that the representational practices through which schools come to be known as elite are deeply imbricated in the history and cultural politics of the nation.

The desirability and elite status of Anglocentric discourse within particular schools is understood within 'histories and geographies of choice in different places' (Gulson and Webb 2012, p. 697). The persistent reproduction of aspects of the English public schools and their emphases on discipline, personal cultivation and age-based hierarchies of entitlement, in Australia signifies traditional values associated with 'quality' schooling. As social semioticians and discourse analysts have shown, elite independent schools accrue status in the Australian market through the use of signifiers that gesture towards an English imperial history and tradition that occupies a rarified space within Australia's 'public habitat of images' (Rose 1999, p. 86).

The status of elite schooling is continually reiterated through linguistic and visual rhetorics of exclusivity and social power. In church-affiliated schools, these rhetorics often draw on religious writings, ecclesiastical language and visual iconography, underscoring claims of educational quality and moral ascendancy (Saltmarsh 2005, 2007). The pervasiveness of these rhetorics in school histories and promotional materials is a significant means by which symbolic power is both implied and conferred in the form of 'consecrated' entitlement (Bourdieu 1996). The allure of entitlement accounts in no small part, I would suggest, for the seemingly unshakeable appeal of elite independent schools to Australian consumers, and for the enduring way in which these schools – unlike elite schools in the other sectors – have come to define elite schooling in Australia. Here, in one of the world's most culturally diverse nations, the purchase of such schooling functions as a means of symbolically acquiring whiteness with which 'Englishness' is tacitly associated (Saltmarsh 2005, 2007). In Australia, to be 'ruling class' by virtue of elite education and social status, has typically implied being interpellated as already 'English', already 'white', already 'superior', hence called to enter the field of power.

Drawing on feminist poststructuralist theories, for example, scholars interested in impression management practices have argued that the portrayal of masculinities and femininities in school promotions is an important means by which the social class location of elite schools is articulated through normative gender discourse. Depictions of masculinity in elite school prospectuses draw on market rhetorics that privilege 'the association of elite masculinity with notions of individual success, competition and prowess – "hard men" superimposed on the social world they inhabit' (Gottschall et al. 2010, p. 28). By comparison, discourses of appropriate and desirable femininities are reiterated through tropes of nature in elite girls' school promotions. These tropes construct notions of the feminine middle-class subject as simultaneously 'at risk' and vulnerable to 'outside influences', while also empowered through discourses of 'social and moral interconnectedness as "naturally" feminine' (Wardman et al. 2013, p. 293).

Others have analysed school promotions that take up discourses of 'altruism, inclusivity, equity and highmindedness' (Windle and Stratton 2013, p. 211) as a commodified form of benevolent bodily dispositions. Claims to equity have an exchange value in the education marketplace, constructing 'a moral quality attached to individuals and schools through the promotion of ethical commitments that are compatible with socially exclusive enrolments' (ibid., p. 211). Organisational rhetorics have 'significant currency in the context of the contemporary cultural politics of education' (McDonald et al. 2012, p. 2), and have 'helped to reify choice in the market lexicon in education in Australia and elsewhere' (ibid., p. 16). Through such analyses, studies of representational practices contribute to understandings of the ways in which elite education's discursive truth claims come into being and function in the perpetuation of systemic raced, gendered and social class inequalities (Wardman et al. 2010, 2013, Gottschall et al. 2010, McDonald et al. 2012, Windle and Stratton 2013).

The second research orientation that informs the Australian research, introduced above, is concerned with the processes that perpetuate social class inequality. Connell's landmark work in the 1970s, for example, argued that Australia's stratified system of schooling, in which high-status private schools catered for a distinctive minority drawn from an 'occupational and economic elite' (1977, p. 158) contributed to significant, wide-ranging social inequality. Although it is no longer the case that only a small minority of students is served by high fee-paying independent sector schools (ABS 2010, 2013), educational sociologists have continued to identify mechanisms by which social stratification is entrenched through elite education.

For example, the drift of middle-class families away from public education is cited as an example of the ways that 'socio-educational advantage (SEA) and disadvantage are compounded' (Kenway 2013, p. 286) under the intensification of market-based ideologies.

Sociological explanations for these disparities informed by the work of Pierre Bourdieu (Bourdieu 1996, Bourdieu and Passeron 1977/2000) point to concerns about the ways that elite schooling not only contributes to structural inequalities, but does so through appeals to the anxieties and desires of middle-class parents. Elite education is seen as cultivating the 'habitus of advantage' (Koh and Kenway 2012, p. 334), offering educational consumers ongoing opportunities for the accrual of social, cultural and financial capital (Ball and Vincent 2001, Vincent and Martin 2002, Ball 2003).

Qualitative research approaches, the third research orientation identified in this chapter, build on and extend understandings of the production of elite social subjects. Recent Australian studies have drawn on a range of theoretical perspectives to explore how subjectivities are discursively and performatively produced in the context of elite school settings (Hatchell 2004, Charles 2007, 2010, O'Flynn and Petersen 2007, Allan and Charles 2014). This body of work draws on ethnographic and discourse analytic methodologies and poststructuralist theories of subjectivity, and is interested in the place of schooling as a context within which particular kinds of subject positions are made available, promoted and rendered possible (O'Flynn and Petersen 2007).

In several studies, gendered middle-class performativities are shown to be profoundly shaped by the experience of attending an elite school, as accounted for through personal biographies, family and school contexts (Maxwell and Aggleton 2014). For some, neoliberal discourse in elite schools establishes and reiterates selfhood as a kind of project to be actively up-skilled, developed and subsequently produced by the enterprising 'self as port-folio' (O'Flynn and Petersen 2007, p. 468). These discourses invite elite school students to actively engage in ongoing processes of accomplishment situated within the gendered and classed norms that are valued and promoted both at home and in school (Maxwell and Aggleton 2013, Allan and Charles 2014).

Recent ethnographies of elite girls' schools have been interested in understanding inconsistencies within discursive formations around gender and social class (Allen and Charles 2014). Inconsistencies abound in a rapidly changing, mediatised global world, and schools must find ways of balancing a traditionally conservative ethos with emerging consumer expectations in order to maintain their market relevance. Thus, despite the entrenchment of individualism and competition, there is an expectation that elite schools will provide opportunities for service and community activities necessary for producing 'well-rounded' students (Allan and Charles 2014). Thus, alongside idealised versions of the passive feminine schoolgirl subject so frequently depicted in school promotional materials (Wardman *et al.* 2010, 2013), there are expectations that elite schools will produce confident, determined girls who are empowered to achieve and take responsibility for themselves and their futures (Forbes and Lingard 2013).

In current neoliberal conditions, 'middle-classness is produced through education practices, particularly concerning the ability to be a mobile, entrepreneurial and cosmopolitan subject' (Allan and Charles 2014, p. 335). These issues have also been explored through a multi-sited multinational ethnography led by Jane Kenway and colleagues interested in the ways that elite schools around the world respond to globalization in their preparation of future leaders (Koh and Kenway 2012, Kenway and Koh 2013, Epstein 2014, Kenway and Fahey 2014, McCarthy et al. 2014, Rizvi 2014). Bourdieu's work provides a theoretical framework for much of their analyses, which are focused on the historical, contextual and institutional specificities that are involved in the formation of global elites. These studies explore how elite schools foster and maintain their own particular cultures embedded in time and place.

Final thoughts

There are a number of important contemporary motivators for research on elite education. To date, research has largely focused on elite schooling's role in reproducing social inequality, and on the ways in which subjectivities are produced within elite institutions. My initial interest in such questions emerged in the form of a doctoral study concerned with high-profile incidents of sexual violence that occurred in the boarding house of one of Sydney's most prestigious boys' schools (Saltmarsh 2005). At the time, very few Australian studies had focused explicitly on elite schools, and fewer yet on violence in such settings. What emerged from that work was a critique of the ways that the elitist, hierarchical and imperialist traditions that have typified elite schooling in Australia coalesce with market ideologies of choice and competition. In so doing, I argued, they produce symbolic, systemic and embodied forms of violence that all too often remain absent from the gaze of researchers and the general public.

The research discussed here contributes much to foundational literature focused on elite schooling's role in the production and perpetuation of social class dissymmetries in Anglophone nations such as Australia. However, its general inattention to elite forms of schooling beyond the independent sector seems to gesture towards another kind of blind-spot, in which wealthy Anglocentric schools built on imperialist traditions tend to dominate the ways in which elite schooling has come to be defined in both popular and scholarly contexts. Yet elite schooling in both public and non-government sectors offers a provocation to examine more closely how choice, competition and selectivity across and within all sectors might feature in producing new and evolving forms of elitism. More needs to be known about how processes of social stratification, marginalisation and exclusion operate in all elite schools, as well as the theoretical and methodological implications of researching these various contexts.

References

Allan, A. and Charles, C. (2014). Cosmo girls: Configurations of class and femininity in elite educational settings. *British Journal of Sociology of Education*, 35(3), 333–352.

Angus, L. (2013). School choice: Neoliberal education policy and imagined futures. *British Journal of Sociology of Education*, 36(3), 395–413.

Australian Bureau of Statistics (2010). *Schools, Australia 2010*, Report 4221.0. Belconnen, ACT: Commonwealth of Australia.
Australian Bureau of Statistics (2011). *Private school numbers continue to grow*. Belconnen, ACT: Commonwealth of Australia. Available at http://www.abs.gov.au/ausstats/abs@.nsf/mediareleasesbytopic/EE9BB88C2B9B9738CA2579C700118E7E?OpenDocument (accessed 2 June 2015).
Australian Bureau of Statistics (2013). *Schools, Australia 2013*, Report 4221.0. Belconnen, ACT: Commonwealth of Australia.
Australian Government. (2012). *Australia in the Asian Century White Paper*. Canberra, ACT: Commonwealth of Australia.
Australian Government. (2013). *Australia – educating globally: Advice from the International Education Advisory Council*, Canberra, ACT: Commonwealth of Australia. Available at https://internationaleducation.gov.au/International-network/Australia/InternationalStrategy/theCouncilsReport/Documents/Australia%20%E2%80%93%20Educating%20Globally%20FINAL%20REPORT.pdf (accessed 5 June 2015).
Ball, S. (2003). *Class strategies and the education market: The middle classes and social advantage*. London & New York: RoutledgeFalmer.
Ball, S. and Vincent, C. (2001). New class relations in education: The strategies of the 'fearful' middle classes. In J. Demaine (Ed.), *Education sociology today*. London, Palgrave.
Bourdieu, P. (1996). *The state nobility: Elite schools in the field of power*. Cambridge: Polity Press.
Bourdieu, P. and Passeron, J. (1977/2000). *Reproduction in education, society and culture*. London: Sage.
Campbell, C. and Sherington, G. (2006). *The comprehensive public high school: Historical perspectives*. New York: Palgrave.
Campbell, C. and Proctor, H. (2014). *A history of Australian schooling*. Crows Nest, NSW, Allen & Unwin.
Campbell, C., Proctor, H. and Sherington, G. (2009). *School choice: How parents negotiate the new school market in Australia*. Crows Nest, NSW: Allen & Unwin.
Charles, C. (2007). Digital media and 'girling' at an elite girls' school. *Learning, Media and Technology*, 32(2), 135–147.
Charles, C. (2010). Complicating hetero-femininities: Young women, sexualities and girl power at school. *International Journal of Qualitative Studies in Education*, 23(1), 33–47.
Connell, R. (1977). *Ruling class, ruling culture: Studies of conflict, power and hegemony in Australian life*. Cambridge: Cambridge University Press.
Connell, R.W. (2003). Working-class families and the new secondary education. *Australian Journal of Education*, 47(3), 235–250.
Cookson, P. and Persell, C. (2010). Preparing for power: Twenty-five years later. In A. Howard and R. Gaztambide-Fernández (Eds.), *Educating elites: Class privilege and educational advantage* (pp. 13–30). Lanham, MD: Rowman & Littlefield.
Epstein, D. (2014). Race-ing class ladies: Lineages of privilege in an elite South African school. *Globalisation, Societies and Education*, 12(2), 244–261.
Forbes, J. and Lingard, B. (2013). Elite school capitals and girls' schooling: Understanding the (re)production of privilege through a habitus of 'assuredness'. In C. Maxwell and P. Aggleton (Eds.), *Privilege, agency and affect* (pp. 50–68). Basingstoke: Palgrave Macmillan.
Fort Street High School. (2014). *Welcome to Fort Street High School*. Available at http://www.fortstreet.nsw.edu.au/ (accessed 2 June 2015).
Gaztambide-Fernández, R. (2009). What is an elite boarding school? *Review of Educational Research*, 79(3), 1090–1128.
Gottschall, K., Edgeworth, K., Hutchesson, R., Wardman, N. and Saltmarsh, S. (2010). Hard lines and soft scenes: Constituting masculinities in the prospectuses of all-boys elite private schools. *Australian Journal of Education*, 54(1), 18–30.
Gulson, K. and Parkes, R. (2009). In the shadows of the mission: Education policy, urban space, and the 'colonial present' in Sydney. *Race Ethnicity and Education*, 12(3), 267–280.

Gulson, K. and Webb, P.T. (2012). Education policy racialisations: Afrocentric schools, Islamic schools, and the new enunciations of equity. *Journal of Education Policy*, 27(6), 697–709.

Hatchell, H. (2004). Privilege of whiteness: Adolescent male students' resistance to racism in an Australian classroom. *Race Ethnicity and Education*, 7(2), 99–114.

Ho, C. (2011). 'My School' and others: Segregation and white flight. *Australian Review of Public Affairs: Digest*. Available at http://www.australianreview.net/digest/2011/05/ho.html (accessed 2 June 2015).

Howard, A. and Gaztambide-Fernández, R. (Eds.). (2010). *Educating elites: Class privilege and educational advantage*. Lanham, MD: Rowman & Littlefield.

Kenway, J. (2013). Challenging inequality in Australian schools: Gonski and beyond. *Discourse: Studies in the Cultural Politics of Education*, 34(2), 286–308.

Kenway, J. and Koh, A. (2013). The elite school as 'cognitive machine' and 'social paradise': Developing transnational capitals for the national 'field of power'. *Journal of Sociology*, 20(10), 1–19.

Kenway, J. and Fahey, J. (2014). Staying ahead of the game: The globalising practices of elite schools. *Globalisation, Societies and Education*, 12(2), 177–195.

Kenway, J., Fahey, J. and Koh, A. (2013). The libidinal economy of the globalising elite school market. In C. Maxwell and P. Aggleton (Eds.), *Privilege, agency and affect: Understanding the production and effects of action* (pp. 15–31). Basingstoke: Palgrave Macmillan.

Koh, A. and Kenway, J. (2012). Cultivating national leaders in an elite school: Deploying the transnational in the national interest. *International Studies in Sociology of Education*, 22(4), 333–351.

McCarthy, C., Bulut, E., Castro, M., Goel, K. and Greenhalgh-Spencer, H. (2014). The Argonauts of postcolonial modernity: Elite Barbadian schools in globalising circumstances. *Globalisation, Societies and Education*, 12(2), 211–227.

McDonald, P., Pini, B. and Mayes, R. (2012). Organizational rhetoric in the prospectuses of elite private schools: Unpacking strategies of persuasion. *British Journal of Sociology of Education*, 33(1), 1–20.

Marginson, S. (1997). *Educating Australia: Government, economy and citizen since 1960*. Cambridge: Cambridge University Press.

Maxwell, C. and Aggleton, P. (2013). Becoming accomplished: Concerted cultivation among privately educated young women. *Pedagogy, Culture and Society*, 21(1), 75–93.

Maxwell, C. and Aggleton, P. (2014). The reproduction of privilege: Young women, the family and private education. *International Studies in Sociology of Education*, 24(2), 189–209.

Millburn, C. (2011). Fears over 'white flight' from selective schools, *Sydney Morning Herald*, 17 October. Available at http://www.smh.com.au/national/education/fears-over-white-flight-from-selective-schools-20111016-1lro2.html (accessed 5 June 2015).

O'Flynn, G. and Petersen, E. (2007). The 'good life' and the 'rich portfolio': Young women, schooling and neoliberal subjectification. *British Journal of Sociology of Education*, 28(4), 459–472.

Proctor, H. (2011). Masculinity and social class, tradition and change: The production of 'young Christian gentlemen' at an elite Australian boys' school. *Gender and Education*, 23(7), 843–856.

Rizvi, F. (2014). Old elite schools, history and the construction of a new imaginary. *Globalisation, Societies and Education*, 12(2), 290–308.

Rose, N. (1999). *Powers of freedom: Reframing political thought*. Cambridge: Cambridge University Press.

Rowe, E. and Windle, J. (2012). The Australian middle class and education: A small-scale study of the school choice experience as framed by 'My School' within inner city families. *Critical Studies in Education*, 53(2), 137–151.

Saltmarsh, S. (2005). *Complicit institutions: Representation, consumption and the production of school violence*. PhD diss., Macquarie University, NSW.

Saltmarsh, S. (2007). Cultural complicities: Elitism, heteronormativity and violence in the education marketplace. *International Journal of Qualitative Studies in Education*, 20(3), 335–354.

Saltmarsh, S. (2008). Disruptive events: Elite education and the discursive production of violence. *Critical Studies in Education*, 49(2), 113–125.

Symes, C. and Meadmore, D. (1996). Force of habit: The school uniform as a body of knowledge. In E. McWilliam and P. Taylor (Eds.), *Pedagogy, technology, and the body*. New York: Peter Lang.

Symes, C. and Preston, N. (1997). *Schools and classrooms: A cultural studies analysis of education, second edition*. Melbourne: Longman.

Symes, C. and Meadmore, D. (Eds.) (1999). *The extra-ordinary school: Parergonality and pedagogy*. New York: Peter Lang.

Synott, J. and Symes, C. (1995). The genealogy of the school: An iconography of badges and mottoes. *British Journal of Sociology of Education*, 16(2), 139–152.

United Nations Educational, Cultural and Scientific Organisation (UNESCO) (2009). *Investing in cultural diversity and intercultural dialogue*. Paris: UNESCO.

Vincent, C. and Martin, J. (2002). Class, culture and agency: Researching parental voice. *Discourse: Studies in the Cultural Politics of Education*, 23(1), 108–127.

Wade, M. and Khaicy, G. (2013). Catholics mark Liberals' turnaround (September 21), *Sydney Morning Herald*. Available at http://www.smh.com.au/federal-politics/political-news/catholics-mark-liberals-turnaround-20130920-2u5hf.html (accessed 2 June 2015).

Wardman, N., Hutchesson, R., Gottschall, K., Drew, C. and Saltmarsh, S. (2010). Starry eyes and subservient selves: Portraits of 'well-rounded' girlhood in the prospectuses of all-girl elite private schools. *Australian Journal of Education*, 54(3), 249–261.

Wardman, N., Gottschall, K., Drew, C., Hutchisson, R. and Saltmarsh, S. (2013). Picturing natural girlhoods: Nature, space and femininity in girls' school promotions. *Gender and Education*, 25(3), 284–294.

Weis, L. and Cipollone, K. (2013). 'Class work': Producing privilege and social mobility in elite US secondary schools. *British Journal of Sociology of Education*, 34(5–6), 701–722.

Windle, J. (2009). The limits of school choice: Some implications for accountability of selective practices and positional competition in Australian education. *Critical Studies in Education*, 50(3), 231–246.

Windle, J. and Stratton, G. (2013). Equity for sale: Ethical consumption in a school-choice regime. *Discourse: Studies in the Cultural Politics of Education*, 34(2), 202–213.

4

'PRIVATE SCHOOLS IN THE PUBLIC SYSTEM'

School choice and the production of elite status in the USA and Canada

*Rubén Gaztambide-Fernández
and Julie Garlen Maudlin*

In 2013, the conservative education scholar Chester Finn noted the decline of private education in the USA. Finn's assertion is supported by the most recent data from the US National Center for Education Statistics (NCES), which reports that private school enrolment in pre-kindergarten to grade 12 decreased by one million students between 2002 and 2012, with the percentage of all students enrolled in private school decreasing by three points (Kena *et al.* 2014). Yet, Finn (2013) points out, '*elite* private institutions are doing just fine, many besieged by more applicants than ever before. The wealthiest Americans can easily afford them and are ever more determined to secure for their children the advantages that come with attending them' (para. 8, emphasis in original).

The fact that highly selective private schools continue to thrive, in conjunction with the gradual decline of enrolment in low-selectivity, lower status private institutions and the reluctance of those schools to admit to declining student numbers, says Finn, serves to mask the endangered status of private education in the USA. Finn points to the contrasting increases in numbers attending charter schools as a particularly telling trend. Charter schools are publicly funded schools that are exempt from certain state and/or local regulations and governed by the accountability standards stated in their charters. These schools represent the greatest increase in public school enrolments over the past decade. Between 2000 and 2012, the number of students enrolled in US public charter schools rose from 0.3 million to 2.1 million, with the percentage of public school students attending charter schools increasing from 0.7 to 4.2 per cent (Kena *et al.* 2014). Finn suggests that this trend might signal the inevitable demise of traditional private education, which 'becomes unaffordable, unnecessary, or both,... as more viable options for students and families present themselves' (para. 4).

The increase in the number of students attending charter schools is the result of a trend, with similar patterns across the USA and Canada, in favour of school choice policies that seek to give parents more control over their children's education by supporting a greater variety of school types and allowing students to attend schools outside their demarcated school zones. The last decade has brought about a plethora of innovative school programmes intended to provide choices to families who might want a different kind of schooling experience from that provided in mainstream, comprehensive schools. These include magnet programmes, initially intended as a strategy for desegregating public schools in large cities by attracting white parents back into mostly black urban schools. More recently, these schemes involve charter schools with special programmes, alternative schools in Canada and other within-school educational programmes, such as the International Baccalaureate. Such programmes have become a 'viable' educational alternative to minimally selective or open admission private schools, which as Finn argues have become an expensive and not very cost-effective way to achieve elite status.

While the proportion of students enrolled in private schools in Canada is only half of that in the USA, holding steady at around 5 per cent, a marked increase in the number of (small and mostly religious) private schools in urban areas such as Toronto has been accompanied by an increase in options and choice schemes in public schools. These emerging policies, along with a nationwide decline in the number of school-aged children could potentially pose, for Canadian independent schools, the same challenge that US private institutions seem to be facing.

This raises the question of the extent to which publicly funded educational alternatives are increasingly meeting the needs previously catered to by private schools. This, in itself, would not be a new phenomenon. The expansion of public school systems in both countries after 1850 brought with it significant if somewhat contradictory changes to the independently operated and locally supported chartered academies that provided schooling opportunities during the seventeenth and eighteenth centuries. These academies were part of a widespread movement that reached beyond growing urban regions to many towns, and included schools that served freed slaves, women and Indigenous communities (Beadie and Tolley 2002). Many of the early private academies, however, catered primarily to the children of newly established merchants and landowners and the few that survive today are considered to be among the most elite (and wealthy) private independent schools. Most of these academies were modelled after the British public schools, imitating their pastoral landscapes and neoclassical architecture, merging a curriculum driven by the 'classics' with a more pragmatically oriented vocational education that deliberately sought to produce a national elite through their links to elite universities. Yet, their 'elite' status and their role in the production of an elite upper class did not fully emerge until well into the nineteenth and through the early parts of the twentieth century, when their contemporary character and social role as elite private schools was crystallised (Gaztambide-Fernández 2009a).

After 1850, the number of independent chartered academies drastically decreased, as publicly funded schools began to serve the purpose of educating a growing population. Yet, the most elite of these schools, which were primarily boarding schools in the USA and day schools in wealthy cities in both the USA and Canada, grew in size and many went through significant transformations in terms of curriculum as well as their base of prospective families. This was driven by the emergence of new elites, as new markets developed following the industrial revolution. Levine (1980) has argued, in fact, that the survival and transformation of what today are considered the most elite private schools was driven by the need to consolidate the social and cultural links between the old (and declining) industrial elite and the new (and rising) banking elite at the turn of the twentieth century.

To a large extent, private schools have continued to be considered the mainstay of elite schooling, providing educational alternatives for affluent families and building strong ties with elite universities, while remaining sheltered from mainstream educational policy and, to some extent, from the public pressures to become more equitable and accessible. Paradoxically, as the economic gap between the most affluent sectors of US and Canadian society continues to widen, the demands for the most selective (and most expensive) private schools continues to grow and elite private schools are experiencing record numbers of applications, while also continuing to grow their endowments. As both the competition for and the cost of an elite private education continue to grow, private schools that cannot claim such elite status appear to have become less attractive, and parents who previously sought out an alternative to mainstream public education in the private sector, now seem to have turned (back) to public schools to provide more affordable, while no less exclusive, educational programmes. Thus, as it relates to questions of elite schooling, the proliferation of choice schemes within public school systems raises the question of how these alternatives are implicated in continued economic stratification through practices and policies that benefit those who already enjoy economic privileges while effectively limiting options for most students through patterns of exclusion. Since private schools have historically reinscribed certain privileges by providing educational and professional opportunities to students who are already at a significant advantage over their public school peers, could it be that school choice alternatives are functioning in a similar way within the public system?

In her recent study of school choice options in Vancouver, British Columbia, Ee-Seul Yoon (2013) found that prospective parents at one of the highest performing public schools considered it a 'private school in the public system' (p. 91). This phrase was also echoed across specialised arts programmes in urban public schools in Canadian cities (see Gaztambide Fernández 2010), which have been documented to serve students who enjoy economic and other social class privileges (Parekh 2013). These patterns suggest that a comprehensive understanding of elite schooling requires attention to how certain sectors of the population mobilise economic, social and cultural resources to secure access to high-status educational opportunities within public schools. This is particularly important if we are to understand whether and how these 'private schools in the public system' are, in effect, undermining or promoting equitable opportunities and outcomes for students in the USA and Canada.

To that end, this chapter examines the development of school choice initiatives in both nations and explores the processes of elite education as they relate to what we term the 'publification' of elite schooling, through which the production of eliteness is expanded beyond the traditional context of private education to include elite public school programmes. Drawing on examples of both specialised arts programmes in Canada and high-performing urban charter schools in the USA, we examine new patterns of exclusion operating through the discourse of choice that make inequality much less visible and actively misrecognise privilege and social advantage. Finally, we consider what these elite public school programmes reveal about elite schooling more broadly.

School choice in the USA and Canada

Neoliberal reforms, which have taken hold in both the USA and Canada over the last two decades, have emphasised, among other things, the expansion of education markets and promoted local control of school districts, corporate-sponsored takeovers of failing schools and increased educational choices, including privately run but publicly funded charter schools. Mobilising a market-oriented approach to education that seeks to 'sell' school alternatives to educational consumers, these neoliberal regimes have also perpetuated discourses of 'talent', 'interests' and 'passions' (Gaztambide-Fernández et al. 2013) to mask initiatives that have ultimately increased segregation within education.

In the USA, talent and interest-based discourses of choice became especially prominent in the 1970s and 1980s, when many systems implemented magnet schools in an attempt to promote racial integration and attract or retain white, middle-class students (Fleming 2012). Magnet schools usually feature a special theme or content focus, but are typically governed by a local school district (Davis 2013). Such open enrolment options are now available in nearly half of all US school districts and serve approximately 15 per cent of the public school population (Davis 2013). In recent years, however, the initial integrative aims of magnet programmes have to some extent receded, as increased political and financial support has shifted toward charter schools (Siegel-Hawley and Frankenberg 2012). Charter schools, while serving a significantly smaller portion of the population, have shown continued growth since first emerging in the 1990s, with enrolment increasing each year. While most of these students are coming from traditional public schools, 'charter schools are pulling large numbers of students from the private education market' (Buddin and Cato Institute 2012, p. 1). Charter schools, while available in 41 US states and in the District of Columbia, are primarily an urban phenomenon.

While national school enrolment patterns are more difficult to establish in Canada due to a lack of oversight at the federal level and significant inconsistencies in how provincial governments and local school boards collect and disseminate data, there is evidence that Canada has seen similar trends in the growth of public school options. Davies and Aurini (2011) surveyed a large sample of Canadian parents to determine how many engage in school choice and for what reasons. Based on their findings, Davies and Aurini (2011) estimated that 32 per cent of Canadian families chose a school other than a standard public school, but this figure included publicly funded religious schools, with the specialised public school programmes only accounting for a very small figure (less than 1 per cent). Davies and Aurini concluded that most Canadian parents are already engaging in some form of school choice, including residential selection and use of performance indicators. Research in Vancouver and Toronto, two of the largest and most diverse Canadian cities, suggests that school choice schemes and alternative school programmes within public schools appear to be playing a significant role in furthering unequal access to educational resources by providing high-status educational opportunities premised on exclusion (Gaztambide-Fernández et al. 2013, Parekh 2013, Yoon 2013).

Specialised arts programmes provide a special case for examining the development of Canadian school choice options that share similar features with US magnet and charter schools. These programmes first emerged in Canada in the 1960s within vocational schools, where the visual arts were emphasised in technical training on design and illustration (Gaztambide-Fernández 2010). Fine arts programmes modelled on US magnet schools began to appear in the 1980s (Graham 1983). However, in contrast to the original integrative mission of US magnet schools, these programmes were established primarily to address the needs of talented students, for whom such options might provide new opportunities and possible futures (Graham 1983, Gaztambide-Fernández et al. 2014). Specialised arts programmes in Canada seem to share many characteristics of contemporary magnet schools in the USA, including the recruitment of students outside their home catchment or school district as well as the use of various admissions procedures, including testing and interviews/auditions for selecting students.

Elite status and the 'publification' of elite schooling

Shifting attention to the role of public schools in providing elite education opportunities requires us to be more specific about what precisely we mean by 'elite' educational programmes. The term elite always operates as a classificatory term, even when used as a noun (i.e. 'the elite'), which typically implies an answer to the question: the elite what? As an adjective, the term elite functions as a marker of superior distinction (e.g. an elite athlete, an elite military unit, an elite bank robber, etc.). The term comes from the Latin *eligere*, the same root as the word 'elect', suggesting that the elite are 'the chosen', as Karabel (2005) suggests in his historical study of admissions policies at Yale, Princeton and Harvard. To be elite means to be chosen, not just by anyone or any place, but by other equally chosen – or equally elite groups, institutions, or organisations with the power and high status to confer such status and enforce such choices.

Studies of the production of elite status have focused on the role of highly selective private schools in the formation of the power elite (Cookson and Persell 2008; Gaztambide-Fernández 2009b; Maxwell and Aggleton 2013). Studies of elite schools tend to draw upon theories of social and cultural reproduction, such as the work of Bourdieu and Passeron (1977), to explain the relationship between education, families and the transference of social class position, which perpetuates inequality and exclusion. In Bourdieu's thesis, cultural and social capital, including the skills, tastes, language, mannerisms and credentials particular to a social class, along with economic resources, are essential to the reproduction of inequality, which is clear in the ways in which elite private schools control access through admission policies and tuition prices that reflect economic and educational inequalities. However, this focus on the relationship between economic resources and elite status suggests a conflation between elite and private and an assumption that the terms are equivalent. This conflation is problematic because not all private schools are elite and not all elite schools are private.

The limited, linear process of generational transference of social status implied by social reproduction theory fails to account for the experience of students who do not come from upper-class backgrounds but achieve elite status nonetheless. It also suggests that attendance at these schools guarantees not only cultural but also some form of financial capital, yet the production of elite status is a more complex process. While social class is technically defined exclusively by economic resources, elite status groups are more specifically defined by high-status knowledge and cultural modes that are connected to various kinds of privilege, not just economic, but also connected to categories of gender and race in important ways (Gaztambide-Fernández 2009b).

Understood in this way, elite status can be achieved by what a group does, what its members own and by the kinds of social markers of distinction they have accumulated and the relative significance of the status symbols they are able to mobilise. This is important for elite educational programmes, including elite private schools and elite programmes in public schools, because it means that elite status depends on institutional arrangements and unequal access to resources, but also specific discursive arrangements, symbolic practices and, much more subtle but equally important, the production of particular affects, such as what Gaztambide-Fernández et al. (2013) describe as 'the sense of entitlement'. Elite status, in other words, is not a given, but an accomplishment; it must be actively produced. That is, eliteness is not a *fait accomplit* – it is a process that must be achieved.

A conceptualisation of eliteness as a process not exclusively dependent upon economic resources is particularly important for understanding the production of elite status in public schools because most, although not all of these schools, by virtue of being public, reflect a higher level of economic diversity than do private institutions. Interestingly, Petrilli and Scull (2010) found that 'private public schools', which they define as schools that serve virtually no students from low-income and working-class families, are attended by more children than charter schools. In some major metropolitan areas, such schools are ubiquitous, indicating a high degree of socioeconomic segregation, as these schools are almost exclusively found in wealthy urban or suburban enclaves with clearly defined geographic borders. By contrast, charter schools in the USA and specialised arts schools in Canada, typically draw students from a wider area that extends beyond residential schools zones, thus – at least in principle – attracting a more diverse student population. This apparent socioeconomic diversity is important to the specific ways that elite status is produced in public schools of choice because that diversity promotes the idea that individual effort, rather than legacy or wealth, is a means of achieving social and economic success. This discourse operates to disguise the ways in which students at these schools are socialised into elite status. Furthermore, racial diversity, as we will later demonstrate, does not guarantee socioeconomic integration, and in fact the 'recruitment' of poor and minority students by selective schools can even operate to downplay systemic socioeconomic inequalities by perpetuating the myth that elite social status is achieved through individual effort.

The prevalence of such private public schools in the USA can be called a kind of 'publification' or public sponsoring of elite schooling. This process of publification involves institutional arrangements, discursive repertoires, affective distinctions and the enforcement of boundaries to actively produce elite status. To understand how publification is operating to produce elite status within public schools today it is crucial to make a distinction between schools in general and specific educational programmes, some of which are occasionally located within schools that may or may not have achieved elite status. Moreover, one way in which publification operates to produce inequality through discursive repertoires is via the 'common sense' idea that we all have the same choices available and could presumably choose high-status educational programmes for our children if we so desired. What such arguments ignore, of course, are the structural inequalities that shape whether and how one not only comes to pursue certain passions or talents, but also how one comes to identify something as a passion or a talent (Gaztambide-Fernández et al. 2013). The pervasive individualism premised in how choices are imagined under neoliberalism make invisible how choices are already a manifestation of structuration (Ball et al. 1996, Cookson 1995). Inequality is also produced through other implicit mechanisms of publification, such as the ostensibly unintentional exclusion of disadvantaged students from having access to certain kinds of choices within public schools. Lauen (2007) notes that school choice research has consistently found that disadvantaged students are less likely to exercise school choice. What this suggests is that, despite the rhetoric of choice as the great equaliser, structural forces play a significant role in determining who is able to access certain kinds of choices.

Public school 'choices' and the five Es of elite education

Shifting analyses of elite education from private to public schools requires a framework for understanding the production of elite status which does not imply that elite institutions simply confer status in some straightforward manner, like a credential or a degree. Rather, elite status requires the staging of a complex process that does not simply assign eliteness as a status category, but that involves the constitution of particular subjectivities. That is, the formation of elite subjects requires processes of identification that are imbricated within broader dynamics of exclusion in which race and gender intersect in complex ways with economic resources, yielding a highly stratified and hierarchical structure of 'unequal distinctions' (Gaztambide-Fernández 2009b).

For Gaztambide-Fernández (2009b), the production of elite status requires five interrelated and co-producing processes – 'the five Es' of elite education: exclusion, engagement, excellence, entitlement and envisioning. Because elite status is, by definition, exclusive, opportunities to achieve it must be made scarce by delimiting who has access and who does not. Sometimes exclusion is institutionalised through admissions processes that may involve testing or other demonstrations of deservedness, and at other times it operates in subtle ways, by making demands of participants that are unachievable due to barriers like language, lack of transportation, or even basic lack of information. Elite educational programmes must also have a bounded definition of what it is that makes them elite and that sets the terms of engagement for those who are able to achieve inclusion. While sometimes the terms of engagement can be general, such as academic excellence, most of the time elite educational programmes have some way of narrowing their area of expertise, such as mathematics and science or the arts in the case of some magnet schools (Finn and Hockett 2012). Students are then expected to demonstrate excellence in order to affirm belonging, which they do always under the threat of potential exclusion when high standards are not met. As such, exclusion is not just a stage in the process, but it is a perpetual part of the production of elite status that must be avoided at all costs. Constantly demonstrating excellence through engagement under the ever-present threat of exclusion is key for the production of a sense of entitlement that becomes integrated into the affective structures of those involved. This sense of entitlement is then projected into the future through the ability to envision elite futures, a process that began even as students started to consider joining elite programmes, which required them to have the ability to see themselves in whatever ways such programmes described their students.

Based on these five Es, we propose an operational definition of elite educational programmes as institutional schemes that are premised on some form of *exclusionary* mechanism based on discursively relevant criteria, that provide access to educational *engagement* with opportunities deemed important by certain high-status groups or audiences, and through which those chosen are to demonstrate *excellence* and deservedness, which in turn produces the necessary sense of *entitlement* to opportunities and to *envisioning* particular kinds of futures also deemed desirable within dominant orientations to and conceptions of economic and social success. We argue that we do not really advance our understanding of elite education if we try to define a priori which schools are elite, but rather we need to look at the specificity of how elite status is produced and transferred through social and cultural mechanisms – processes that may vary not only by nation, but also by social groups competing for particular forms of status.

Not all public school choice programmes are elite, of course, yet the ones that have achieved relative high status and are chosen by parents who would otherwise choose private schools reveal interesting aspects about the specificity of how elite status is produced within them. To illustrate this, we focus on two examples, the first of which is drawn from a larger study of public school specialised arts programmes in Canada and the USA (Gaztambide-Fernández 2010). The Toronto

School for Creative and Performing Arts, or CAPA (a pseudonym), is widely considered an 'elite' performing arts school within the district. In Toronto, a recent analysis of the demographic characteristics of schools reveals that specialised arts programmes in general – whether as whole schools or programmes within schools, are largely serving students who already enjoy high levels of economic, social and cultural capital (Parekh 2013). Of course, when students and teachers at CAPA are faced with this reality, the response is quite simple; the students did not choose the school because they are affluent, but because they are artistic, and they were not chosen because they were wealthy, but because they have talent. Yet a close examination of the process of *exclusion* through the fairly elaborate admissions process, as well as the ways in which exclusion through admissions processes is justified, reveals strong patterns of inequality being produced through institutional practices based on discourses of talent, passion and commitment. These discourses have the effect of masking privilege in the production of elite status in order to justify inequalities that could otherwise be explained through social class differences (Gaztambide-Fernández et al. 2013). What is key in the case of CAPA – and likely true for other publicly funded choice programmes – is that exclusion is not operationalised directly through verifiable markers like grades or test scores or even money (since it is a public programme) – but through intangible and ephemeral notions like talent and, importantly, specific affects, like the proper demonstration of 'passion'.

The second case, the Gwinnett School of Mathematics, Science and Technology (GSMST), a public charter school in Lawrenceville, Georgia, USA, provides an example of the ways in which exclusionary mechanisms can operate even within a school featuring seemingly 'fair' admission processes. The school, which is located in the third most populous county in the state of Georgia and lies within the Atlanta metropolitan area, was ranked by the *US News and World Report* as the third best public high school in the nation. In Georgia, all charter schools are required by law to use a lottery process for admission if there are more applicants than slots available at the school. Because any student residing within the Gwinnett County Public School zone is eligible to register for the admission lottery, one might expect that the demographic make-up of the school would reflect that of the county as a whole. However, the disparities are startling. In 2014, the distribution of the school population included 40 per cent Asian, 23 per cent Black/African American, 22 per cent White, and 10 per cent Hispanic/Latino (Bray and Dees 2014). In addition, 34 per cent of the students were considered economically disadvantaged based on their eligibility for free or reduced cost lunch programmes. By contrast, countywide demographics were reported by the Governor's Office of Student Achievement (GOSA 2014) as 10 per cent Asian, 32 per cent Black/African American, 28 per cent White, 26 per cent Hispanic/Latino. The percentage of economically disadvantaged students in Gwinnett County is 59 per cent. Clearly, in spite of the 'random' admission process, the ethnic and socioeconomic make-up of the school fails to reflect countywide demographics.

Proponents of school choice might well justify the demographic disparity by pointing out that certain students may not be interested in the school's mathematics, science and technology focus, or perhaps do not feel academically prepared for the rigorous curriculum. Certainly, this could play a role in deterring disadvantaged students from exercising the option to apply, but considering that there are no performance-based admission standards, fear of failure or lack of interest seems like an oversimplification. It is clear that there are a number of important mechanisms in the lottery registration process that operate to exclude disadvantaged students. While admission is, in fact, open to all eighth grade students who reside within the Gwinnett County Public School (GCPS) zone, they must complete a multiple-step process to enter the lottery, including attendance at a parent meeting and completing a form online. A verification form must then be printed or filled out in person at an information meeting. Parents must therefore have a valid email address and at least one valid phone number in order for the registration to be processed. Thus, the 'open' registration process assumes levels of information, access, transportation and communication that may not be available to many Gwinnett County students, the majority of whom are economically disadvantaged.

Once admitted into these schools, the students *engage* with pedagogical and curricular opportunities that further define the programme as elite, and in the case of CAPA and other specialised arts programmes this manifests itself both in the academic and in the artistic training the students receive. In the case of elite boarding schools, what marks them as elite is not only the vast curricular offerings available, but the very particular pedagogical approaches that produce the dispositions required to be 'at ease' within contexts defined by privilege. At CAPA, this involves very traditional conceptions of music, dance training and visual arts (which reflect the dominant hierarchies of cultural goods, with Western European practices at the top).

At GSMST, students are expected to engage 'through a unique, challenging, and integrated curriculum with a focus on mathematics, science, and technology that will result in a world-class education' ('Lottery Application 2' 2013). Students are also expected to embrace a career-oriented mindset that is fostered through the school's active partnerships with business and industry. In fact, all students are expected to participate in at least two internships with external organisations, often private companies. However, in addition to the stated focus on career readiness, college admission is highly prioritised, as evidenced by the high levels of participation in Advanced Placement (AP) courses. In 2012–13, 70 per cent of GSMST students took one or more AP courses, compared to 31 per cent of all GCPS high school students (Bray and Dees 2014). GSMST also boasts scores on college entrance exams, including SAT and ACT, that are significantly higher than local, state and national averages.

Of course, to achieve elite status the students must not only *engage* with this curriculum, which involves locating oneself within a high-status curricular hierarchy, they must also demonstrate *excellence*, lest their status come into question. And here there is an important difference between private elite schools where, as Gaztambide-Fernández (2009b) argues, there are almost limitless opportunities to be excellent at something, and elite educational programmes in public schools. Within the latter, the need for specialisation and limited resources encroach on the range of possible ways to be 'excellent' available to students, which exacerbates the feelings of anxiety that shape the experience. At CAPA, ways to demonstrate excellence are narrowly prescribed by the European classical standards and mainstream practices within the dominant institutions of the arts. Students must demonstrate mastery within these prescribed practices, and it is through the image of successful ballet dancers, classical musicians, gallery shows and Broadway musicals that the school builds a public image as an elite performing arts high school.

Similarly, at GSMST, a discourse of excellence is embedded throughout the information the school provides to construct its public image. For example, parents are reminded on the online lottery application that it is the school's mission to 'nurture the talents and high potential' of its students and provide a curriculum that 'will result in a world-class education' ('Lottery Application 2' 2013). The 2013–14 *Accountability Report* also lists a wide range of accolades, including local, state and national honours that no doubt contribute toward a school environment where excellence is not only encouraged, but expected (Bray and Dees 2014).

The ability to enact excellence within the parameters defined by the institutions is central to the production of a specific kind of affective orientation; the sense of entitlement (Gaztambide-Fernández et al. 2013). This sense of entitlement can be understood as the feeling that one belongs somewhere, that one deserves something, a sentiment that is expressed through students' belief in their own agency and which is crucial for their ability to envision themselves succeeding in other elite spaces beyond their schooling experience. At CAPA, for instance, most students asserted their desire to attend private universities in the USA or the UK, and the school mobilised the high numbers who did leave Canada to pursue higher education in the USA as a way to make claims about elite status. Meanwhile, at GSMST, being in a school that has been recently ranked third nationally leads students to articulate visions for their futures that include statements, reported in a local media story, such as 'I'm ready for college on a whole (other) level. I don't think college is ready for me actually', by one student, who had already been accepted to and received scholarships from some of the top colleges in the US (WSB-TV 2013). Another student, in this same article, reported that she planned to pursue a double major in computer science and engineering, with a goal of obtaining a PhD in robotics. The required internships with local companies also serve an important role in allowing the students to construct imagined futures.

Elite status beyond private education

The emerging school choice initiatives in the USA and Canada pose many questions regarding the production of elite status beyond private education. The cases that we offer here are but two of many similar schools, all of which vary widely in their particular missions, demographics and geographic contexts. Each of the schools provides unique insights into the way that elite status is being produced by interrelated and co-producing processes through which the 'publification' of elite schooling is advanced and conceptions of eliteness are being expanded beyond the taken-for-granted context of private education to include elite public school programmes.

Rather than offering here a comprehensive analysis of 'private schools in public systems', in this chapter we have sought to highlight the ways in which exclusion operates through discourses of choice in ways that are less overt and perhaps more insidious than the exclusions that produce privilege and social advantage in highly visible elite private institutions. Of course, the intervention we offer here is merely a starting point and a call for further investigation into the ways that discourses of school choice, which purport to enhance educational opportunities for all students, actually operate to produce eliteness and institutionalise the exclusion of disadvantaged students. The processes that we have examined here support Gillborn's (2005) assertion that while such injustices might not be the intended goals of education policy, the inequity is not incidental: 'The patterning of racial advantage and inequity is structured in domination and its continuation represents a form of *tacit intentionality* on the part of white powerholders and policy-makers' (p. 485, emphasis in original).

The question of the production of elite status can only be answered fully when we are able to account for the wide range of circumstances through which different status hierarchies are (re)produced while accounting for the specific modes through which certain groups and individuals come to occupy superordinate positions within those hierarchies. This requires asking questions that move beyond merely whether the institutional context is defined as elite or whether the particular group formation under analysis is itself 'an elite'. We might instead, within particular circumstances, ask what hierarchies are at stake within a given institution or social geography, and attempt to understand how elite status is achieved within those hierarchies. To put this simply, wealth alone does not an elite make, and one does not become elite just because one wins the lottery (including the charter school admission lottery). In every instance, elite status must be sought, it must be produced, it must to some extent be struggled over, and the subtlety and complexity of this process is illuminated in particular ways when we look at contexts in which such status is more or less precarious, precisely because this precarity brings the process into relief, while at the same time requiring that it become more hidden.

References

Ball, S. J., Bowe, R. and Gewirtz, S. (1996). School choice, social class and distinction: The realization of social advantage in education. *Journal of Education Policy*, 11(1), 89–112.

Beadie, N. and Tolley, K. (Eds.). (2002). *Chartered schools: Two hundred years of independent academies in the United States, 1727–1925*. New York: Routledge.

Bourdieu, P. and Passeron, J. C. (1977). *Reproduction in education, society and culture*. Beverly Hills, CA: Sage.

Bray, IV and Dees, D. (2014). *Accountability report*. Available at http://gsmst.org/gsmst_web/sites/default/files/file/pdf%20files/2013/GSMST_Issued%202013-14_FINAL2.pdf (accessed 3 June 2015).

Buddin, R. and Cato Institute. (2012). The impact of charter schools on public and private school enrollments. *Policy Analysis*, No. 707.

Cookson, P. W. (1995). *School choice: The struggle for the soul of American education*. Yale University Press.

Cookson, P. W. and Persell, C. (2008 [1985]). *Preparing for power: America's elite boarding schools*. New York: Basic Books.

Davies, S. and Aurini, J. (2011). Exploring school choice in Canada: Who chooses what and why? *Canadian Public Policy*, 37(4), 459–477.

Davis, J. (2013). *School choice in the states: A policy landscape*. Report of the Council of Chief State School Officers.

Finn Jr., C. E. (2013). Why private schools are dying out. *The Atlantic*. Available at http://www.theatlantic.com/national/archive/2013/05/why-private-schools-are-dying-out/275938/ (accessed 3 June 2015).

Finn Jr., C. E. and Hockett, J. A. (2012). *Exam schools: Inside America's most selective public high schools*. Princeton, NJ: Princeton University Press.

Fleming, N. (2012). Magnets adjust to new climate of school choice. *Education Week*, 31(30), 1–17.

Gaztambide-Fernández, R. (2009a). What is an elite boarding school? *Review of Educational Research*, 79(3), 1090–1128.

Gaztambide-Fernández, R. (2009b). *The best of the best: Becoming elite at an American boarding school*. Cambridge, MA: Harvard University Press.

Gaztambide-Fernández, R. (Ed.). (2010). *Specialized arts programs in the Toronto District School Board: Exploratory case studies* (Report of the Urban Arts High Schools Project, Phase 1: Exploratory Research 2007–2009: Technical Research Report). Toronto, ON: Centre for Urban Schooling, Ontario Institute for Studies in Education, University of Toronto. Available at http://hdl.handle.net/1807/30018 (accessed 3 June 2015).

Gaztambide-Fernández, R., Cairns, K. and Desai, C. (2013). The sense of entitlement. In C. Maxwell and P. Aggleton (Eds.), *Privilege, agency, and affect* (pp. 32–49). London: Palgrave Macmillan.

Gaztambide-Fernández, R., VanderDussen, E. and Cairns, K. (2014). 'The mall' and 'the plant': Choice and the classed construction of possible futures in two specialized arts programs. *Education and Urban Society*, 46(1), 109–134.

Gaztambide-Fernández, R., Saifer, A. and Desai, C. (2013). 'Talent' and the misrecognition of social advantage in specialized arts education. *The Roeper Review – A Journal on Gifted Education*, 35(2), 124–135.

Gillborn, D. (2005). Education policy as an act of white supremacy: Whiteness, critical race theory and education reform. *Journal of Education Policy*, 20(4), 485–505.

Governor's Office of Student Achievement (GOSA) (2014). *Report card*. Available at http://gosa.georgia.gov/report-card (accessed 3 June 2014).

Graham, D. (1983). Schools for the arts. *Education Canada*, 23(2), 22–26.

Karabel, J. (2005). *The chosen: The hidden history of admission and exclusion at Harvard, Yale, and Princeton*. Boston, MA: Houghton, Mifflin.

Kena, G., Aud, S., Johnson, F., Wang, X., Zhang, J., Rathbun, A., Wilkinson-Flicker, S. and Kristapovich, P. (2014). *The condition of education 2014* (NCES 2014-083). U.S. Department of Education, National Center for Education Statistics. Washington, DC. Available at http://nces.ed.gov/pubsearch/pubsinfo.asp?pubid=2014083 (accessed 3 June 2015).

Lauen, D. L. (2007). Contextual explanations of school choice. *Sociology of Education*, 80(3), 179–209.

Levine, S. B. (1980). The rise of American boarding schools and the development of a national upper class. *Social Problems*, 28(1), 63–94.

'Lottery Application 2' (2013). Retrieved from http://www.gsmst.org/gsmst_web/?q=lottery_application (accessed 11 November 2014).

Maxwell, C. and Aggleton, P. (Eds.). (2013). *Privilege, agency, and affect: Understanding the production and effects of action*. London: Palgrave Macmillan.

Parekh, G. (2013). *Structured pathways: An exploration of programs of study, school-wide and in-school programs, as well as promotion and transference across secondary schools in the Toronto District School Board*. Research Report 13/14-03, Toronto: TDSB.

Petrilli, M. J. and Scull, J. (2010). *America's 'private' public schools*. Washington, DC: Thomas B. Fordham Institute. Available at http://files.eric.ed.gov/fulltext/ED511401.pdf (accessed 3 June 2015).

Siegel-Hawley, G. and Frankenberg, E. (2012). *Reviving magnet schools: Strengthening a successful choice option. A research brief*. Los Angeles: University of California Civil Rights Project/Proyecto Derechos Civiles. Available at http://escholarship.org/uc/item/5sv7r6cr (accessed 3 June 2015).

WSB-TV. (2013). 'Gwinnett School Ranks Among Top 3 in Nation'. Available at http://www.wsbtv.com/news/news/local/gwinnett-school-ranks-among-top-3-nation/nXT2y/ (accessed 3 June 2015).

Yoon, E.-S. (2013). Being chosen and performing choice: Young people engaging in imaginative and constrained secondary school practices in Vancouver, BC, Canada. University of British Columbia (unpublished doctoral dissertation).

5

THE FUTURE OF ELITE RESEARCH IN EDUCATION

Commentary

Stephen J. Ball

On the whole, educational researchers are not good at 'remembering elites', although there has been a recent flurry of interest in elite education. Generally speaking, the primary focus of educational research has tended to follow a 'downward' gaze to concentrate on social disadvantage, rather that what Aguiar (2012) calls 'studying up'. For very good reasons educational researchers have been preoccupied with explaining disadvantage and the negative consequences of educational inequalities rather than trying to understand and explain advantage.

However, in the last 20 years, following the lead of Pierre Bourdieu, there has been a growing interest in 'studying across' to examine the 'middle classes'. This body of work has attended to the ways in which the middle classes – the plural indicates recognition of diversity and difference within the middle class – go about reproducing their capitals and assets and the methods of their deployment in the field of education (Brantlinger 2003, Vincent and Ball 2006, Vincent et al. 2012) (Ball, 2003). This aside, Savage and Williams (2008, p. 2) write about a 'glaring invisibility of elites' in sociological research generally, although they do acknowledge the history of 'traditional elite theory' (p. 3) within sociology.

In the time since those comments were made there is certainly evidence of more 'remembering' and a greater visibility of elites in social research – for example the work of Mike Savage and his colleagues at the ESRC Centre for Research on Socio-Cultural Change. The title of the Centre is significant and telling – the attention to 'remembering' has been driven by, and made necessary by, social and economic changes which research has been compelled to take into account.

Lifestyle flamboyance and public displays of excess by elites of all sorts are now very visible in the media, and glaring and increasing wealth and income inequalities, in the context of global economic crisis and austerity policies, are now subject to political attention and social commentary. Andrew Sayer's recent book *Why we can't afford the rich* (2014), is one example of this new attention to the wealthy and the political and economic implications of their wealth. He explains in a recent blog piece:

> The recent economic crisis didn't just happen and the rich were pretty instrumental in the making of it. The globalisation of economies from the 1970s onward weakened labour in the old industrialized countries, allowing big firms to engage in a race to the bottom for cheap labour, low taxes, and lax environmental and employment regimes. Deregulation of finance allowed a bonanza in the growth of mechanisms of wealth extraction, which we are now paying for in austerity.
>
> With wealth goes power: political power. We've seen a rise of the rich in politics and the overshadowing of democracy by plutocracy. The global rich and big business are increasingly funding, infiltrating and dominating governments, and rigging the rules of the economy in their favour.[1]

The term *elites* is very widely and imprecisely used and is a descriptor in a whole range of social fields, including now in relation to sport. Both in a technical and semantic sense the word elite is a problem for social researchers – what exactly do we mean when we use it? That problem is evident in a number of ways in this volume and these chapters.

Elite is often elided with privilege, elite schooling with private schooling, or even in some cases we are back to talking about the affluent middle class as an 'elite'. The boundary between the middle class and the elite is difficult to determine, and their lifestyles and arenas of social action are not always distinct. The term 'elite' is a floating signifier. There is clearly no single or agreed usage or definition of the term in the chapters that form Part I of this volume.

In part, the fluidity of the concept signals the importance of differences in local and national histories and traditions – that is to say, elites are different and differently constituted and understood in different places, as Saltmarsh notes Chapter 3. There is a relativity to elite status and there is a geography of elites – in a number of senses. Nationally, elites tend to cluster in particular localities, almost by definition – Forbes and Weiner note this in Scotland. In some circumstances they seek to distance themselves from 'others', in part to preserve their exclusivity, in part to protect their advantages. In the UK, over the past two centuries the locus of elites has shifted from primarily rural settings to being now mainly an urban phenomenon. Gaztambide-Fernández and Maudlin write about how the curricula of elite schools have changed to reflect these changes in the constitution and location of elites.

More generally, contemporary elites are clustered in 'global cities'[2] and there is a concomitant growth in schools which specifically serve their post-national educational requirements. In a related sense, we can distinguish between national and global elites. There are those whose social reproduction is located firmly within national systems of education and those who move their children between countries for education. The form of education which each group seeks may also be different. These chapters primarily address the former – national elites.

Spatial mobility also raises questions about identity and perspective, or rather the extent of *disidentification* of elite groups from local and national senses of 'belonging'. These might come together in a form of what Savage *et al.* (2005) call 'elective belonging' on the one hand, as opposed to a 'diasporic identity' on the other. That is to say, some elite fractions are involved in 'transnational practices' (Sklair 1991) and move between 'global cities' and might be understood as what Bauman (1991) calls *globals*, who, he argues, are literally 'not of this world'. Furthermore, Bauman suggests that globals lead a precarious, liquid life and, in this globalised, mobile and postmodern world, the category of home is problematised.

Drawing on Heller's (1995) essay on home, Bauman highlights the differences between those who are locally tied, who may experience their home as a prison, and those (the globally mobile) 'who can dissolve whatever constraints a real home may impose' (Bauman 1998, p. 91). It follows from this that these are people 'for whom the nation works less well as a source of resonance and for whom nation is replaced by transnational ties and ... such ties may entail a kind and a degree of tuning out, a weakening personal involvement with the nation and the national culture' (Hannerz 1996, pp. 88–89).

Over and against this, mobile elites, although continually travelling and therefore constantly on the move, find for themselves or build isolated and exclusionary private spaces – gated communities, exclusive hotels and restaurants, private islands. In a similar vein, Elliott and Lemert (2006) write about 'global spaces, individualist lives' and a 'new age of individualism' within which 'people desperately search for self-fulfillment and try to minimise as much as possible inter-personal obstacles to the attainment of their egocentric designs' (p. 3) in the 'polished cities of the west', as they call them.

In some cases, Elliott and Lemert (2006) suggest, it may be that 'the conflict between globalisation and identity has led to the kind of "hollowing out" of people's emotional intimacies' (p. 7), to the extent to which emotions also have a geography. For such globals, experience is constructed on the edge of 'a disappearance of context' (p. 13). Social and political commitments, responsibility and social obligations towards others may all be eroded. Nonetheless, Savage *et al.* (2005) make the point that 'the precise form and nature of global connections depends strongly on the precise field of practice that is being studied' (p. 207).

What these chapters point out is the need to distinguish elites spatially and within different circuits of social relations, social fields and educational settings. As in other areas of research, we have to be able to think both about structures and flows, and stability and mobility. Location is important but perhaps not decisive. Elites have to be understood both within and beyond national class structures.

The so-called 'elite' schools addressed in these four chapters are primarily rooted in and reproduce national histories and traditions, in contrast to some elite schools that situate themselves within more detached sensibilities and seek to inculcate cosmopolitan identities and perspectives. Obviously, day schools and boarding schools may differ in this respect. Even so, some aspects of tradition and forms of schooling in Australia and North America are 'borrowed' from the English 'public' school system – Gaztambide-Fernández and Maudlin mention the pastoral landscape and neoclassical architecture of elite American schools which model themselves on British archetypes – but these forms and traditions are also re-worked locally and 'mashed up' with other influences. Maxwell and Aggleton's chapter offers a comparative historical analysis of the construction of elite education in England, which has in many cases been transported around the world.

To some extent in these chapters and in other research there are slippages between *the schooling of elites* and *elite schooling*, that is between the idea that elite schools recruit students from elite families and the idea that elite schools are part of the formation or production of elites – that they are, in effect, vehicles of social mobility into elite status and a means of access to elite 'opportunities' in the labour market and elsewhere. A slippage between social mobility and social reproduction. Saltmarsh refers to this in relation to non-Anglo families in Australia. Students in the latter schools may rely more heavily on the accumulation of cultural assets for elite status than the former. However, it would be a mistake to give too much emphasis to school in elite formation and reproduction. There are other sites of importance.

It is almost certainly the case that these mobility and reproduction functions are performed differently by different schools, but some schools may undertake both. Gaztambide-Fernández and Maudlin indicate in their case studies the variation in 'missions, demographics and geographical contexts' of schools. On the other hand, the Scottish private schools discussed by Forbes and Weiner seem to share a particular form and style of 'bookish' schooling.

In other words, some elite schools are more exclusive than others; there are different circuits of elite schooling. This is often reflected in the scale of fees. In England, Cheltenham Ladies' College charges up to £34,302 for boarding, while fees are £32,280 at Marlborough, £32,490 at Westminster and £32,067 at Eton College. In all, the average boarding fee now stands at £27,600. A more modest but high-performing private day school in England would be charging £4,000 a term. In the abstractions of class analysis and in the qualitative focus on strategies and perspectives of the dominant social groups, it is easy to lose sight of the wealth of elites, or at least some sorts of elites, and to neglect the basic role played in their lifestyle, identity and social relations by the exclusive possibilities provided by such wealth. Social researchers are not good with money. Elite formation and reproduction rest heavily on the ability to pay, even elite sport is defined primarily these days in financial terms. We only occasionally glimpse the material aspects of the elite class in the pages of this collection but clearly elite membership and social identities are, as in the past, constructed in relation to certain forms of consumption – fashion labels, fast cars and exclusive eating. 'Taste' and distinction are not cheap.

However, as noted already, there are the inherent conceptual and empirical problems involved in distinguishing the elite from other relatively advantaged groups, and in identifying the commonalities and differences between elites of different kinds – cultural, political, economic and sporting. It is worth reiterating the disclaimer made by Savage and Williams (2008, p. 9) in their introduction to the collection of papers *Remembering elites*. They say:

> We are best off sidestepping the debate about precise definitions of elites, to pose the issue in a somewhat different way, where our attention is directed in the first instance, towards how the wealthy have prospered and regrouped in contemporary financialized capitalism.

This also underlines the point that elites change – the recent history of Russian elites is a case in point. Savage and Williams argue that 'the continued rhetorical identification of elites with "old boy networks", the "establishment" or "inner circles" is deeply unhelpful' (p. 15). Even the constitution of business elites is subject to change – for example the very recent emergence of '.com' billionaires has changed the make up of the *Fortune 500* and *Sunday Times* 'rich lists' quite dramatically.

As with other class groups, we perhaps need to distinguish between the new and the established, as in Luna Glucksberg's research.[3] An important cultural distinction is identified between these two groups – members of the new elite group, she finds, tend to be more preoccupied with material items and are acutely conscious of the potential for downward mobility, while the established elite tend to have less regard for material items and instead place greater value on high culture pursuits and social connections. In effect, the new elites have to work harder at their eliteness.

'Eliteness', therefore, appears in a diverse array of constellations and spaces of practice. Status and advantage have to be worked at and maintained, and done 'correctly' in order to ensure their preservation.

In a different sense, we also need to be alert to the diversity and heterogeneity of elites and elite research needs to be intersectional – that is, it needs to explore dynamically the complex interplay of wealth and power with gender, race and sexuality. Among others, Maxwell and Aggleton (2010, 2014) and Forbes and Lingard (2013) attend specifically to the formation and reproduction of elite girls and Saltmarsh picks this up in her chapter. These categories and their attendant identities play a role in shaping lived experience differently, even among elites.

Khan's (2011) book *Privilege: The making of an adolescent elite at St. Paul's School*, examines a process of elite-making which is much more open in terms of gender and race than previously but which, nonetheless, in its effects, contributes to the ramification of old inequalities. Saltmarsh's chapter alludes to this too. The young people in Khan's study are very much at ease with their privileges and display a clear sense of entitlement and of the naturalness of difference, both in terms of material advantages and social fate – perhaps evidence of the 'egocentric designs' noted above – and this is what Forbes and Lingard (2013) call *assuredness*, or what Maxwell and Aggleton (2013) have termed *surety*. These young people do not question their privileges; they indulge them. On the other hand, Kahn's research portrays an elite which is capable of crossing boundaries and participating in diverse cultural forms – they are aware of their status but also see the world as a playground of possibilities which can be enjoyed and leveraged.

As noted already, the elite class is increasingly dynamic in its structure, as emphasised by the findings of Savage *et al.* (2013) and by Kahn's research. Again, this makes the matter of definition more difficult but also more important. Furthermore, relative fluidity and dynamism pose certain perceived dangers for those in the elite class: there is a degree of churn or precarity in elite status.

This also raises new issues for research and Friedman's research,[4] for example, draws on Bourdieu's concept of habitus to explore the emotional experience of performing class. Friedman's study of movement into the elite classes, addresses the emotional experience of mobility between classes and into the elite, and the symbolic baggage that people carry in the navigation of class. The research of Kenway et al. (2013) takes this further by drawing attention to what they call 'the sale of affective flows' (p. 21). What they are referring to in particular is the global market in elite 'desires' that links together anxiety, lifestyle and affect. Elite schools construct themselves as one such object of desire and are nodes at which flows and emotions come together.

The issues, questions and problems adumbrated above suggest three imperatives for further research. First, the need, as highlighted already, for researchers to take more seriously the differences within and between elites, especially differences in terms of localism as against cosmopolitanism, and the contribution of education to identity formation in relation to these different orientations. Second, the need to attend more closely to the complex and changing relationships between the global education market and elite formation, the ways in which this dynamic drives processes of differentiation and reproduction. Third, the need for more research studies which 'get close' to the 'work' of social reproduction and the performance of eliteness within families and educational institutions. Research on elites, therefore, must always be relational, and 'studying up' in these ways can contribute to our understanding of the role of education in growing social inequality, economic polarisation and global social change.

Notes

1 See https://policypress.wordpress.com/2014/11/25/fact-we-cant-afford-the-rich/ (accessed 3 June 2015).
2 See http://www.saskiasassen.com (accessed 3 June 2015).
3 See http://stratificationandculture.wordpress.com/2013/10/12/qualitative-approaches-to-the-study-of-elite-practices-lse-workshop-28th-november/ (accessed 3 June 2015).
4 See https://twitter.com/samfriedmansoc (accessed 3 June 2015).

Acknowledgement

This chapter draws upon, but significantly extends, a number of ideas discussed in Ball, S. J. (2015). Elites, education and identity: An emerging research identity. In A. van Zanten, S. J. Ball and B. Darchy-Koechlin (Eds.), *Elites, privilege and excellence: The national and global redefinition of educational advantage* (pp. 233–240). London: Routledge.

References

Aguiar, L. L. M. (2012). Redirecting the academic gaze upward. In L. L. M. Aguiar and C. J. Schneider (Eds.), *Researching amongst elites: Challenges and opportunities in studying up.* (pp. 1–27). Farnham, Surrey: Ashgate.
Bauman, Z. (1991). *Modernity and ambivalence*. Oxford: Polity Press.

Bauman, Z. (1998). *Work consumerism and the new poor*. Buckingham: Open University Press.
Brantlinger, E. (2003). *Dividing classes: How the middle class negotiates and rationalizes school advantage*. London: Routledge.
Elliott, A. and Lemert, C. (2006). *The new individualism: The emotional costs of globalisation*. London: Routledge.
Forbes, J. and Lingard, B. (2013). Elite school capitals and girls' schooling: Understanding the (re)production of privilege through a habitus of 'assuredness'. In C. Maxwell and P. Aggleton (Eds.), *Privilege, agency and affect* (pp. 50–68). Basingstoke: Palgrave Macmillan.
Hannerz, U. (1996). *Transnational connections*. London: Routledge.
Heller, A. (1995) 'Where are we at home?'. *Thesis Eleven*, 41, 1–18.
Kahn, S. R. (2011). *Privilege: The making of an adolescent elite at St. Paul's School (Princeton Studies in Cultural Sociology)*. Princeton, NJ: Princeton University Press.
Kenway, J., Fahey, J. and Koh, A. (2013). The libidinal economy of the globalising elite school market. In C. Maxwell and P. Aggleton (Eds.), *Privilege, agency and affect* (pp. 15–31). Basingstoke: Palgrave Macmillan.
Maxwell, C. and Aggleton, P. (2010). The bubble of privilege. Young, privately educated women talk about social class. *British Journal of Sociology of Education*, 31(1), 3–15.
Maxwell, C. and Aggleton, P. (2013). Becoming accomplished: Concerted cultivation among privately educated young women. *Pedagogy, Culture & Society*, 21(1), 75–93.
Maxwell, C. and Aggleton, P. (2014). The reproduction of privilege: Young women, the family and private education. *International Studies in Sociology of Education*, 24(2), 189–209.
Savage, M. and Williams, K. (Eds.). (2008). *Remembering elites*. Oxford: Blackwell.
Savage, M., Bagnall, G. and Longhurst, B. J. (2005) *Globalisation and belonging*. London: Sage.
Savage, M., Devine, F., Cunningham, N., Taylor, M., Li, Y., Hjellbrekke, J., Le Roux, B., Friedman, S. and Miles, A. (2013) A new model of social class? Findings from the BBC's Great British Class Survey Experiment. *Sociology*, 47(2), 219–250.
Sayer, A. (2014). *Why we can't afford the rich*. Bristol: Policy Press.
Sklair, L. (1991). *Sociology of the global system*. Baltimore, MD: The Johns Hopkins University Press.
Vincent, C. and Ball, S. (2006). *Childcare, choice and class practices*. London: Routledge Falmer.
Vincent, C., Rollock, N., Ball, S. and Gillborn, D. (2012). Being strategic, being watchful, being determined: Black middle-class parents and schooling. *British Journal of Sociology of Education*, 33(3), 337–354.

PART II
European perspectives
Similarities and differences in Scandinavia, France and Germany

6
A SOUND FOUNDATION?

Financial elite families and egalitarian schooling in Norway

Helene Aarseth

Introduction

While globalisation and increased competitiveness are assumed to encourage strategies to secure privilege among elite parents, Norwegian elites still tend largely to educate their children in the non-selective, state comprehensive school system. In this chapter, I explore a possible compatibility, and even mutual enrichment, between the mode of socialisation practised by financially elite families and the egalitarian school system in Norway. Drawing on findings from a study of families in which at least one parent was employed in investment banking or financial intermediary services, I describe a perceptible and perhaps unexpected earnestness in their take-up of non-selective, mixed ability schooling.

I argue that egalitarian schooling may in fact fit well with the everyday emotional investments and modes of socialisation that emerge in these families as they encounter an increasingly marketised and radicalised competitiveness in the workplace. More specifically, I suggest that the non-competitive and 'all inclusive' school system provides a feeling of safety and 'holding' in everyday life for both the family and the neighbourhood community. This sense of holding not only provides 'a shelter from the storm' but serves equally as a sound foundation from which to nurture the ability to produce the 'fitness' and 'strength' required to participate in the insecure and ruptured world of finance.

Elites and egalitarian schooling in Norway

Although not unaffected by the forces of globalisation and a heightened emphasis on competition and achievement, Norwegian society has, generally speaking, no private schooling sector, no educational market dynamics, and no elite education system.[1] The concept of the *enhetsskolen* or 'one school for all' has been a significant element in the construction of Norwegian social democratic welfare state policies.

The basic principle is one of state-funded, non-selective, comprehensive education, in which pupils are not streamed according to ability until age 16. In addition, pupils attend the school that is nearest their home (Welle-Strand and Tjeldvoll 2002). Secondary education, either vocational or academic, is obligatory and the admission requirements to academic secondary schools are highly inclusive.[2] An explicit and important political aim has been to use schooling as an equaliser, by combining high-quality education relevant to each individual with the promotion of equal opportunities for all, irrespective of individual abilities and circumstances (ibid.). Today, there is general agreement, however, that this principle has not been successfully implemented. In recent decades, the positive correlation between parents' educational level and students' academic achievement has remained largely unchanged (Bakken and Elstad 2012).

Comprehensive schooling should be seen as an important part of a more wide-ranging egalitarian orientation that is evidenced in the comparatively low levels of economic inequality in the Scandinavian countries. For historical reasons, this egalitarianism is perhaps particularly strong in Norway. Having spent time under Danish and Swedish rule, Norway has not had a large upper class of its own, as the elite has tended to be associated with foreign power. Arguably, intellectual endeavours have been afforded relatively low status compared to more practical virtues and material production (Skarpenes and Sakslind 2010). Egalitarian values are strongly supported by the middle classes (ibid.). Furthermore, across all classes, Norwegian parents have been found to put the primary emphasis on the importance of being a 'sound human' ['et gagns menneske'], cherishing adaptability and sociability above other virtues (see, for example, Haldar and Wærdahl 2010, Stefansen and Aarseth 2011).

However, Norway has not been unaffected by forces of globalisation and liberalisation at the end of the twentieth century – within both the economic and educational spheres. The so-called PISA shock (a reaction to the results of the Programme for International Student Assessment, when Norwegian pupils only got average scores in OECD's ranking of pupil competences in reading, mathematics and science), instigated a shift in education policy towards a more visible pedagogy that emphasised more measurable outcomes and national ranking of schools. While some of the humanist and social democratic intentions associated with the 'one school for all' ideal could be argued to now take the form of 'a paradise lost' (Welle-Strand and Tjeldvoll 2002, Antikainen 2006), these values still command considerable public support. Thus, when the Norwegian royal family recently moved their children from the local comprehensive to an International School, this decision provoked a national outcry.

Also, in recent decades, Norway has seen a growth in the proportion of people considered to be part of the financial elite (Hansen 2012). More than other groups, the economically privileged have started to buy properties in particular school catchment areas. Thus, in the capital city Oslo it is now possible to identify privileged enclaves or sanctuaries with a high density of economic capital (Ljunggren and Andersen 2014). While the children of these families still attend their local comprehensive, non-selective state school, these school catchment areas are becoming increasingly homogenous (as also observed by van Zanten, 2005 in France). In this chapter, I explore further how this comprehensive, non-selective school system fits with the modes of socialisation of families who are part of this financial elite group.

Heightened anxieties and increased investment in competitiveness?

Globally, economic elite fractions can be depicted as agents of a heightened competitiveness and increased orientation to instrumentalisation in education (Brown 2000, van Zanten 2005, Au 2008). Economic elites could be argued to profit from increased standardisation and high-stakes testing as they are able to pay for private lessons and exam preparation courses (Ball 2003, van Zanten 2010). At the same time, they could also be understood as driving self-energising processes which intensify competition between groups, thereby spurring heightened anxieties and fears of failure (Brown 2000).

What kinds of emotional consequences arise from this intensified competitiveness in schooling and work? Savage and Williams (2008) have argued that deregulation and the increased globalisation of markets since the end of the last century have had the effect of financialising the constitution of elite groups (Kahn 2012). These changes have destabilised elites previously confident about their 'sense of place' (McDowell 1997). With a growing competitive individualism, a shift from meritocratic to market roles (Brown 2000) and an increasing fragility of position, profound ruptures and upheaval have been experienced by elites, seriously affecting the everyday working lives of those in finance, investment and banking as well as the upper strata of corporations – notably, CEOs and board members (McDowell 1997). Intensified competitiveness also implies an increased urge to be strong, vigorous and bold; in short, a heightened urge to succeed. Thus the 'amalgam of dread and confidence' (Ball 2003, p. 4) [3] that has characterised the upper middle classes in late modernity is likely to affect the economic upper class as well.

In recent research on the role of the family as 'the heartland of the formation of classed subjects' (Vincent and Ball 2006, p. 68), this heightened anxiety is seen to drive parents to invest strategically in their children. Preferred strategies include a willingness to trade well-being for school achievement (Reay 2000, Walkerdine et al. 2001), a manic enrolment in enrichment activities (Vincent and Ball 2007), and an instilling of cosmopolitan competence that should enable children to have a sense that 'the world is my home' (Weenink 2008). At a more general level, the aim is to nurture the confident and entitled self (Lareau 2002, Vincent and Ball 2006), with a 'sense of one's place' (Vincent and Ball 2006, Ottosen 2009), and with a feeling of continuity and surety (Maxwell and Aggleton 2014). Involvement in dense social networks of 'taste communities' enables privileged people to see themselves in relation, and in a superior position, to others (Ball 2003, p. 65).

Recently, this literature emphasising anxiety-driven strategies to ensure success has been supplemented, and challenged to some extent, by research that has highlighted parents' concern for their children's well-being in the present, not just strategically looking towards the future (Irwin and Elley 2011). Parents have been found to emphasise the need for intimacy as a form of enrichment (Stefansen and Aarseth 2011), or to promote a form of *concerned* rather than concerted cultivation focused on finding a 'balanced approach to life and learning' (Maxwell and Aggleton 2013, p. 82). Here, feelings of familiarity and homeliness are not only seen as a means to securing entitlement and distinction, but are equally understood as a source of well-being (Maxwell and Aggleton 2014). This feeling of familiarity may nurture a sense of surety and continuity that in turn may increase chances of success, but it is fundamentally driven by the concern to balance the costs of competitiveness. In short, elite parents may be nurturing competitiveness alongside a compensatory concern for security and a sense of continuity. Overall, however, the literature suggests that competitiveness and 'fear of falling' permeates the educational system; the question is to what extent parents are 'playing the game' or seeking to modify it.

In Norwegian society there appears to be a relative lack of the kind of existential drama related to academic achievement and social reproduction that is reported in other European countries, such as Britain and France (Skarpenes and Sakslind 2010). In this chapter, I will explore how the Norwegian comprehensive school perhaps fits with the modes of socialisation among financial elite parents, who might be expected to be particularly susceptible to the requirements of a fast-moving and globalised capitalism.

The research study

This chapter draws on an in-depth study of 13 families with children aged between six and 18 years. In all, 22 parents were interviewed. The interviewees live in parental couples characteristic of Norway's economic elite, in which the father holds a senior position in the expanding group of financial intermediaries that make up a large part of the capitalist class (Savage and Williams 2008, Kahn 2012). The male interviewees work as investors, proprietors, board members or as partners in consultancy or law firms that provide financial services. With relatively few exceptions, they started their career in the City of London or in other world cities. Currently, they live in the 'privileged enclaves' of Oslo where other equally economically resourced families have chosen to reside. These neighbourhoods seem to be carefully chosen for the particular schools that serve them. Four of the families in the study were dual-career families where the male partner works in finance and the female partner holds a position as CEO. In the remaining families, the mother's main occupation was as a homemaker, although quite a few combined this with part-time flexible work, including work–life-balance counselling, arts and craft teaching, interior decorating or, alternatively, managing small investment companies. Thus, a majority of the interviewed parents are reminiscent of what Vincent and Ball (2006, p. 6) have characterised as 'City men and flowery women' families. They practise a distinctly gendered family culture that stands out in the broader Norwegian context, where only 4 per cent of women consider themselves 'house wives' (Kitterød and Rønsen 2011), and where the professional middle classes in particular tend to embrace a dual-career/dual-carer family model (Kitterød 2000, Aarseth 2007).

The focus of this study was how these parents experience their everyday lives at work and within the family. Data were collected through free-association narrative interviews (Hollway and Jefferson 2000) in order to explore the interpretative schemes and 'emotional investments' through which interviewees perceived the world. However, I departed from Hollway and Jefferson's (2000) idea that our investments in the world are primarily driven by the need to defend ourselves against threatening emotions (Aarseth, forthcoming). Instead, I combined this psychoanalytically inspired method with hermeneutic readings of Bourdieu's theory of practice (Crossley 2001, McNay 2004, Martin 2011). In particular, I sought to focus on the emotional investments that emerge in the dialectic encounter with certain field requirements: a particular 'feel for the game' or a 'socialised desire' that makes agents susceptible to certain requirements (Bourdieu and Wacquant 1992, Bourdieu 2000). Thus, I was not seeking to record the deliberate motives and reasons for making particular choices but the emotional investments or, as I call them, the 'enchanted perceptions' informed by un-conscious and pre-conscious fantasies that drive certain practices and orientations. More particularly, I focused on the relationship between the interviewees' enchanted perceptions of field requirements, their 'situated experience of oughtness' (Martin 2011, p. 252) at work on the one hand, and their perceptions of the requirements of everyday parenting, or their 'mode of socialisation' (Bernstein 1977), on the other. How do they experience the world of finance and how do their 'enchanted perceptions' of everyday life in the family relate to this? And how does all this 'fit' with understandings of comprehensive schooling in Norwegian society?

In the trenches – enchanted perceptions in the field of finance

When the financial intermediaries in my study talked about their work, I got the feeling that they were discussing taking part in a running race. Success was seen to depend on a strong will and being goal-focused. The overall maxim appeared to be that they needed to 'keep focused' and be prepared to make sacrifices, by 'going for the gold medal', or 'completing the race they had embarked on'. Chris likened his job to taking part in a contest. He recounted that in his youth he had, somewhat unexpectedly won a gold medal in an international tennis championship: 'They all said that I had no chance of making it. But I just decided that I was going to win, and I just focused on that goal, and I made it.'

The suggestion throughout such narratives was that being determined to win would almost release some sort of superhuman powers when it counted the most. In order to achieve this, there was a sense that you must be willing to sacrifice a lot and to keep entirely focused on your goal. Parents therefore talked about 'going for it' and the importance of never hesitating. Ann, one of the female CEOs, emphasised the need to 'always say yes, or else you're out'. Furthermore, interviewees talked about hesitation or any moment of self-doubt signalling an end to your chances of reaching your goal, or winning the so-called race. Alex, a male fundraiser said, 'It is about being visible and strong. Strong and visible. If you are invisible and careful, then you haven't got a chance in this business.'

The interview stories also included plenty of war metaphors. Fredric talked about 'lines of fire' and Ann about 'being in the trenches'. Catherine described how they had recently been in 'a real storm' where the chairman of the board in her husband's law firm had tried to 'totally destroy him'. She suggested that the problem lay in being challenged by someone about, or for, your business – 'you start to doubt yourself'. She explained that the only way she had survived those 'horrendous, horrendous' months during which her husband's position as partner was under threat, had been to hang on, 'you know you just hang on, and you don't let go'. Thus, these stories emphasise not only the importance of competing, fighting and winning, but also, critically, being emotionally resilient. You go for gold, you stay in the race, and you hang on.

However, within the interview stories reference was also made to a constant fear of falling. This is a game in which the stakes are high and the fall may be unpredictable and brutal. Some talked about a sense of uneasiness due to lack of security. You might be fired if the 'financial results are not satisfactory', or if the company is bought by another company. For these families (the men in particular) there appeared to be a sharp line between winning and losing, success and failure – you either win or you are defeated and lose. Many also expressed the feeling of having no one to lean on. Despite many of these couples having other resources to rely on if their businesses collapsed or they were fired (not to mention the generous support they would be eligible for from the prosperous Norwegian welfare state), their subjective and enchanted perceptions meant they felt as if they were 'in the trenches' and constantly at risk of being 'total failures'. Some interviewees mentioned suicide among neighbours or friends. Alex referred to a friend who recently killed himself and he related this act to a 'feeling of being a total failure' and of 'losing *everything* you have'. It seems that this ceaseless pressure to win, and the concomitant fear of losing, fuels the 'organised strivings' (Martin 2011) of these financial intermediaries. It is to the particular 'fit' between these families' 'enchanted perceptions' of the game and their everyday socialisation practices that I will now turn.

Preparing for the race

An overall aim of everyday life for these families was to provide their children with 'a good start' so as to be able to compete in the 'race' (Aarseth 2014a). 'To me, the most important thing is that the children thrive and that they get the best possible foundation so that they may accomplish as much as possible in their life', said Maria. To prepare their children for the race, considerable emphasis was put into different ways of pursuing schoolwork. Schoolwork was lent an air of seriousness and weight, with children described as being 'engaged and clever' at school. But parents such as Lilly and Maria acknowledged that to be such 'requires effort'. Such a narrative was particularly evident among the homemaker mothers. Afternoons appeared to be focused on their children's schoolwork well 'into the evening'. Maria underlined how they have set 'a standard' for schoolwork. To quite a few of the parents this standard was to 'aim for gold' (i.e. the top marks). 'If you have the capability to get an A, you just don't go for a B,' Lilly explained. Children were expected 'go for it' and 'push their limits'. Lilly told the story about how her son's friend had been disappointed by his B-grade on a recent exam, although he had worked really hard in preparation and followed all the curriculum content expected by the teacher. But, Lilly explained, 'you cannot expect to get an A when you just do what is expected. Teachers set out what is expected for the average pupil, not what it will take to get an A'.

There was a sense in the interviews that families perceived comprehensive schooling as somewhat lacking in ambition, and that they would have liked to have a more specialised and elite schooling for their children, had it been available. There were quite a few references to the 'standard' of the state school being somewhat average. Although the local school is 'a really good school', said Charlotte, there will always be 'some teachers who have certain shortcomings'. Thus, for many mothers, their goal was to compensate for any such shortcomings within the school. Catherine, who had a German upper-class family background, considered Norwegian education to be a little too *laissez faire*. She continued, since 'they get so much freedom at school' I have 'taken that role on of being a little bit more strict than I would have perhaps naturally liked to be'.

However, far more noticeable was the way that many of the parents interviewed did *not* perceive the state schooling system as impeding their children's ability to 'push their limits' and 'go for gold'. Instead, parents suggested that being educated in an institution where 'everybody is included' and 'accepted for who they are' as Julia formulated it, plays an important role in providing the 'good start' they crave for their children.

Fitness and resilience

Linked to the sporting analogies made when discussing their employment, parents emphasised fitness when discussing their children's orientation to schoolwork, whereby children should have 'a healthy mind in a healthy body'. Achieving this required protection from 'disturbing elements' such as computer games and social media. Therefore, time spent in front of the computer and the television was strictly limited in most of these families; with noticeably more restrictions than reported in a study of parents from the culturally elite fractions of Norwegian society (Stefansen and Aarseth 2011, Aarseth 2014a).

Another key consideration for these parents was their children's physical health. Here, nutritious food was seen as crucial – 'getting them to eat their broccoli', as Catherine expressed it – as well as the necessary amount of sleep, time spent outdoors and engagement in sports. With only a few exceptions, children from these families were involved in several sports at a competitive level.[4] Sport was, as Thomas pointed out, 'a really healthy way to be together with other children'. Mothers therefore worked to create optimal conditions for their children to excel in their athletic pursuits, by for instance preparing healthy meals and serving them at the right time of the day before training or competitions. Parents also stressed the need to acquire a healthy and resilient body so that their children would be physically 'fit for fight'. Critically, this resilience and fitness was also believed to be associated with their psychological well-being.

The sense of belonging and safety

These families live in the catchment areas of 'really good' local comprehensive schools, and in neighbourhoods where other families with similar socioeconomic circumstances are concentrated. Many of the interviewees, for example Tina, explained that they wanted to live in 'exactly this neighbourhood', and that they 'always knew that this is where they would move when they became parents'. Some parents had themselves been raised in the same areas and Charlotte told me that 'almost everyone had eventually moved back there' when their own children were born. In particular, they highlighted the *Gemeinschaft* they felt within their community – it was a place where 'everybody knows everybody' and where, as Margaret underlined, the children can 'walk in and out of each other's houses and gardens'.

Generally, the homemaker mothers were heavily involved in their local communities. They were usually members of the parent forum at the local school, arranging summer parties or class expeditions, and heavily involved in the running of their children's after-school activities. Some mothers also helped to run a parent-led 'homework assistance club', and others facilitated Sunday school at the local church. All but one of the women interviewed who were stay-at-home mothers, were heavily involved in their local neighbourhoods – Tina explained, 'most people around here probably know who I am'.

Such a connectedness with community meant that the mothers, as Tina, had 'a fairly good overview of the different families and who belongs to whom'. Such involvement was partly motivated by a kind of philanthropy. 'It is very important that there is someone that actually has the time to engage in the community,' Lilly explained. 'There are actually some people out there who are having a hard time, and who need someone.' Such an investment in their neighbourhood had become an important part of these mothers' own life projects (Aarseth 2014b). These particular mothers felt a keen need to ensure that everyone felt included – as Lilly pointed out, 'if everyone from time to time would just say something nice and ask them [other people] to pop over to their home to see them, if only from time to time, . . . they [other people] would perhaps start to feel more included'. Such sentiments were linked to the importance of living in a setting where people could lean on one another and 'be part of something'. Such an emphasis on inclusiveness and care for 'the human side' of relationships may not only be motivated by an ideological desire to compensate for their underlying belief in the survival of the fittest, but may also be seen as a critical requirement for prospering in their particular life situation.

The importance of living in a close and inclusive neighborhood was particularly emphasised in the narratives of parents who had children who were not seen as so 'engaged and clever', or who had had particular health problems or who had faced other kinds of challenges, such as severe asthma or epilepsy. For instance, Margaret, whose son was diagnosed with ADHD, stressed that he has been included, made to feel 'part of the crowd'. 'Here, [in the neighbourhood] we have all these things that knit them together, but at [the secondary school located in the city] they end up hanging around in the streets, you know'. The local community is seen as having a nurturing effect, in contrast to the 'world out there'. 'They [the children] are very safe here', Lilly emphasised, 'there is a really safe and good environment around here'. Julia pointed out that the school is 'right down the street', and there is only 'a safe little path between our house and the school'.

This emphasis on safety and belonging points to a more general sensitivity observed in mothers' narratives concerning the need for protection of 'the human side'. Here, the local school, as these mothers see it, also provides their children with 'sound attitudes' and 'raises them to be good people'. To be a good person with clear values seemed to be linked to features of the Norwegian school system that were seen as enabling a feeling of being included and part of a bigger whole that is not based on competitive individualism. Since all the children already knew each other in the local neighbourhood, there was no need for them 'to position themselves', as Julia explained, and therefore no need for them to 'try to demonstrate that they are someone they are not'.

Another recurring theme in the interviews was the contrast drawn between 'life in the City of London' where many had started their careers, and the 'calmness' and safety of their lives in Norway. Most would never have contemplated raising their children in London or another big city, as these places were experienced as chaotic, stressful and exhausting. Children, it was felt, should grow up in a safe neighbourhood, surrounded by a green environment, with 'sound virtues'. 'In London, everything was about how much money you made and how successful you were', explained Tina.

More generally, parents seemed eager to protect their children from an overly competitive environment and an emphasis on 'material values'. They wanted their children to experience a 'normal' Norwegian childhood. A couple of the fathers talked about the importance of their children growing up oblivious to their privileged economic position, and so were careful to protect them from money issues and avoided conspicuous consumption. However, in Norway, for reasons of transparency, information given to the tax authorities is publicly available. This is juicy stuff for the newspapers, who each year print the lists of those with the highest income and capital. Fredric, one of the fathers, would probably be on that list and would have preferred that his children remained ignorant of the family's economic status. He felt uneasy about the day when his children's classmates would be old enough to read these lists: 'I am really, really dreading that day', he said, suggesting that this would be the day when his children would eventually be deprived of their childhood innocence. Significant to my research was the urgent need that these parents expressed in their narratives to draw a line between the 'innocence' of childhood and the very real anxieties they experienced of winning or losing in the world of finance – their chosen employment sector.

Enhancing the dialectic of belonging and competing?

An overall aim of the everyday socialisation practices of these financially elite families was to provide their children with 'a good start'. A good start required two separate forms of investment. On the one hand, parents emphasised the importance of competitiveness, determination and of having the desire to succeed, to perform and to push oneself to the limit. In their narratives, these stories to some extent echoed the heightened perceptions of life in finance – an urge to compete and to 'hang in there', to 'go for gold' and 'complete the race you have started'. On the other hand, parents seemed to have developed a more 'enchanted perception' of the importance of building a sound foundation on which this particular orientation towards succeeding could be nurtured. Such a foundation was best secured through a focus on health and fitness, as well as an emphasis on ontological security and psychological well-being. Initially, children required protection from 'the rat race' and the chance to grow up in a space where they did not need to position themselves, remaining 'safe' from the threat of failure. In order to provide such a childhood, parents invested heavily in their local community or sanctuary to create a place where everyone knew one another and felt included.

Although comprehensive schooling – the norm in Norway – was largely seen as meeting the needs of the 'average' pupil, it was nonetheless not thought to impede their children's ability to 'push the limits' and 'go for gold', arguably because it played such a critical part in creating a safe community. Thus, the local comprehensive school, without high-stakes testing and processes focused on tracking the winners and losers, was a critical component of the sound foundation parents were seeking to provide for their children – a safe distance away from the more gruelling rat race that lay ahead. Being institutions in which 'everybody is included' and 'accepted for who they are', the local schools could therefore be understood as an extension of the 'sanctuary' that deepened children's (and parents') sense of belonging and inclusion, so crucial for 'the good start' in life yearned for by these economically elite families.

There is much evidence to indicate that these parents expect that their children will eventually leave the sanctuary and go abroad to study and work. But the sanctuary remains a critical part of preparing their children for late life. In the enchanted perceptions of these parents, the safe, nurturing and holding properties of the local school and community are precisely those components that will facilitate the production of fitness and power which will prepare children to be able to successfully negotiate the competitiveness that will be required of them in their future lives. These narratives of financial elite parents stand in stark contrast to findings from a comparable study among academic elite parents (Stefansen and Aarseth 2011, Aarseth 2014a). Among these academic elite couples, the aim of parenting seemed focused more on developing children's ability to enjoy learning through perpetrating an 'enriching intimacy' (Stefansen and Aarseth 2011).

Perhaps the heightened perceptions of the need for a sound foundation among these financial elite parents can be further understood in light of Norwegian culture and history. Only few of these interviewees were descended from 'old bourgeois families', the majority coming from upwardly mobile middle-class families (typically engineers who had done well economically in the expanding economy of the postwar decades). Consequently, they did not experience the 'sense of place' and rootedness that can emerge from family networks and properties 'that have always been there' as expressed, for instance, by Lamont's (1992) upper middle class interviewees in France. The couples from the Norwegian economic elites more likely mirror what Lamont depicts as the US maxim of 'hard work' and 'fitness'. They orient themselves to what could perhaps be coined an 'instant rootedness' that is, a sense of connection that does not rely on 'things that have always been there' but rather on the possibilities of building security and safety in the here and now.

Overall, the research described here suggests that the claim that is more or less implicitly made in some of the literature – namely, that increased competitiveness among the elites spurs an intensified call for more of the same – may not always hold true. From this study I would suggest that there exists a mutual dialectic between increased radical individualism among elites and a call for new spaces that can hold and can provide a feeling of safety. Non-selective, comprehensive schooling in countries such as Norway could be one mechanism that facilitates such a holding function.

Notes

1 Private schools are only permitted when they offer a distinct and approved pedagogic alternative to state-funded, comprehensive education. In the main cities, international schools (French, US and German) attract some elite parents. Also, a handful of Steiner schools and Montessori schools attract some members of the cultural and economic elites respectively, but they are not elite educational institutions. Moreover, in spite of an increase in the number of Norwegian students attending elite universities abroad, the total number is still fairly small (according to Aftenposten June 2014, 131 Norwegian students attended eight of the best-known UK and US elite universities 2013/2014) There is little evidence that these students originate primarily from the elite groups represented here.
2 In the largest cities, such as Oslo, admission requirements are also differentiated according to the number of applicants, so that the most popular schools have higher requirements.
3 The expression is taken from Lewis and Maude (1950, p. 273).
4 There was little mention of cultural activities such as playing a musical instrument, singing in a choir, doing ballet or other forms of cultural enrichment (Vincent and Ball 2007). This could be indicative of a lack of cultural interests among the economic elite in Norwegian society. A recent study conducted among music students concluded that the chances of attending higher musical education are higher if you come from a working class background than if you come from the economic elite (Madsen 2013).

References

Aarseth, H. (2007). Between labour and love: The re-erotization of homemaking in egalitarian couples. *NORA, Nordic Journal of Feminist and Gender Research*, 2–3, 133–143.

Aarseth, H. (2014a). Lyst til læring eller fit for fight? Middelklassens læringskulturer. [Desire for learning or fit for fight? Middle class modes of socialization]. In Harriet Bjerrum Nielsen (Ed.), *Forskjeller i klassen* [Classed differences]. Oslo: Scandinavian University Press.

Aarseth, H. (2014b). Finanskapitalismens kjønnsromantikk. [The genderromantic of finance capitalism: A study of business elite families in Norway]. *Tidsskrift for kjønnsforskning* [Norwegian Journal of Gender Research], 3–4, 203–218.

Aarseth, H. (forthcoming). Eros in the field? Bourdieu's double account of socialized desire. *Sociological Review*.

Antikainen, A. (2006). In search of the Nordic model in education. *Scandinavian Journal of Educational Research*, 50(3), 229–243.

Au, W. (2008). Between education and the economy: High stakes testing and the contradictory location of the new middle class. *Journal of Education Policy*, 23(5), 501–513.

Bakken, A. and Elstad, J. I. (2012). *For store forventninger? Kunnskapsløftet og ulikhetene i grunnskolekarakterer.* [The educational reform and achievement inequalities]. Rapport 7/12. Oslo: Nova.

Ball, S. (2003). *Class, strategies and the education market: The middle classes and social advantage.* London: RoutledgeFalmer.

Bernstein, B. (1977). *Class, codes and control, Vol. 3* (2nd edition). London, Routledge and Kegan Paul.

Bourdieu, P. (2000). *Pascalian meditations.* Cambridge: Polity Press.

Bourdieu, P. and Wacquant, L. J. D. (1992). *An invitation to reflexive sociology.* Cambridge: Polity Press.

Brown, P. (2000) The globalization of positional competition? *Sociology*, 34(4), 633–653.

Crossley, N. (2001) *The social body: Habit, identity and desire.* London: Sage.

Haldar, M. and Wærdahl, R. (2010). Teddy diaries: A method for studying the display of family life. *Sociology*, 43(6), 1141–1150.

Halrynjo S. and Lyng, S. T. (2010). Fars forkjørsrett – mors vikeplikt? Karriere kjønn og omsorgsansvar i eliteprofesjoner. [Fathers' priority – mothers' duty to give way? Gender, career and childcare in elite professions.] *Tidsskrift for samfunnsforskning* [Journal of Social Research], 2, 249–280.

Hansen, M. N. (2012). Om konsentrasjonen av formue i Norge over tid. [On the changes in fortunes in Norway.] *Søkelys på arbeidsmarkedet*, 29(3), 213–223.

Hollway, W. and Jefferson, T. (2000). *Doing qualitative research differently: Free association, narrative and the interview method.* London: Sage.

Irwin, S. and Elley, S. (2011). Concerted cultivation? Parenting values, education and class diversity. *Sociology*, 45(3), 480–495.

Kahn, S. R. (2012). The sociology of elites. *Annual Review of Sociology*, 38, 361–377.

Kitterød, R. H. (2000). Hus- og omsorgsarbeid blant småbarnsforeldre: Størst likedeling blant de høyt utdannede. [Division of labour within the family: A more equal division among highly educated couples.] *I Samfunnsspeilet*, No. 5, 34–47. Oslo: Statistisk sentralbyrå.

Kitterød, R. H. and Rønsen, M. (2011). Husmor i likestillingsland. Hvem er hjemmearbeidende i dag? [Homemaker in a country of gender equality.] *Samfunnsspeilet* No. 1. Oslo: Statistisk sentralbyrå.

Lamont, M. (1992). *Money, morals, and manners: The culture of the French and the American upper-middle class.* London: University of Chicago Press.

Lareau, A. (2002). Invisible inequality: Social class and childrearing in black and white families. *American Sociological Review*, 67(5), 747–776.

Lewis, R. and Maud, A. (1950). *The English middle classes.* London: Phoenix House.

Ljunggren, J. and Andersen, P. L. (2014). Vertical and horizontal segregation: Spatial class divisions in Oslo, 1970–2003. *International Journal of Urban and Regional Research* (available online 22 December 2014).

Madsen, A. (2013). En musikalsk overklasse? En kvantitativ studie av rekrutteringen til høyere utøvende musikkutdanninger. [A musician upper class?] Unpublished MA thesis, Department of Sociology and Human Geography, University of Oslo.

Martin, J. (2011). *On the explanation of social action*. Chicago, IL: University of Chicago Press.

McDowell, L. (1997). *Capital culture: Gender at work in the city*. London: Wiley.

McNay, L. (2004). Agency and experience: Gender as a lived relation. *Sociological Review*, 52, 2, 173–190.

Maxwell, C. and Aggleton, P. (2013). Becoming accomplished: Concerted cultivation among privately educated young women. *Pedagogy, Culture and Society*, 21(1), 75–93.

Maxwell, C. and Aggleton, P. (2014) . The reproduction of privilege: Young women, the family and private education. *International Studies in Sociology of Education*, 24(2), 189–209.

Ottosen, M. H. (2009). A sense of one's place: Residential experiences among working and upper class inhabitants, *Sosiologisk tidsskrift*, 17(1), 41–69.

Reay, D. (2000). A useful extension of Bourdieu's conceptual framework? Emotional capital as a way of understanding mothers' involvement in their children's education. *Sociological Review*, 48(4), 568–585.

Savage, M. and Williams, K. (2008) Elites: Remembered in capitalism and forgotten by social sciences. *The Sociological Review*, 56(1), 1–24.

Skarpenes, O. and Sakslind, R. (2010). Education and egalitarianism: The culture of the Norwegian middle class. *The Sociological Review*, 58(2), 219–243.

Stefansen, K. and Aarseth, H. (2011). Enriching intimacy: The role of the emotional in the 'resourcing' of middle-class children. *British Journal of Sociology of Education*, 32(3), 389–405.

van Zanten, A. (2005). New modes of reproducing social inequality in education: The changing role of parents, teachers, schools and educational policy. *European Educational Research Journal*, 4(3), 155–169.

van Zanten, A. (2010). The sociology of elite education. In M. W. Apple, S. J. Ball and L. A. Gandin (Eds.), *The Routledge international handbook of the sociology of education* (pp. 329–339). Abingdon, UK: Routledge.

Vincent, C. and Ball, S. J. (2006). *Childcare, choice and class practices: Middle-class parents and their children*. London: Routledge.

Vincent, C. and Ball, S. J. (2007). Making up the middle-class child: Families, activities and class dispositions. *Sociology*, 41(6), 1061–1077.

Walkerdine, V., Lucey, H. and Melody, J. (2001). *Growing up girl: Psycho-social explorations of gender and class*. London: Palgrave.

Weenink, D. (2008). Cosmopolitanism as a form of capital: Parents preparing their children for a globalizing world. *Sociology*, 42(6), 1089–1106.

Welle-Strand A. and Tjeldvoll, A. (2002). The Norwegian unified school: A paradise lost? *Journal of Education Policy*, 17(6), 673–686.

7
ELITE EDUCATION IN SWEDEN
A contradiction in terms?

Mikael Börjesson, Donald Broady, Tobias Dalberg and Ida Lidegran

To talk about elite education in Sweden may sound like a contradiction in terms since Sweden is known as one of the most egalitarian societies in the world. Today, in spite of the rapid growth of economic inequalities over recent decades, Sweden boasts one of the most egalitarian distributions of income and wealth. However, growing differences in income, wealth and housing have been accompanied by profound changes at the policy and ideological level, as the old Social Democratic slogan of 'increased equality' is no longer threaded through national discourse as it used to be.

The Swedish educational system has undergone a parallel transition. For most of the twentieth century, widening access policies were pursued with great success (Lindensjö and Lundgren 2000). Even today, tuition fees cannot be charged at school or university level (except to students from outside the European Union). Furthermore, everyone who gains entry to an upper secondary school or higher education institution is entitled to apply for grants or loans to cover most of their living expenses.

Another aspect of what has been called the 'democratisation' of the educational system has been greater homogenisation in the structure of education. In the early 1970s, a comprehensive form of primary education, *grundskolan*, for all children up to the age of 14 was put in place across Sweden. This put an end to the former division that existed between the *folkskola* for the 'common people' (quite literally) and the *läroverk* (upper secondary grammar school) to which the affluent classes sent their children. At the same time, all institutions in the upper secondary education sector were merged to create a single type of school – *gymnasieskolan*. Later, in 1977, the diverse tertiary (as well as some upper secondary) educational provision was amalgamated into a single organisation – *högskolan* – comprised of universities, the newer university colleges and the many institutions providing vocational training (such as for primary school teachers). The effect of these changes was that social class advantage was no longer pursued via different educational tracks, but processes of social differentiation became more acute *within* each educational level.

Due to the homogenisation and expansion of the system, the overall level of educational attainment within the Swedish population rose, and the effect of social class origin on outcomes was reduced, up until the 1980s. However, the 1990s witnessed important transformations in Swedish education policy, whereby a shift from democratisation and equity to a focus on competition, performance, efficiency and audits emerged. Both Social Democratic (1982–1991, 1994–2006, 2014–) and right-wing (1991–1994, 2006–2014) governments have promoted the progressive differentiation, marketisation and privatisation of schooling. One example of such a policy shift has been the widespread implementation of the school vouchers system. Under this programme, each school receives its resources directly from the state budget, calculated on the basis of the number of pupils on its roll. Families are free to apply to any school of their choice. Private schools are allowed to operate on a for-profit basis. Thus, a growing proportion of venture capitalists are investing in the business of education, while schools owned by the municipalities have adapted to the same market logic in order to compete for pupils.

Higher education in Sweden has, to date, been less affected by the shift towards privatisation, although the principles of New Public Management have been forcefully introduced and steps have been taken towards new forms of 'academic capitalism' (cf. Slaughter and Leslie 1997, see also Rider *et al.* 2013). However, with very few exceptions, universities and other post-secondary education institutions are still owned by the state. Successive governments' attempts to create an academic market have been met with resistance (Börjesson, forthcoming).

These transformations of the educational system have had important consequences for the relative value of education and for the educational strategies adopted by various social groups. The increasingly complex educational landscape found today in Sweden includes a growing number of institutions at compulsory and secondary levels, as well as a greater number of tracks and study programmes at all levels. Having the knowledge and resources to navigate this new world has advantaged the cultural fractions of the middle classes, who have used their close relationship to the educational system to manoeuvre their way through it.

Three definitions of elite education

It is helpful to differentiate between three definitions of elite education when thinking about current education provision in Sweden.

The first is a *meritocratic* definition involving the recruitment of students based on academic merit. Merit other than scholarly achievement may be valid in some cases, for example in gaining entry into art schools. In addition, those programmes and institutions that are most selective also follow this principle in their recruitment of teachers and principals, thereby multiplying the effects of selection: the 'best' students receive the 'best' teachers (Bertilsson 2014). The most significant effect of the meritocratic selection process is probably the peer effect – where ambition, high attainment and sustained effort are seen as the norm.

A second definition of elite education is a *social* one that denotes elite schools or programmes as those that contribute to the intra-generational reproduction of current dominant groups. Here it is important to differentiate between the reproduction of elites and the reproduction of the upper classes (Baltzell 1995, pp. 6–7).[1] By 'elites' we simply mean groups that occupy dominant (formal and informal) positions within the overall field of power or within different fields, such as the economic, political, academic or artistic fields. An individual belongs to an elite on the basis of his or her individual position and merits. For elite groups it is crucial to reproduce and strengthen the specific forms of capital that they possess (political capital within the political elite, and so forth). In contrast, the upper class is defined in relation to the social space, i.e. the class structure, and has no need to reproduce specific types of capital (political, artistic, etc.) but simply to retain or strengthen a dominant position within the social structure. In Western societies, the most important division within the upper classes tends to separate those who are wealthier in terms of economic capital (the financial and industrial bourgeoisie) from those who are more dependent for their position on cultural capital and the educational system (scholars, artists, intellectuals, etc.). In between these two groups we find groups of professionals with a more balanced portfolio of capitals (higher civil servants, engineers, lawyers and medical doctors) (Bourdieu 1979, pp. 139–144). Additionally, it is of some importance how the nobility and the royal family fit into this picture. In recent years, the nobility have become more dependent on the formal educational system for educating their children. The Swedish royal family, for instance, now makes use of the elite segment of the educational system to educate its younger members. The school attended by a royal prince or princess is seen by the public as perhaps the most obviously socially elite institution.

A third definition is a *functional* one, according to which elite institutions are understood as sites for the formation of tomorrow's dominant agents. Obvious examples include the Royal Institute of Art, for careers within the fine arts, or the Stockholm School of Economics, which produces graduates who enter the economic field. Elite education in this functional sense also operates at the lower tiers of the educational system, whereby certain high-profile schools and programmes prepare their students to gain entry into sought-after and exclusive programmes at higher levels of the system.[2] Here, we can distinguish between elite schools and programmes that have a more general orientation and more specialised schools and programmes. An example of the latter occurs within art education where attendance at certain upper secondary schools or *folkhögskolor* is central to successfully gaining entry into the most prestigious art schools at the tertiary level.

These three definitions are intertwined, of course. Thus, programmes that are highly selective in terms of scholastic ability tend to recruit their students from families belonging to social elites and/or the upper classes, and often offer effective preparation for future success in the educational system and beyond. In this chapter we argue that there is evidence to suggest that the overall expansion of the educational system has led to a growing overlap between the three definitions of elite education, as well as growing competition over the scarce resources that are assembled, refined and legitimated through elite schools and programmes.

Sweden's elite educational

Within a system that has attempted to homogenise and democratise education, the boundary between elite and mass education has been less obvious than in many other countries. In Sweden, there exists no sharp cleavage between types of institutions, such as, for example, in France between, on the one hand, the *grandes lycées*, the *classes préparatoires* and the *grandes écoles* and, on the other hand, the ordinary *lycées*, *universités* and other institutions; or in the UK between the Russell Group universities (including Oxford, Cambridge and the London School of Economics) and other universities. The Swedish system is, in certain respects, more similar to the German one, comprised of a variety of universities and a few small specialised institutions. Neither does the Swedish system display the kinds of binaries more likely to be found in the US system, with elite education being associated with the private sector and mass education with the public. In fact, in Sweden, as in France, elite institutions are typically owned by the state or by municipalities.

However, there are some schools in Sweden that are denoted as elite. Although the old *läroverk* – grammar schools that educated those primarily aspiring to undertake further studies at university – were invaded by the middle classes during the twentieth century, the ancient 'cathedral schools' and some other well-established *läroverk* in the larger cities have managed to retain a process of selective recruitment, prioritising the cultural fraction of the upper middle class and upper class. Furthermore, a few private boarding schools based in rural Sweden have served as important sanctuaries for the sons, and later also for the daughters, of the economic fractions of the upper classes, including the most affluent families within the Swedish nobility, the *nouveaux riches*, and those executives and diplomats living abroad. The oldest of these boarding schools, Lundsbergs Skola, was established in 1896 by a leading Swedish industrialist and was modelled on English public schools such as Eton College, Rugby and Harrow. From the beginning, it placed a strong emphasis on athletic training and sports, including rowing, alongside a strong commitment to the cultivation of manners (Sandgren 2012).

Wealthy and upper class families have also favoured some of the private upper secondary schools like Carlssons Skola and Enskilda Gymnasiet, both established at the beginning of the twentieth century in the most sought-after neighbourhoods in Stockholm. A relative latecomer to this group of schools is the private Viktor Rydberg Gymnasium, opened in 1994 in the most affluent suburb of Stockholm, Djursholm. Today this gymnasium also runs two more schools in central Stockholm. Furthermore, the ancient Tyska Skolan (The German School, founded in 1612) and the Franska Skolan (The French School, 1862) educate many students from non-Swedish families together with members of the Swedish elites. Similarly, schools offering the International Baccalaureate (IB) have also been seen as an elite group, though with their growing popularity and the increase in number of schools offering the IB, the cohort of students recruited has become socially less exclusive than previously (Palme 2014).

The history of the development of tertiary education in Sweden in the late nineteenth and early twentieth century has shaped how elites are formed through education. At this point in time, higher education became an essential prerequisite not only for the clergy and the civil servant corps, but also for other elite groups. What is today understood as the field of 'higher education' emerged out of the two ancient Swedish universities (Uppsala, founded in 1477, and Lund, founded in 1666) and the two more modern *högskolor* (university colleges) in Stockholm (1878) and in Gothenburg (1891). Alongside these universities sat an array of specialised educational institutions, some which later became critical sites for the formation of elites: the Royal Institute of Technology (Kungliga Tekniska högskolan) founded in 1827; Chalmers Tekniska högskola founded in 1829; the Karolinska Institutet founded in 1810, and the Stockholm School of Economics (Handelshögskolan i Stockholm) founded in 1909.[3] To this list should be added a couple of specialist institutions in Stockholm that grew out of the most prominent training academies for painters, musicians and other artists. This category includes the Royal Institute of Arts (Kungliga Konsthögskolan), with its roots in the eighteenth century Royal Art Academy, and the Royal College of Music (Kungliga Musikhögskolan), dating back to the late eighteenth century and the Royal Academy of Music. Today, all these specialised institutions have a very selective recruitment process, meaning they occupy a prominent position not only in the educational system but also in their respective social fields. The Karolinska Institutet, for example, is by far the most important site for scientific medical research in Sweden, and coordinates the designation of the Nobel laureates in medicine.

There are important differences between elite institutions depending on which part of the educational system they are in – compulsory, upper secondary or tertiary. At the compulsory level, the most distinctive function of the elite institutions is to provide pupils with a general education, and to socialise them into the culture of the affluent classes. Extra-curricular activities are stressed as crucial for schooling, as is the development of a moral character. These schools also provide excellent learning environments. At the upper secondary level, the programme structure creates a division between general programmes preparing students for higher education, and more vocational-oriented programmes that aim to prepare students for entrance into specific occupations. Elite institutions at this level tend to emphasise the importance of general education programmes, and especially the natural science track, although exceptions do exist, such as in certain vocational art programmes. Finally, in the higher education segment of the elite educational system, a larger degree of specialisation is found and field-specific capital tends to become more important. However, there is still an emphasis on socialising students into a more general elite culture within these high-status institutions. At the larger universities, for instance, there are associations, such as the student 'nations' (a very important kind of fraternity in the old universities), sports teams, and student political parties that have the effect of bringing students from different educational programmes together and thus developing the basis for a wide-ranging social network.

To complete the picture of elite education in Sweden, we need to add a number of institutions that sit outside the main educational system that are significant for the education of current and future elites. One of these is the Tolkskolan (the Armed Forces Interpreter Academy) which has provided training in languages to (almost exclusively) men, who then go on to hold a variety of elite positions within fields as diverse as business, politics, administration, diplomacy, journalism and academia. Another example is the diplomat programme run by the Ministry of Foreign Affairs, which only recruits 20 candidates a year and offers a direct route to a diplomatic career. Furthermore, within the private sector, large multinational corporations have their own trainee programmes, about which little is known, but which are clearly of significance for developing careers in business and engineering. For families belonging to the dynasties of banking and industry, training to be an officer in the army reserve has almost become a mandatory start for an aspiring career. Finally, for most of the twentieth century, political and administrative elites, especially those connected to the Social Democratic Party, have followed the courses at *folkhögskolor* and the blue collar unions' own training programmes.

Four ways to study elite education

It is possible to distinguish four main approaches in sociological research on elite education. First, and probably most common, are studies focusing on one particular institution, often examining the history of these settings chronologically (see, for instance, Trumpbour 1989, Muxel 2003, Scot 2011). Second, some research has focused on a set of elite institutions. Such studies may examine the entire elite educational space within a country, such as the work undertaken by Pierre Bourdieu and Monique de Saint Martin (1987) in their seminal work on the *grandes écoles* of France. Alternatively, the focus might be on a certain type of schools, such as those offering the IB (Dugonjic 2014), or US and English preparatory schools (Cookson and Persell 1985). A third category of research takes a broader focus, in which different kinds of elite institutions and programmes are studied by situating them within a national (or international) educational system. Our own endeavours may perhaps be best viewed as fitting within this category. Finally, some studies have focused on the formation of elite education tracks, in which linkages between institutions at different levels are examined. Thus, in their study of preparatory schools, Cookson and Persell (1985, pp. 167–189) emphasise the links between these schools and the most prestigious universities.

When it comes to studies of Swedish elite education, contributions to date are fairly meagre. Given the strong focus on 'democratisation' in Swedish educational policy and the domination of so-called 'welfare sociology' within the social sciences, it is perhaps not surprising that there has been a lack of sociological research on elite education. There do exist a few historical studies of specific schools or institutions,[4] as well as some more general studies of elites, in which education is just one aspect of what is examined. There have also been some studies which have mapped the educational pathways pursued by those currently in elite positions, but these tend to focus on the type, the level or number of years of education rather than on a more in-depth examination of the role education itself plays in reproducing or securing an elite position.

The Sociology of Education and Culture (SEC) research unit at Uppsala University where we work has, however, been studying elite education in some depth for the past 25 years.[5] In the remainder of this chapter we will share some of the findings from our research, focusing in particular on the national and regional spaces within upper secondary education, and placing the analysis of these within the educational system as a whole.

Mapping educational spaces

In order to focus in on elite institutions and study programmes, as well as the educational strategies of elites groups, we have tried to 'map' relations within the space of secondary education. Our approach is inspired by the work of Bourdieu and de Saint Martin (1987; also Bourdieu 1989) – in line with the third approach to studying elite education introduced above. Drawing on large data sets that contain individual-level information on the entire population of Swedish school pupils, higher education students and teachers from the past 30 years – and utilising concepts such as capital, strategies and fields and Geometric Data Analysis (GDA, see Le Roux and Rouanet 2004, 2010) – we have been able to identify a clear and remarkably stable pattern of social differentiation over the past three decades.

Figure 7.1 has been created by means of a simple correspondence analysis (CA), a technique within GDA. This structure of the upper secondary education space is derived by using information on the social origin and gender of all Swedish pupils at this level within a particular timeframe. We distinguish between 64 categories: sons of lawyers, daughters of police officers, and so on. The position of each educational institution/programme is determined by the characteristics of the pupils enrolled in it. If institutions/programmes exhibit a similar pattern of recruitment – approximately the same proportions of daughters of librarians, sons of farmers, and so on – they are neighbours on the map, if not they are further apart. Into these spaces, we then project supplementary variables such as, for example, pupils' grades from compulsory school, which enables us to compare elites in the social sense with elites in a more meritocratic sense.

Elite programmes/courses/institutions are identified as those found in the upper compartments of the map, that is, in the regions characterised by a strong concentration of highly recognised assets, especially inherited (from the parental home) cultural and educational capital. We regard those as sites for elite education, whether they are commonly perceived as such or not. Elite education is shown to be the most selective in terms of not only inherited resources, but also acquired educational capital in the form of high grades. Thus, in Sweden, we are able to consider elite education drawing on both 'social' and the 'meritocratic' definitions, by analysing data on inherited as well as acquired symbolic and material resources. Due to limitations on the statistical data available, it is more difficult for us to examine the elite educational system drawing on the third definition – that is, on 'functional' aspects of such education – as available data only document current assets possessed by pupils. Future work should examine closely whether having received a certain kind of elite education does in fact translate into elite careers in the future.

The constructed space of upper secondary education in Sweden (Figure 7.1) is based on data on pupils' gender, social origin, and the school and the programme where they are enrolled. The population is all pupils ($n = 370,000$) in the second grade of upper secondary between 1997 and 2000. The space takes on a triangular shape. At the base, where vocational programmes are located, the 'horizontal' distance is substantial between those programmes populated predominantly by boys and those by girls. Here the amounts of inherited as well as acquired capitals are small. At the top of the triangle we find the sons and daughters from families in higher social classes concentrated – especially from social groups such as university teachers, medical doctors and lawyers, whose positions have been secured through possession of a significant amount of educational and cultural capital – in various science programmes, the IB and some social science programmes. The same general structure is mirrored regionally and at local level.

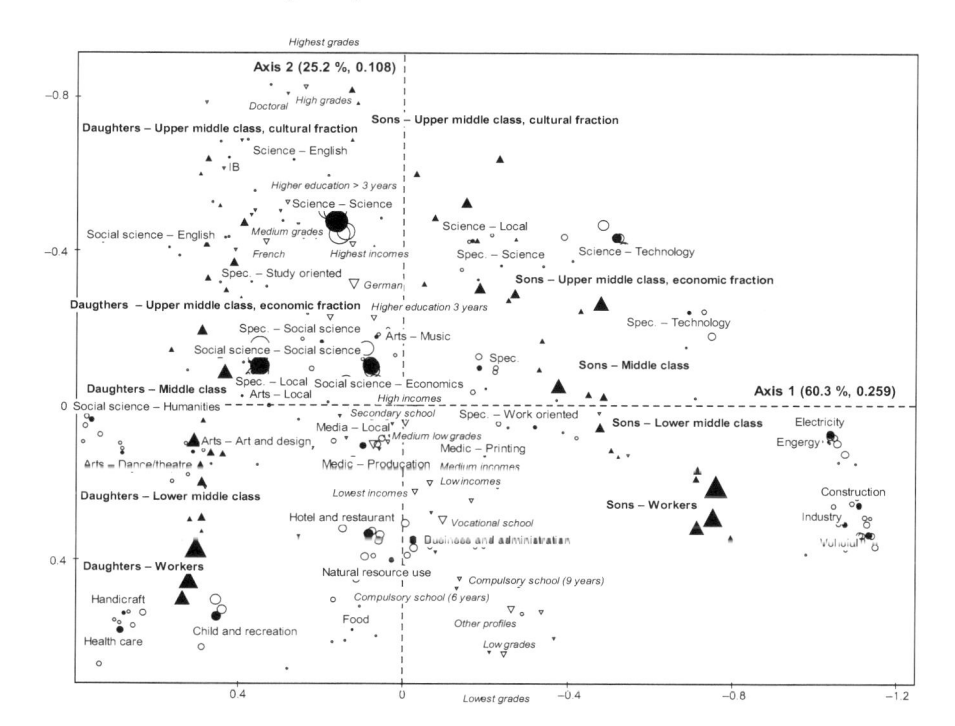

FIGURE 7.1 The space of upper secondary education in Sweden, 1997–2000

Note: Simple correspondence analysis, the plane of axes 1 and 2. Active variables are educational programme, and the pupils' social origin combined with sex.

Focusing on the regions, the significance of specific schools emerges. Thus, in upper secondary education in Stockholm, for example, we find that the public institutions in the inner city (most notably Östra Real, Norra Real, Kungsholmens Gymnasium and Södra Latin) and in the affluent suburbs (for example, Hersby Gymnasium, Danderyds Gymnasium and Saltsjöbadens Samskola) occupy the most dominant positions, attracting the largest proportions of pupils from homes with high levels of educational, cultural and economic capital (Palme 2008, Forsberg, forthcoming). These institutions are often the *läroverk* built at the turn of the twentieth century as bastions of learning, whose architecture includes grandiose entrances, voluminous staircases, impressive auditoriums and classrooms with high ceilings. A few independent schools, located in the same neighbourhoods, including Viktor Rydberg Gymnasium, Enskilda Gymnasiet, Tyska Skolan and Franska Skolan, also occupy dominant positions within the field of upper secondary education in Stockholm.

In Uppsala, by contrast, three larger public institutions dominate the space of upper secondary education, the two traditional former *läroverk* – Katedralskolan and Lundellska Skolan – and the newly established Rosendals Gymnasium. There are no private alternatives to these three top schools (Bertilsson 2014), a feature that sets Uppsala (a university city strongly dominated by culturally propertied groups) apart from Stockholm, where economic power is much more prominent (Lidegran 2009) and private schools have a stronger foothold (Forsberg, forthcoming).

By relating the meritocratic structure to the social one, we can clearly see the overlapping logics. The pupils endowed with the highest grades from compulsory schooling are found in the top of the space, where the sons and daughters of the cultural fraction of the upper and upper middle classes dominate. It is also in this part of the space that the natural science programme, where graduates have the highest average grades, is located. In this sense, the educational system is used to reproduce meritocratic capital: high initial grades are converted to high output grades. Most successful in this conversion are pupils originating from the groups that are most affluent in educational capital which is true for different geographic contexts (Lidegran 2009).

Finally, we need to consider recent transformations within upper secondary education and the implications these have for the production and reproduction of elites. Whereas during the post-war years, upper secondary education was largely for the cultural fractions of the upper middle class and the upper class, since the 1990s almost everyone now attends the *gymnasium*, with nearly 90 per cent of pupils at the end of their schooling now being eligible to apply for a higher education place. This means that particular social groups have to plan this part of their children's education trajectory more strategically in order to ensure they remain able to secure any advantages. Our analysis shows that the most general kind of university programme, the science programme, has become increasingly important in this respect, and that those groups most dependent on the educational system for their social position are actively pursuing high grades within the science programme as part of their strategy for social reproduction.

Conclusion

During the second part of the twentieth century, Sweden was regarded as one of the most egalitarian societies in the world. Despite differences in income, wealth, housing, and so forth having increased rapidly over the past three decades, Sweden is still more egalitarian than most. The same could be said about the Swedish school system, which, between the 1930s and late 1980s, underwent a unification that ended the former division between the *folkskola* for the general population and the *läroverk* (upper secondary grammar school) for the more affluent classes, especially those from the cultural fractions. Higher education too was unified when the old universities and almost all other forms of post-secondary training were incorporated in 1977 into *högskolan*. Furthermore, no tuition fees are permitted at any level of the educational system within Sweden. It might therefore sound like a contradiction in terms to speak of elite education in Sweden.

However, for both traditionally dominant groups and the rising new upper middle classes, a successful education has gradually become more and more necessary (though, of course, not in itself sufficient) as a vehicle for securing their dominant positions. This implies that both upper secondary and higher education have to an increasing degree been internally restructured by social and meritocratic factors to advantage these groups. Thus, although the Swedish system appears to be a democratic, homogeneous system, it in fact always has and still does contain elite institutions and programmes.

At the primary and secondary level, the most selective public schools and some of the private institutions (such as the boarding schools for the upper classes) could be understood as comprising an elite segment in this schooling space. Then, in upper secondary, natural science programmes, the IB and some social science programmes have been found to be those most likely to be pursued by dominant groups, but also central to securing educational advantage. With few exceptions, most notably the boarding school Lundsberg in the woods of Värmland, all elite institutions are found in the metropolitan areas, including the traditional university towns of Uppsala and Lund, but concentrated in the Stockholm-Uppsala region.

We have found it helpful to differentiate between three definitions of elite education: a *meritocratic* one (dominance of students with very high grades or other valuable credentials), a *social* one (overrepresentation of children from the upper middle class, the upper classes and various elite groups) and a *functional* one (formation of the elites of tomorrow, or preparation for the entrance to elite programmes and institutions at higher levels in the educational system). We argue that there is evidence that the overall expansion of the educational system has created an increasing overlap of elite education according to all three definitions, while at the same time leading to intensified competition over the scarce resources that are assembled, refined and legitimated at elite schools and programmes.

The net effect of these factors is an increasingly complex educational market at all levels of the system in which meritocratic and social elites share and struggle over this space. This is perhaps most visible at the upper secondary level where there is intense competition between very different kinds of schools. In the largest but also smaller cities with learned traditions, there are the old public *läroverk* that favour meritocratic selection, whereby students from the cultural fractions of the higher social classes are advantaged. In the affluent areas of Stockholm, Gothenburg and Malmö, there is a small segment of private schools (day or boarding), attended by the economic fractions of the upper class, the nobility and the royalty. Additionally, alongside these elite schools, is a growing body of newly established private schools, run by commercial enterprises, who in many cases proclaim themselves to be elite schools. The contradiction here is that it is more profitable for their owners, in reality, to offer mass education, as the state pays schools for each pupil on the school roll.

Our research suggests that the divide between 'social' and 'meritocratic' elite education seems to be reducing, since the most highly ranked schools and programmes are becoming more socially *and* meritocratically selective. We anticipate that the Swedish educational landscape will experience some interesting struggles over the coming years, as social groups and elite institutions continue to fight for dominance in a system where credentialism is being challenged due to grade inflation, and where economic power holds little sway since the state funds the education of each pupil directly, regardless of the school or higher education institution they attend.

Notes

1 There are, of course, relationships between the elites and the upper classes. Upper class families tend to emerge from individuals who acquire elite positions that are then reproduced over time. Moreover, even if the upper classes have shared interests, they are divided into competing fractions, usually closely related to different fields.
2 The US prep schools (Cookson and Persell 1985), the British public schools (Sutton Trust 2008; Williams and Filippakou 2010), and the French *classes préparatoires* (Bourdieu 1989) are perhaps the most obvious examples.
3 The academisation of elite education has not always been a smooth affair. For example, journalists were hesitant about the establishment of institutes for journalism in the 1950s (Gardeström 2011), and within fine arts there is a strong belief that formal education is not the most appropriate form of training to foster creativity (Edling 2012).
4 See, for example, Larsson (2005) on the Swedish military academy, Engwall (2009) on the Stockholm School of Economics, and the most recently published volume on the history of Uppsala University (Frängsmyr 2010). For a valuable analysis of an important Swedish elite institution and its role in elite production and reproduction, see Florin and Johansson's (1993) study of the Swedish *läroverk* (upper secondary grammar school) in the late nineteenth century.
5 See www.skeptron.uu.se/broady/sec/ (accessed 7 June 2015).

References

Baltzell, E. D. (1995 [1958]). *Philadelphia gentlemen: The making of a national upper class.* New Brunswick, NJ: Transaction Publishers.
Bertilsson, E. (2014). *Skollärare. Rekrytering till utbildning och yrke 1977–2009.* Diss. Uppsala: Uppsala universitet.
Bourdieu, P. (1979). *La distinction: Critique sociale du jugement.* Paris: Éditions de Minuit.
Bourdieu, P. (1989). *La noblesse d'État: Grands corps et grandes écoles.* Paris: Éditions de Minuit.

Börjesson, M. (forthcoming). Oraison funèbre du modèle suédois. Trois dimensions de la marchandisation de l'enseignement supérieur. In C. Charle and C. Soulié (Eds.), *La dérégulation académique. La construction étatisée des marchés universitaires dans le monde.* Paris: Syllepse.

Bourdieu, P. and de Saint Martin, M. (1987). Agrégation et ségrégation. Le champ des grandes écoles et le champ du pouvoir. *Actes de la recherche en sciences sociales*, 69, 2–50.

Cookson, P. W. and Persell, C. H. (1985). *Preparing for power. America's elite boarding schools.* New York: Basic Books.

Dugonjic, L. (2014) *Les IB schools, une internationale élitiste. Émergence d'un espace mondial d'enseignement secondaire au XXe siècle.* Diss. Paris: EHESS.

Edling, M. (2012). Att förbereda för rummet av möjligheter: om skolornas antagning, fria utbildning och starka fältberoende. In M. Gustavsson, M. Börjesson and M. Edling (Eds.), *Konstens omvända ekonomi: tillgångar inom utbildningar och fält 1938–2008* (pp. 67–81). Gothenburg: Daidalos.

Engwall, L. (2009 [1992]). *Mercury meets Minerva. Business studies and higher education: The Swedish case.* Stockholm: Stockholm School of Economics.

Florin, C. and Johansson, U. (1993). *Där de härliga lagrarna gro. Kultur, klass och kön i det svenska läroverket 1850–1914.* Stockholm: Tidens förlag.

Forsberg, H. (forthcoming). *Kampen om eleverna. Gymnasiekolors och familjers tillgångar och strategier på gymnasiefältet i Stockholm, 1992–2011.* Diss. Uppsala: Uppsala universitet.

Frängsmyr, C. (2010). *Uppsala universitet 1852–1916.* Uppsala: Uppsala universitet.

Gardeström, E. (2011). *Att fostra journalister. Journalistutbildningens formering i Sverige 1944–1970.* Diss. Göteborg: Daidalos.

Larsson, E. (2005). *Från adlig uppfostran till borgerlig utbildning. Kungl. Krigsakademien mellan åren 1792 och 1866.* Diss. Uppsala: Uppsala universitet.

Le Roux, B. and Rouanet, H. (2004). *Geometric data analysis: From correspondence analysis to structured data analysis.* Dordrecht, Boston, London: Kluwer.

Le Roux, B. and Rouanet, H. (2010). *Multiple correspondence analysis.* London: Sage.

Lidegran, I. (2009). *Utbildningskapital. Om hur det alstras, fördelas och förmedlas.* Diss. Uppsala: Uppsala universitet.

Lindensjö, B. and Lundgren, U. P. (2000). *Utbildningsreformer och politisk styrning.* Stockholm: Liber.

Muxel, A. (2003). *Les étudiants de Sciences Po. Leurs idées, leurs valeurs, leurs cultures politiques.* Paris: Presses de Sciences Po.

Palme, M. (2008). *Det kulturella kapitalet. Studier av symboliska tillgångar i det svenska utbildningssystemet 1988–2008.* Diss. Uppsala: Uppsala universitet.

Palme, M. (2014). *'The International' in Swedish upper secondary education.* Unpublished paper presented at the International Colloquium Transnational capital and Transformation of the elites. Paris.

Rider, S., Hasselberg, Y. and Waluszewski, A. (Eds.). (2013). *Transformations in research, higher education and the academic market.* Dordrecht, New York: Springer.

Sandgren, P. (2012) *Emulating Eton: The paradox of elite boarding schools in the social democratic utopia.* European University Institute, Department of History and Civilization, unpublished paper.

Scot, M. (2011). *La London School of Economics & Political Science. Internationalisation universitaire et circulation des savoirs en sciences sociales 1895–2000.* Paris: PUF.

Slaughter, S. and Leslie, L. L. (1997). *Academic capitalism: Politics, policies, and the entrepreneurial university.* Baltimore, MD: Johns Hopkins University Press.

Sutton Trust (2008). *University admissions by individual schools.* London.

Trumpbour, J. (Ed.). (1989). *How Harvard rules: Reason in the service of empire.* Boston: South End Press.

Williams, G. and Filippakou, O. (2010). Higher education and UK elite formation in the twentieth century. *Higher Education*, 59(1), 1–20.

8
ELITE EDUCATION IN GERMANY?
Trends, developments and challenges

Ulrike Deppe and Heinz-Hermann Krüger

In this chapter we offer an overview of recent research on elite education in Germany. First, the conditions and educational developments that led to the present situation in Germany are described. Second, we outline the principal research concerns and theoretical assumptions our research group is engaging with in studying current trends and mechanisms of elite education. Third, we consider a number of recent changes in educational provision, outlining the creation of elite tracks within the secondary and tertiary sectors. Finally, we consider a future research agenda on elite education in Germany, discussing both the theoretical and the methodological challenges that arise as part of this work.

Elite education without elite educational institutions? Conditions and historical pathways in Germany

Historically, the field of secondary and tertiary education in Germany has not recognised the presence of educational institutions that might be regarded as explicitly 'elite' in their character (Hartmann 2001, p. 183). Until relatively recently, German universities were deemed in public discourse to be fundamentally equal in terms of the degrees and graduate certificates awarded by each institution (Teichler 2007, p. 24, Kreckel 2010, p. 242). Nevertheless, distinctions between universities and schools have long existed. For instance, some Gymnasiums were established long ago during the Renaissance and early modern period. In addition there are prestigious Jesuit schools, the Saxonian *Fürstenschulen* and their successors, and the Prussian *Landesschulen*. These were originally founded as schools run by the church or by monarchs, and largely seen as responsible for training the clergy or state officials respectively. Within the university sector too there have always been differences in status linked to amount of research undertaken at a given institution and whether they have an international reputation, such as the Humboldt University of Berlin, the University of Heidelberg or University of Tübingen.

The dismantling of a system previously perceived to be equal began as early as 1810, when Humboldt, a German philosopher and government functionary, created the *Humanistic Gymnasium* (Kreckel 2010, p. 242). This led to further reforms in the nineteenth century when three types of schools were introduced at the secondary level – the *Volksschule*, the *Realschule* and the *Gymnasium* (Drewek 1997, p. 197). This change resulted in the Gymnasium school-leaving certificate – the *Abitur* – becoming the only recognised qualification for entrance into university (Deppe *et al.* 2015, p. 1). Thus, within Germany, academic segregation occurs in most federal states (*Bundesländer*) from the age of ten (Zymek 2009, 2014).

At the beginning of the nineteenth century, the first modern research universities, funded by government, were also established in Germany. Modelled on the Humboldt University of Berlin, which was founded in 1810, these higher education institutions combined research and teaching, rather than focusing solely on tuition as had previously been the case. Graduating from one of these newer research universities was expected to lead to career trajectories within state institutions and other professions, such as law, medicine and engineering, and so forth. As the connecting link between the Gymnasium and university, the *Abitur* was an essential qualification for those wishing to enter higher education (Kreckel 2010, Deppe *et al.* 2015).

Over the past two decades, the situation has changed. Now, young people can obtain the *fachgebundene Hochschulreife*, a subject-specific higher education entrance qualification, acquired by attending 'vocational' Gymnasiums, which provides access to subject-specific *Fachhochschulen* and universities (Trautwein and Neumann 2008, pp. 487f.). This change has allowed those who do not seek, or who are unable, to opt for a more 'academic' education at such a young age to still pursue an educational pathway that may open up possibilities for elite positions in the future (Deppe *et al.* 2015).

Since the beginning of the twenty-first century, there has been a more direct and open discussion about excellence and elite education in Germany (Barlösius 2008, p. 151). With recent findings from the Programme for International Student Assessment (PISA) studies (Baumert *et al.* 2001), statements by the OECD (OECD 2013), and global academic rankings such as the Academic Ranking of World Universities (ARWU) and the Times Higher Education World University Ranking (THE) highlighting the relatively poor outcomes of German schools and universities compared to other countries (van Ackeren 2008), public debate and policy on this issue has increased. Such a focus on 'excellence' and 'elites' is new in Germany, especially with the spectre of elites in the Third Reich still influencing German sensibilities (Krüger *et al.* 2012, p. 328, also Rust 2005).

The German government has pushed forward a number of recent reforms in response to concerns raised by these international assessment exercises, such as PISA. A specific initiative on 'gifted pupils' (KMK 2003, Section D) included the expansion of schools and particular departments within these to cater for gifted and high achievers (Ullrich 2014, p. 182). The Federal German government and the federal states also launched a so-called 'Excellence Initiative' in 2005, aiming to foster cutting-edge research centres within universities (Ullrich 2014, Deppe *et al.* 2015). There has also been growth in private secondary and tertiary institutions in Germany (Deppe and Kastner 2014, Ullrich 2014). These developments pose further questions about the perceived egalitarian nature of the 'education system in Germany, which assumed the equality of educational certificates and institutions', and re-emphasise the emergence of 'vertical distinctions at each educational level' (Krüger *et al.* 2012, p. 328).

Research into elite education in Germany is very limited (Krüger *et al.* 2012, pp. 333f., exceptions include Kalthoff 2006, Helsper *et al.* 2008, Ullrich and Strunck 2012). Ullrich and Strunck (2012), for instance, have documented aspects of the private education sector, but have not focused on elite education. Meanwhile, Gibson and Helsper (2012) have explored how certain schools make symbolic claims about being elite. The emergence of international schools in Germany has received a little more attention, along with the children who attend them (Hornberg 2010, Bates 2012, p. 263, Hallwirth 2013, Krüger *et al.* 2014a). Within German higher education, research has examined the impact of the Excellence Initiative, described above (Bloch *et al.* 2008, Leibfried 2010, Hartmann 2011, DFG and Wissenschaftsrat 2012). However, with the establishment of the Mechanisms of Elite Formation in the German Education System research unit (based at the Martin Luther University Halle-Wittenberg and funded by the German Research Foundation) in 2011, a more concerted focus on elite education, across the education phases and sectors, has begun to emerge.

Mechanisms of elite formation in the German education system – key research questions and theoretical approaches

Our own research to date has focused on a number of central questions on elite education. First, we have examined how discourses about elites and excellence in tertiary education filter through into discussions about other aspects of education within policy and other public fora. Second, we have focused on how concerns about excellence and elite education are shaping parental educational strategies. Third, we have mapped educational pathways and transitions into and between elite educational institutions, examining what factors shape the choices made. Fourth, we have explored the recruitment processes for teaching professionals in such institutions, as well as the development of institutional norms and practices. Given the newness of this field of research in Germany, the research unit has so far adopted a broadly qualitative approach to researching these questions.

Our theoretical starting point lies in the concepts of 'elite' and 'excellence', which require further definition (Krüger *et al.* 2012, p. 330). Similar to Lukes' characterisation of the concept of power, the terms 'elite' and 'excellence' are 'ineradicably evaluative and essentially contested' (Lukes 2005, p. 9). For ourselves, however, the concept of elite is 'associated with social hierarchy and social status', while the notion of excellence is 'linked to outstanding achievements' (Krüger *et al.* 2012, p. 330; see also Wasner 2004, Maaz *et al.* 2009, Ricken 2009). Elite education is underpinned by 'processes of distinction open to hierarchic interpretation in the upper segment of the education system' (Krüger *et al.* 2012, p. 332). Elite education refers, first, to the models of justification that legitimise vertical distinctions in the education system; second, to practices that bring about these distinctions; and, third, to individual and institutional self-images that count on them (ibid.).

In much of our work, we draw on the concept of *elite formation mechanisms* advocated by Hedström (2008). This framing embraces a structurally meaningful and socially constructionist perspective (Tufte 2010). We have taken four elite education mechanisms as the starting point for our research, linked to processes of social negotiation, social construction and institutionalisation, that offer greater insight into elite education: (i) choice strategies by families and individuals, (ii) recruitment and selection procedures of elite institutions, (iii) processes of distinction engaged in by these institutions and (iv) the ways in which collective identities are formed within institutions but also by those attending these and the extent to which this leads to a homogenisation of expectations, values and practices (Krüger *et al.* 2012, pp. 332ff.). The following section summarises some of the key findings from our research to date.

Elite education in secondary and tertiary education

Gymnasiums in Germany

Although there is no history in Germany of clearly identifiable elite secondary schools, the past ten years have seen a significant change in the processes of differentiation in secondary schooling, which has simultaneously been accompanied by processes of vertical differentiation in institutions of higher education. Driving these developments has been a focus on the promotion of gifted students in Gymnasiums and a large increase in demand for a Gymnasium education. The number of pupils visiting a Gymnasium rose from approximately 30 per cent in 1992 to more than 40 per cent in 2011 (Deppe *et al.* 2015). In many cities today, over half of all pupils will attend this more academic type of school. This change, alongside the expansion of the private school sector, means that Germany now has more obvious market-like structures shaping education (Ball 2006, Bellmann and Weiß 2009, Zymek 2009). Our analysis of Gymnasiums across Germany, has identified five discrete types:

1. prominent traditional Gymnasiums, like the prestigious Prussian and Saxonian *Fürstenschulen* and their successors (Flöter 2009), or traditional Gymnasiums specialising in classical philology (*Humanistic* Gymnasiums);
2. Gymnasiums funded by the Protestant or Catholic Church;

3   Gymnasiums driven by progressive educational philosophies, mainly sponsored by private organisations;
4   state Gymnasiums that focus on providing an education to particularly gifted children or seeking to develop specific talents, such schools include those with a particular focus on the natural sciences, music or art and elite sports;
5   a growing category of bilingual Gymnasiums (particularly in large urban settings) and international schools, which have a globally oriented curriculum and provide internationally recognised school-leaving certificates, such as the International Baccalaureate (Ullrich 2014).

The latter two types of schools have most recently emerged within the German context.

Quantitative and qualitative studies have shown that a common feature across all five Gymnasium categories is that their main cohorts are comprised of children from socially privileged families (Standfest *et al.* 2005, Helsper *et al.* 2008). Interestingly, these are not always the groups of students who achieve the highest academic outcomes. A quantitative secondary analysis of PISA data from 2001 indicated that only half of the German Gymnasiums under review and attended by socially privileged pupils performed highest in the competence tests used by PISA (Maaz *et al.* 2009, p. 221). Furthermore, with the exception of 'elite sports schools', these Gymnasiums do not use the term 'elite' in their public profiles (Helsper *et al.* 2014, Krüger *et al.* 2014a). Interviews with senior managers in the upper secondary education system suggest that the term 'elite' is only deemed appropriate if it is associated with meritocracy and excellence in terms of academic outcomes. In German public discourse more generally, the term 'elite' is seen as taboo, not only because of the country's history of national socialism, and communism in eastern Germany, but also through its connection with financial and economic elites and processes of social inequality (Krüger *et al.* 2014a).

Not only is the term 'elite' largely missing from public discourse and the narratives offered by pupils, parents and educational professionals, but we have found little evidence of processes promoting exclusivity during the selection and recruitment of students. At the end of Year 5 of primary school, children move into secondary education. The selection practices we have analysed are very heterogeneous – from standard tests, with more specialised exams for specialist Gymnasiums (in mathematics, natural science or sports), to a written application and interview process for faith-based Gymnasiums and international schools. Although having the financial means is often a necessity when applying to a private institution, such as one of the growing number of international schools, it is seldom openly expressed as such (Krüger *et al.* 2014b). Furthermore, the availability of scholarships suggests publicly that access to these schools is relatively open, though this may not be the case (ibid.). Our research shows that at exclusive Gymnasiums there appears to be an overall tendency to prioritise the use of standardised and quantifiable procedures of selection. Nevertheless, despite attempts to appear meritocratic in their approach, as in other contexts, economic and/or social capital continue to be of central importance in determining who successfully gains entry into these exclusive spaces.

Distinctions within German tertiary education

Within the tertiary sector, reforms aimed at vertical differentiation have taken place since 2004. Through the Excellence Initiative (which runs until 2017 with a budget of over €4 billon), the German federal government hopes to develop a small group of top-level research universities which will train a new generation of outstanding scientists and raise the international profile of German universities more generally, thereby enhancing their global competitiveness. Forty universities have so far been awarded the status of being 'elite', with 11 of these having been unofficially designated 'elite universities' (Deppe *et al*. 2015). In other universities, particular research clusters or graduate schools have been identified as elite centres or departments (DFG and Wissenschaftsrat 2012). Thus, Berlin's Humboldt University and Free University as well as Ludwig Maximilian University and TU Munich are now widely recognised as elite universities, while particular disciplines such as social sciences at the universities of Frankfurt or Bielefeld are considered to be high status/elite. The remaining 70 German universities are seen not to merit such a title (Deppe *et al*. 2015).

Alongside these processes of stratification within the state-funded higher education sector, Germany has experienced significant growth in the establishment of private universities. While this development has further embedded market-like conditions within the higher education sector, only 5 per cent of any given cohort starting an undergraduate degree currently attend one of the 90 private universities in Germany today. These private institutions tend to focus on training people for senior management positions in the field of economics and politics (Bloch *et al*. 2014) – arguably providing a similar function to the French *grandes écoles*.

Research has found that the ten to 20 most well-endowed research universities have found that the elite status awarded via the Excellent Initiative has extended their income and prestige further (Münch 2007, 2011, Hartmann 2011). Research examining the experiences of university students enrolled on courses in the departments understood to be elite according to the Excellence Initiative, or private university degree courses, has found that a sense of differentiation is primarily generated by through the positive rankings which their institutions are awarded, the international links these universities are increasingly forging and the allegedly highly selective admissions processes they must successfully negotiate (Bloch *et al*. 2014). The selection processes require the submission of extensive application documents, research proposals and interviews. Closer inspection of these selection practices, however, suggests that candidates are required to demonstrate particular forms of social capital to successfully navigate these selection processes. We have found that informal networks between individual candidates and university lecturers at these universities, particularly private universities, increase students' knowledge of how best to shape and present their applications. Furthermore, some selection processes include relatively costly assessment procedures and, in private universities, the high tuition fees mean that, apart from the small number of scholarships available, only students from wealthier backgrounds can access these educational opportunities (Bloch *et al.* 2014).

Conclusion – further perspectives for research on German elite education

Vertical differentiation in upper secondary and higher education has increased significantly in Germany over the past ten years. In the school sector, this is most noticeable in terms of the number of different types of Gymnasiums that families and young people can choose from – offering different curricula, historical legacies and often homogeneity in the social composition of social groups attending them. Currently, families can choose from more traditional Gymnasiums that have a historical legacy of providing an elite and exclusive education, but there are also schools that have been specifically established to educate 'gifted' children or which provide a bilingual education and the opportunity to obtain internationally recognised qualifications. International schools have been found to be attractive not only to international, professionally mobile parents, but also to wealthy German families (Deppe *et al.* 2015). In future work we intend to examine more closely how the type of Gymnasium attended shapes the aspirations and future educational and career trajectories of its students.

Meanwhile in the German higher education system, the Excellence Initiative has created a small group of elite universities that receive higher levels of funding and which are further attempting to establish distinctive, internationally recognised degree programmes that will train a new generation of excellent scientists, business or public/political leaders (Deppe *et al.* 2015). It will be important to examine how these processes of distinction and stratification continue to develop once the funding for the Excellent Initiative ceases in 2017.

Despite the lack of in-depth research on this area, there is some initial evidence that universities highlighted through the Excellence Initiative have become more popular among secondary school students (Winkler 2014). Through our current research programme, we intend to examine how Gymnasiums encourage and attempt to facilitate access to these universities. Additionally, we are undertaking longitudinal research to examine the career paths of under- and postgraduate students who have studied at these elite institutions (Deppe *et al.* 2015). This research will also include a focus on how social class background, family habitus and the institutions attended shape future career trajectories.

A third central focus for the current work programme of our research unit has been to examine the impact of internationalisation on the German education system as a whole. With internationally recognised graduate certificates and curricula becoming increasingly valuable, it will be important to enquire into how German schools and universities are supporting their students to develop a more transnational outlook, and encouraging opportunities for experiences beyond the country's national borders.

References

Ackeren, I. van (2008). Nationale Spitzenleistungen – internationale Leistungsspitze? In H. Ullrich and S. Strunck (Eds.), *Begabtenförderung an Gymnasien. Entwicklungen, Befunde, Perspektiven* (pp. 37–60). Wiesbaden: VS Verlag.
Ball, S. J. (2006). *Education policy and social class.* London: Routledge.
Barlösius, E. (2008). Leuchttürme der Wissenschaft. *Leviathan*, 36(1), 149–169.
Bates, R. (2012). Is global citizenship possible, and can international schools provide it? *Journal of Research in International Education*, 11(3), 262–274.
Baumert, J. et al. (Ed.). (2001). *PISA 2000. Basiskompetenzen von Schülerinnen und Schülern im internationalen Vergleich.* Opladen: Leske + Budrich.
Bellmann, J. and Weiß, M. (2009). Risiken und Nebenwirkungen Neuer Steuerung im Schulsystem. Theoretische Konzeptualisierung und Erklärungsmodelle. *Zeitschrift für Pädagogik*, 55(2), 286–308.
Bloch, R., Keller, A., Lottmann, A. and Würmann, C. (Ed.). (2008). *Making excellence. Grundlagen, Praxis und Konsequenzen der Exzellenzinitiative.* Bielefeld: Bertelsmann.
Bloch, R., Kreckel, R., Mitterle, A. and Stock, M. (2014). Stratifikationen im Bereich der Hochschulbildung in Deutschland. In H.-H. Krüger and W. Helsper (Eds.), *Elite und Exzellenz im Bildungssystem – Nationale und internationale Perspektiven. Zeitschrift für Erziehungswissenschaft*, Supplement 17, 243–261. Wiesbaden: VS Verlag.
Deppe, U. and Kastner, H. (2014). Exklusive Bildungseinrichtungen in Deutschland. Entwicklungstendenzen und Identifizierungshürden. In H.-H. Krüger and W. Helsper (Eds.), *Elite und Exzellenz im Bildungssystem – Nationale und internationale Perspektiven. Zeitschrift für Erziehungswissenschaft*, Supplement 17, 263–283. Wiesbaden: Springer VS.
Deppe, U., Helsper, W., Kreckel, R., Krüger, H.-H. and Stock, M. (2015) Germany's hesitant approach to elite education. In A. van Zanten, S. J. Ball and B. Darchy-Koechlin (Eds.), *Elites, privilege and excellence: The national and global redefinition of educational advantage* (pp. 82–94). London: Routledge.
DFG and Wissenschaftsrat (2012). Gewonnen und verloren. Die Ergebnisse der Exzellenzinitiative. In *Forschung & Lehre*, 19(7), 553–554. Available at www.forschung-und-lehre.de/wordpress/Archiv/2012/ful_07-2012.pdf (accessed 7 June 2015).
Drewek, P. (1997). Geschichte der Schule. In K. Harney and H.-H. Krüger (Eds.), *Einführung in die Geschichte von Erziehungswissenschaft und Erziehungswirklichkeit* (pp. 183–207). Opladen: Leske & Budrich.
Flöter, J. (2009). *Eliten-Bildung in Sachsen und Preußen: Die Fürsten- und Landesschulen Grimma, Meißen, Joachimsthal und Pforta* (1868–1933). Köln: Böhlau.
Gibson, A. and Helsper, W. (2012). Erziehung und Bildung der 'Auserwählten' – Privatschulen und deren 'Elite'-Anspruch. In H. Ullrich and S. Strunck (Eds.), *Private Schulen in Deutschland. Entwicklungen – Profile – Kontroversen* (pp. 225–246). Wiesbaden: VS Verlag.
Hallwirth, U. (2013). Internationale Schulen. In A. Gürlevik, C. Palentien and R. Heyer (Eds.), *Privatschulen versus staatliche Schulen* (pp. 183–195). Wiesbaden: VS Verlag.
Hartmann, M. (2001). Klassenspezifischer Habitus oder exklusive Bildungstitel als soziales Selektionskriterium? In B. Krais (Ed.), *An der Spitze* (pp. 157–216). Konstanz: UVK.
Hartmann, M. (2011). Funktionale oder vertikale Differenzierung. Die Folgen der Exzellenzinitiative. *Recht der Jugend und des Bildungswesens*, 59(3), 284–296.
Hedström, P. (2008). *Anatomie des Sozialen. Prinzipien der analytischen Soziologie.* Wiesbaden: VS Verlag.
Helsper, W., Brademann, S., Kramer, R.T., Ziems, C. and Klug, R. (2008). Exklusive Gymnasien und ihre Schüler – Kulturen der Distinktion in der gymnasialen Schullandschaft. In H. Ullrich and S. Strunck (Eds.), *Begabtenförderung an Gymnasien* (pp. 215–249). Wiesbaden: VS Verlag.
Helsper, W., Niemann, M., Dreyer, L. and Gibson, A. (2014). Positionierungen zu 'Elite' und 'Exzellenz' in gymnasialen Bildungsregionen. In H.-H. Krüger and W. Helsper (Eds.), *Elite und Exzellenz im Bildungssystem. Nationale und internationale Perspektiven. Zeitschrift für Erziehungswissenschaft*, Supplement 17, 203–219. Wiesbaden: Springer VS.

Hornberg, S. (2010). Internationale Schulen. In H. Ullrich and S. Strunck (Eds.), *Private Schulen in Deutschland. Entwicklungen – Profile – Kontroversen* (pp. 117–130). Wiesbaden: VS Verlag.

Kalthoff, H. (2006). Doing/undoing class in exklusiven Internatsschulen. In W. Georg (Ed.), *Soziale Ungleichheit im Bildungssystem* (pp. 93–123). Konstanz: UVK.

Kreckel, R. (2010). Zwischen Spitzenforschung und Breitenausbildung. In H.-H. Krüger, U. Rabe-Kleberg, R.-T. Kramer and J. Budde (Ed.), *Bildungsungleichheit revisited* (pp. 235–256). Wiesbaden: VS Verlag.

Krüger, H.-H., Helsper, W., Sackmann, R., Breidenstein, G., Bröckling, U., Kreckel, R., Mierendorff, J. and Stock, M. (2012). Mechanismen der Elitebildung im deutschen Bildungssystem. Ausgangslage, Theoriediskurse, Forschungsstand. *Zeitschrift für Erziehungswissenschaft*, 15(2), 327–343.

Krüger, H.-H., Keßler, C., Otto, A. and Schippling, A. (2014a). Elite und Exzellenz aus der Perspektive von Jugendlichen und ihren Peers an exklusiven Schulen. In H.-H. Krüger and W. Helsper (Eds.), *Elite und Exzellenz im Bildungssystem – Nationale und internationale Perspektiven*. *Zeitschrift für Erziehungswissenschaft*, Supplement 17, 221–241. Wiesbaden: Springer VS.

Krüger, H.-H., Keßler, C. and Winter, D. (2014b). Schulkultur und soziale Ungleichheit. Perspektiven von Schulleitungen auf den Elite- und Exzellenzdiskurs. In J. Böhme, M. Hummrich and R. Kramer (Eds.), *Schulkultur – Theoriebildung im Diskurs* (pp. 163–210). Wiesbaden: Springer VS.

Kultusministerkonferenz (KMK) (Ed.). (2003). *Bildungsbericht für Deutschland. Erste Befunde*. Opladen: Leske & Budrich.

Leibfried, S. (Ed.). (2010). *Die Exzellenzinitiative. Zwischenbilanz und Perspektiven*. Frankfurt am Main, New York: Campus.

Lukes, S. (2005). *Power: A radical view* (2nd edition). London: Palgrave Macmillan.

Maaz, K., Nagy, G., Jonkmann, K. and Baumert, J. (2009). Eliteschulen in Deutschland – Eine Analyse zur Existenz von Exzellenz und Elite in der gymnasialen Bildungslandschaft in einer institutionellen Perspektive. *Zeitschrift für Pädagogik*, 55(2), 211–227.

Münch, R. (2007). *Die akademische Elite. Zur sozialen Konstruktion wissenschaftlicher Exzellenz*, Frankfurt am Main: Suhrkamp.

Münch, R. (2011). *Akademischer Kapitalismus*. Berlin: Suhrkamp.

Organisation for Economic Co-operation and Development (OECD). (2013). *Bildung auf einen Blick 2013: OECD-Indikatoren*. Gütersloh: W. Bertelsmann Verlag.

Ricken, N. (2009). Elite und Exzellenz. Machttheoretische Analysen zum neuen Wissenschaftsdiskurs. *Zeitschrift für Pädagogik*, 55(2), 194–210.

Rust, H. (2005). *Das Elite-Missverständnis. Warum die Besten nicht immer die Richtigen sind*. Wiesbaden: Gabler.

Standfest, C., Köller, S. and Scheunpflug, S. (2005). *Lernen – Leben – Glauben. Zur Qualität evangelischer Schulen*. Münster: Waxmann Verlag.

Teichler, U. (2007). *Die Internationalisierung der Hochschulen*. Frankfurt am Main, New York: Campus.

Trautwein, U. and Neumann, M. (2008). Das Gymnasium. In K. S. Cortina, J. Baumert, A. Leschinsky, K. U. Mayer and L. Trommer (Eds.), *Das Bildungswesen in der Bundesrepublik Deutschland* (pp. 467–502). Reinbek: Rowohlt.

Tufte, P. A. (2010). Kritik der Analytischen Soziologie. In T. Kron and T. Grund (Eds.), *Die Analytische Soziologie in der Diskussion* (pp. 225–243). Wiesbaden: VS Verlag.

Ullrich, H. (2014). Exzellenz und Elitenbildung in Gymnasien. Traditionen und Innovationen. In H.-H. Krüger and W. Helsper (Ed.), *Elite und Exzellenz im Bildungssystem – Nationale und internationale Perspektiven*. *Zeitschrift für Erziehungswissenschaft*, Supplement 17, 181–201. Wiesbaden: Springer VS.

Ullrich, H. and Strunck, S. (Eds.). (2012). *Private Schulen in Deutschland. Entwicklungen – Profile – Kontroversen*. Wiesbaden: VS Verlag.

Wasner, B. (2004). *Eliten in Europa. Einführung in Konzepte, Theorien und Befunde*. Wiesbaden: VS Verlag.

Winkler, O. (2014). Exzellente Wahl. Soziale Selektivität und Handlungsorientierungen bei der Wahl von Spitzenbildung im Hochschulbereich. *Zeitschrift für Soziologie der Erziehung und Sozialisation*, 34(3), 1–17.

Zymek, B. (2009) Prozesse der Internationalisierung und Hierarchisierung im Bildungssystem. *Zeitschrift für Pädagogik*, 55(2), 175–193.

Zymek, B. (2014). Ausleseverfahren und Institutionen der nationalen Elitebildung und ihre internationalen Herausforderungen. Eine historisch-vergleichende Skizze zu Frankreich, England und Deutschland. In H.-H. Krüger and W. Helsper (Eds.), *Elite und Exzellenz im Bildungssystem – Nationale und internationale Perspektiven. Zeitschrift für Erziehungswissenschaft*, Supplement 17, 59–79. Wiesbaden: Springer VS.

9
PROMOTING EQUALITY *AND* REPRODUCING PRIVILEGE IN ELITE EDUCATIONAL TRACKS IN FRANCE

Agnès van Zanten

An educational institution can be considered 'elite' if it confers privilege and power on its students (Cookson and Persell 1985, Gaztambide-Fernández 2009, Khan 2011). Such status depends on external factors, notably the social and academic characteristics of its current students, its inclusion in a network of elite institutions and the kinds of professional and political positions or further studies students take up on leaving the institution. It is also granted on the basis of the institution's capacity to define and impose an educational model perceived as relevant to the elite groups (students, parents, agents of other elite institutions, employers) with whom it interacts, and accepted as legitimate by society at large. Elite institutions generally enjoy 'relative autonomy' (Bourdieu and Passeron 1977) and have the material and symbolic resources necessary to alter various parameters in order to pursue their own interests (Karabel 1984). In addition to this, their actions are frequently self-reinforcing. Once an institution's elite status has been secured, those wishing to become members of an 'elite' apply to such an institution; the more candidates who do so, the more selective the institution becomes and the more it imposes its elitist model. This helps reinforce its capacity to hoard available opportunities (Tilly 1998) with respect to access to elite positions, which in turn reinforces its elite image, and thus a 'virtuous cycle' is established.

While elite institutions can be found in many countries, the situation in France is unique for at least three reasons. First, the country has a long history, dating back to the eighteenth century, of a few institutions being consecrated as elite that have managed to preserve this status until the present day. Second, in contrast to other countries where 'elite' and 'private' forms of education may be synonymous (Maxwell 2015), a significant proportion of elite institutions in France were established by the state with the aim of creating a 'state nobility' (Bourdieu 1996; van Zanten and Maxwell 2015). Third, within the French education system there exists a series of distinctive elite or 'high status' tracks (Kingston and Lewis 1990). The focus in this chapter is on these inter-institutional paths between high-status educational institutions.

To analyse the nature and effects of this linking process, I draw on the work of Ralph Turner (1960) and his ideal-type models of 'sponsorship' and 'open competition', which he developed when comparing and contrasting access to elite positions and social mobility in England and the USA. However, I extend Turner's ideas by arguing that both models can co-exist in the same country (see also Noel 1962, Kerckhoff 2001, Naudet 2015), and that three types of agents are involved in the development of sponsorship processes: the state, educational institutions and families. France is characterised by a political, economic and cultural elite whose position and reproduction is strongly dependent on the existence of an elite system of education. In such a context, I argue, an ostensive commitment to 'open competition' in fact remains embedded in old and new forms of sponsorship carried out by these three types of agents.

This chapter comprises four sections. In the first section, I offer a brief history of the creation of elite higher education institutions and highlight the central role played by the *concours* in regulating admissions to them. Next, I examine the role of the state in the constitution of elite educational tracks and other forms of state involvement in the sponsorship of elite education. In the third section, I describe some of the ways in which educational institutions provide a specific kind of sponsorship through their selection and training of students. Finally, I focus on how social groups with cultural and economic capital are able to sponsor their children by both boosting their capacity to win in 'meritocratic competitions' and constructing specific educational trajectories for them.

The institutionalisation of meritocratic competitive examinations

The image of elite higher education institutions in France is symbolically linked to the French revolution and two of the most famous institutions created by the revolutionaries, l'École polytechnique and l'École normale supérieure (ENS). However, some of these 'special training schools', which came progressively to be referred to as *les grandes écoles*, were in fact established earlier by royalty in the seventeenth century for the purpose of training individuals for high-level technical or command positions within the military (Green 2013). Initially, only young men and those of a noble birth or with family links to highly ranked officers were admitted to these specialist military training establishments. Birth and connections were, however, considered insufficient criteria by some, which led to the creation, in the period immediately before the French revolution, of a system of competitive examinations – later known as *concours* – used to select the most able candidates to become state officers and engineers (Belhoste 2002). The revolutionaries did not cast aside such a commitment to elite recruitment and training system. In fact, particularly through the creation of l'École polytechnique in 1794, they chose to extend it, in order to train those required to take on administrative and technical roles in state institutions to support the development and governing of France. However, they sought to ensure that the *concours* should democratise the selection process for elite training and future positions. Holding a public position was declared open to all citizens and selection only possible on the basis of 'merit' (ibid.).

Napoleon and subsequent political regimes encouraged the development of these state-sponsored institutions and of the competitive *concours* at the expense of publicly funded universities which, for historical reasons, were not considered trustworthy or capable of training future high-level state employees. This, in turn, encouraged a process of 'institutional isomorphism' (DiMaggio and Powell 1983) by private providers of higher education that began to emerge from 1870 onwards as a result of economic development. Many of these private higher education institutions (such as the business schools now known under the names of HEC, ESCP Europe or ESSEC) were supported by the industrial and business sectors and later began to acquire a high degree of autonomy and visibility by securing funding from regional chambers of industry and commerce. Their adoption of the *concours* to regulate entry was seen, by the most ambitious of them, as a crucial step in raising their reputation as it allowed them to increase their academic selectivity and to benefit from the sense of 'nobility' bestowed through this meritocratic contest (Bourdieu 1996).

The *concours* progressively became the symbol of a new 'Republican elitism' (Belhoste 2002) in the form of a state-supported form of 'open competition' in which all candidates were put on an equal footing by an examination that focused only on academic performance, with no reference to a candidate's personal characteristics. The *concours* was therefore believed to have eliminated previous forms of sponsorship, based on social rank, associated with the *Ancien Regime* (ibid.). However, research has highlighted that, as in other countries where competitive entry systems also dominate, such as Japan (LeTendre et al. 2006) or where elite higher education institutions have developed diverse procedures to increasingly select their students on the basis of their academic ability, such as England and the USA (Karabel 2005, Zimdars 2010), this form of educational meritocracy has not prevented the reproduction of privilege. In fact, the existing data suggest that processes linked to the reproduction of privilege have, if anything, become more embedded with time. Nowadays, students in the elite higher education tracks in France come predominantly from upper-class families (Baudelot and Matonti 1994) and their presence in these tracks has steadily increased over the past 50 years (Albouy and Wanecq 2003, Euriat and Thélot 1995).

To understand why this is the case, it is useful to focus on the *concours* and its distinctive characteristics. A defining aspect of the *concours* is its function as part of a larger process linking particular state institutions with individual, highly prestigious state-funded *grandes écoles* (Suleiman 1978). In this system, the state effectively delegates the recruitment and training of influential future state employees to specialist educational institutions, a process which has both practical and symbolic consequences. At a practical level, admission to the most prestigious state *grandes écoles* has been traditionally associated with access to the civil service which explains why students who gain admission still today receive a salary for the duration of their study and why the *grandes écoles* offer only a very small number of places per year for new entrants, thereby increasing the level of competition (l'École polytechnique, for instance, only recruits about 400 French students a year and l'École normale supérieure only 200). Although many students entering these *grandes écoles* no longer feel personally committed, nor are they obliged by the institutions or the state, to take up positions as future agents of state administration (van Zanten and Maxwell 2015), this association has been maintained by the institutions to preserve both their legitimacy and their reputation, based on 'scarcity value' in the national context (Veltz 2007). These various features of the *grandes écoles* also highlight the symbolic value attached to the *concours* which, through state sponsorship, confers public recognition of an individual's academic and moral qualities and clearly and definitively distinguishes the 'elect' future dominant agents from 'others' (Bourdieu and Saint-Martin 1987).

The second set of distinguishing features of the *concours* concerns their content. Although there is much variation between *concours* according to field of study and the institutions to which admission is being sought, a common feature is that they simultaneously aim to evaluate students' specialised knowledge of certain fields, 'general culture' (implying a good knowledge of French literature, history and philosophy), mastery of English and other languages, as well as more personal qualities, including now the display of initiative, the capacity to work in groups, self-motivation and other more diffuse personal characteristics (the specificity of which characteristics are foregrounded in the selection process varies a little across institutions). Specialised and general academic knowledge and more personal attributes are typically evaluated separately, through two different types of test – another distinctive feature of the French *concours*. Written exams on academic subjects serve, first and foremost, to select 'admissible' candidates, while later oral and more hybrid-type examinations determine the final set of 'admitted candidates'. Returning to Turner's (1960) work, only the written exams align with the ideal-type in facilitating 'open competition', as examiners mark the written academic outputs allocated to them without knowledge of a candidate's gender or social and economic position. However, during the oral examinations and tests, examiners' judgements can be more heavily influenced by candidates' backgrounds and their 'impression management' strategies (Allouch 2013).

State sponsorship

The existence of the *concours*, and its implications for future employment and social position, has meant that a whole tier of education provision has come into existence to prepare students for these examinations. Before the French revolution, some candidates preparing for the *concours* employed the services of a private tutor, although most took lessons in private boarding institutions, some of which had strong links with the examiners of the *concours*. In both of these systems, financial means were necessary in order to access vital preparatory training. After the revolution, and especially after Napoleon had created a system of public *lycées* in 1802, the situation changed. While private institutions continued to provide residential opportunities and individual academic training in the form of mock oral examinations, additional tuition in science subjects, especially in mathematics, usually the focus of the written exams, was given in special classes created to prepare for the *concours* within the state *lycées* themselves. Later on the situation changed again. The Falloux Law of 1850 paved the way for the expansion of private secondary schools. Some of these institutions offered full preparatory classes. However, most preparatory provision (which by then also included coaching for oral examinations) remained located within the state *lycée* system (Belhoste 2001). The main reasons for the development of this system of preparation were political and institutional. National political and educational authorities wanted to provide a type of support that would strengthen the state's control of the education of elites, as well as links between public institutions, by circumventing universities and downplaying the role of private schools.

The majority of these classes (85 per cent of them in 2014) – now called *classes préparatoires aux grandes écoles* (CPGE) and colloquially known as *prépas*, which comprise a two- to three-year programme of study, based at the *lycées* after the *baccalauréat* – can still be found in the public sector, thereby arguably making them accessible to all students. And yet, recent data provided by the Ministry of Higher Education show that, within the CPGE system, 50 per cent of students have an upper-class background and only 12 per cent come from working-class families (MESR 2012) – figures which have remained relatively unchanged over the past ten years. Thus, it can be argued that economic investment by the state in these elite education tracks represents an inverse form of redistribution favouring wealthier students. This point is further emphasised by the fact that the annual cost to the state of educating a CPGE student is much higher (€15,080) that that of educating students who usually come from more diverse backgrounds and are studying at a public university (€10,770).

An important mechanism through which those with greater economic resources are more likely to gain access to elite higher education tracks derives from the fact that the most elite *classes prépas* are concentrated in the major French cities. Despite government efforts since the 1970s to diversify the location of CPGEs, one-third of all students in preparatory classes remain enrolled in *lycées* located in the Parisian region, especially in the centre of Paris (18 per cent). Meanwhile 20 per cent (21 out of 101) of France's administrative regional *départements* do not have a single *lycée* with a *prépa* attached to them. While a small number of *lycées* offering a CPGE provide boarding opportunities for a few students coming from more regional and rural areas of France, the costs involved in living away from family and place of origin are likely to dissuade lower income students and parents from applying. Furthermore, research has highlighted that students are more likely to choose to enrol in a CPGE if there is one in their own *lycée* (Nakhili 2005), and one might expect this to be particularly the case for students from lower income backgrounds.

The state also indirectly sponsors students from privileged backgrounds and the CPGE system itself through the rules determining access to higher education. A significant factor here is that the CPGEs have always been allowed to select their students, while public universities have had to accept all students who apply to study in them. Another important factor is that access to the CPGEs has traditionally been reserved for students who have followed the academic track in their upper secondary schooling. While a few scientific CPGEs now accept students from technological tracks, the latter only represent 5 per cent of the total CPGE population. Students who, since 1987, have obtained a vocational *baccalauréat* are not even allowed to apply. Such forms of institutional tracking also mean that *prepa* students have very strong academic records, with 13 per cent having 'skipped' a year during preschool or primary school, and the vast majority obtaining their *baccalauréat* with honours (i.e. with a grade point average (GPA) of 14 to 16 out of 20) or high honours (a GPA above 16 out of 20) (MESR 2012).

State educational authorities have nevertheless also taken measures to ensure and expand the implementation of a system of 'open competition' by controlling the procedures for application to these classes. Two main policies are important here. The first concerns the introduction in 2008 of a centralised application system, which does not allow the CPGE to know how students have ranked them, a ploy used to reinforce the 'blindness' of the whole selection process. As a result, CPGEs have now to consider a wider pool of applicants, which theoretically should result in a greater 'diversity' of students being able to apply. The second policy has to do with the content of the applications, which must only include academic information related to a student's grade point average, class rank and comments from their teachers on the last two years of *lycée*, again aimed at reinforcing the anonymity of the process and, therefore, selection based solely on 'merit'. However, as I argue in the next section, educational institutions have found ways to circumvent these state rules.

Institutional sponsorship

Examining what educational institutions do is important because, although the state continues to play a key role in shaping the field of elite education, it delegates the process of admission and training to CPGE headteachers and staff, allowing for institutional interests to emerge. Findings from the EDUC-ELITES project[1] suggest that selection panels in elite public CPGEs use information on feeder *lycées* to reinterpret students' academic results. Until the 1980s, students tended to come from a relatively small number of *lycées*, and so the main difference between applicants was whether they had attended a public or private school. During this time, panel members in state CPGEs tended to discriminate against students from private *lycées* partly because they believed that students' grades in private *lycées* were inflated to satisfy fee-paying parents and partly because they saw these students as members of the economic, conservative and Catholic fractions of the bourgeoisie, whereas teachers working in the public sector were usually from the cultural fractions of the middle classes. After a second wave of massification or 'segregative democratisation'

(Merle 2000) of secondary education in the 1980s, the way in which bias came to operate in the selection process changed to take into account a new influx of students coming from the new public *lycées* created in disadvantaged areas. Now, panels often perceive the academic assessment of students made by teachers working in disadvantaged schools as 'overindulgent', which means they often view the grades awarded as being over-inflated. Panel members also appear to make assumptions about such students' more general capacity to 'fit into' the elite CPGE environment.

This form of institutional sponsorship is even more pronounced in private elite CPGEs which, because they operate partly outside state control, are more able to rely on 'institutional channelling' (Hill 2008) between private *lycées* and private CPGEs, both to counterbalance the institutional tracking between state *lycées* and CPGEs and because of a belief in the superior moral and social qualities of students who come from private secondary schools. However, private CPGEs also aim to recruit 'top-of-the-class' students from public *lycées* as a mechanism through which to maintain their reputation and legitimacy (as not being too socially exclusive). Although a student's academic records remains paramount in the assessment process, the information contained in applications includes students' grade reports as well as an independent evaluation by teachers of a student's motivation and personal qualities, information about parental background and, crucially, a personal statement from the applicant themselves. The purpose of including a fuller set of materials within a student's application is, first, to select students, most frequently from private *lycées* who, despite not having excellent academic results, may exhibit specific qualities considered socially valuable. A second purpose is to facilitate the weeding-out of students, generally from public *lycées*, who are perceived to be too academically oriented to fit into an environment devoted less to the intellectual training of members of the cultural elite (scientists, university professors, writers or artists) but more to the 'all-round' education of academically very able students who plan to occupy positions of power in the private sector and become integrated into the economic elite (Bourdieu 1996, de Saint-Martin 2008).

The existence of the CPGE system has also generated less direct but still powerful sponsorship at the lower levels of education and, most notably, at the *lycée* level. *Lycée* teachers and other personnel tend to shape the aspirations of their students and variously support their entry into elite higher education tracks. An ongoing qualitative study on transitions to higher education that I am presently conducting in four *lycées* suggests that educational agents in the most elite *lycée* systematically present the CPGE as the most desirable and 'natural' track for their students to follow – through brochures, 'open days', parent–teacher meetings, classroom discussions and guidance to individuals. Institutions also tailor advice to students and parents on the best CPGE to apply for and on how to maximise the chances of being selected. In contrast, the most disadvantaged *lycée* in our study promotes applications to non-selective university degrees or two-year vocational higher education institutions and encourages only a very small number of highly academic students to apply to CPGEs, very seldom to the most selective ones. In these *lycées* there is also very little institutional knowledge of how best to 'play the system' when applying for admission to a CPGE (van Zanten 2015b).

At the other end of the track – the transition from the CPGE into a *grande école* – we find different forms of institutional sponsorship, despite the formal commitment to 'open competition' created by the *concours*. A group of around 20 to 30 CPGEs, both public and, increasingly, private ones as well, currently monopolise access to the most prestigious *grandes écoles*. These CPGEs are largely located in old, prestigious *lycées*, often in Paris. The success of such a small cluster of CPGEs and the strong institutional links between these two parts of the elite education track can be understood as becoming self-reinforcing – as a greater the number of students in a CPGE succeed in the *concours*, important knowledge is gained and accumulated over the years, both through students' accounts and from comments received from *concours* panel members and directors of the *grandes écoles* concerning the content of the examination and the evaluation criteria used by the examiners.

'Chartering' (Meyer 1970) or curricular specialisation is also an important feature of institutional sponsorship at this stage. All CPGEs provide a learning environment quite different from that of universities. There are more favourable teacher-ratios in the former, and the curriculum offer includes both broad and in-depth subject coverage; intensive training in problem-solving and writing; large amounts of homework as well as weekly assessment exercises and mock oral examinations; and individualised assessment for each student in relation to academic progress and personal development (Darmon 2013, Daverne and Dutercq 2013, Rauscher 2010). The most prestigious CPGEs go one step further by running 'star classes' for the most academically able students, where the curriculum is directly modelled on the programmes of the most competitive *concours*. These CPGEs also encourage attendance at conferences where students will be exposed to a wide range of experts across different fields of study, and promote involvement, especially within the privately-run CPGEs, in cultural, charitable and religious activities.

Family sponsorship

Beyond, but intersecting with, the different forms of sponsorship in schools and higher education, are forms of family sponsorship which have, for a long time, reinforced these institutional processes. Significant in sustaining the illusion of 'meritocratic elitism' within the French educational system is the fact that historically the image of the *grandes écoles* and the *classes préparatoires* has been associated not with the economic elite but with the cultural fractions of the upper and middle classes. There are two main reasons for this. The first is that, until the 1960s, the most prestigious *grandes écoles* were state-funded. The second is that, because public CPGEs did not charge tuition fees, members of the cultural fractions of the upper and middle classes tended to dominate these tracks. Furthermore, between the 1930s and 1960s, when democratisation of the elite tracks was at its height, a significant proportion of the CPGE students were the sons and daughters of secondary and primary school teachers, many of whom had themselves experienced social mobility through education (Euriat and Thelot 1995, Albouy and Wanecq 2003).

This picture is widely accepted as evidence of a 'class meritocracy' (Power et al. 2003) in France. Unlike the USA, for instance, where the economic fractions of the upper classes have tended to monopolise access to elite positions (Khan 2011) and to draw strong boundaries between themselves and the lower classes (Lamont 1992), the fact that many elite educational institutions in France are state-funded and there exists a lower degree of social closure between the cultural fractions of the upper, middle and lower classes, creates widespread public belief in the social openness of the elite education system. However, this symbolic openness has rather served to hide the fact that these cultural fractions have been very successful in sponsoring their children through the elite education system. This is, first and foremost, due to the fact that their members have high volumes of cultural capital which they can frequently transmit more effectively than other social groups, both because they tend to have more time to spend with their children than, say, managers in the private sector, and because very early on they begin to actively cultivate the 'cultural co-operation' of their children (van Zanten 2013). This last process is also highly effective in 'naturalising' the idea of merit – that is, of making society and children themselves believe that the latter's elite trajectories are primarily the consequence of their own efforts and thus are fully deserved (Tenret 2011). A second dimension is also important here. Many members of these cultural fractions 'know the ropes' and have networks within the education system. This is particularly the case for parents who are teachers themselves. Parents with this knowledge can strategically build successful school trajectories for their children, thereby increasing their chances of succeeding in the *concours* (van Zanten 2013, 2015a).

In the past three decades, however, the influence of economic capital in facilitating access to elite education tracks has increased – partly due to broader transformations within the economy, but also because of changes within the education system itself. The continuing rise in house prices has meant that, increasingly, it is only members of the economic fractions of the upper classes who are able to live in the catchment areas of the most prestigious schools. In addition, it is this group of parents who are most inclined to send their children to be educated in the private sector, which over time has become increasingly academically selective and effective at gaining admission to CPGEs. These parents are also able to buy private tuition for their children and send them on language courses. Cultural resources remain, nevertheless, important and research suggests that students are best served by having a father who is a manager or a highly paid professional and a mother who is a teacher or another kind of 'cultural worker' – allowing the family to draw on significant economic and cultural capitals to sponsor their children's pathway into a future elite position (van Zanten forthcoming).

Conclusion

I have argued throughout this chapter that, although the French authorities managed through an ambitious form of 'open competition' – the *concours* – to abolish traditional forms of direct sponsorship for access to elite positions on the basis of social rank and connections, the *concours* itself, how it has become embedded over time into the way in which dominant agents in different professional sectors (public and private) are selected and the relationships forged between different educational institutions, has produced new forms of sponsorship. These strategies in effect create processes of social closure, which has resulted in the majority of elite positions in French society being held by a fairly homogenous group of individuals. Yet, the strong claim to meritocracy to which the, partly state-funded, system lays claim, is strongly supported by the continuing legitimacy offered by the *concours*.

The role of the state in facilitating or limiting 'open competition' can be understood as ambiguous. On the one hand, it provides free tuition in public CPGEs but, on the other hand, reduces it by the continued concentration of this provision in particular metropolitan areas. Similarly, while the state promotes a system of national applications (in which personal information is not included), it has specified that students following technological and vocational secondary school tracks may not apply. Meanwhile, the elite CPGEs themselves, engage in a complex process of separating 'the wheat from the chaff', through various forms of academic and indirect social selection. Similarly, families with the necessary resources to participate in the complex game of accessing elite status are more able to actively sponsor their children's movement through the system.

Driven by research studies showing the growth of educational inequalities in secondary and higher education in France, and by a heterogeneous group of political leaders, business representatives and directors of some of the most selective higher education institutions, a variety of policies and schemes have been implemented since 2001 to 'open up' and 'diversify' elite tracks through a widening participation agenda. These new developments have generally taken the form of 'compensatory sponsorship' (Grodsky 2007) through different procedures including scholarships, partnerships with disadvantaged schools and additional tutoring. Such efforts actually suggest that access to elite education and future elite positions continues to be perceived by elites themselves as strongly dependent on sponsorship (van Zanten 2010). In other words, elites in post-revolutionary France have managed to sustain over time the social ideal of 'open competition' *and*, through various forms of sponsorship, including sponsoring the promotion of a small number of students from less well-resourced backgrounds into elite education tracks, to closely control their own processes of reproduction.

Note

1 The EDUC-ELITES project was directed by myself, and conducted by a team of ten researchers, with funding from the *Agence national de la recherche* in France. It is a four-year qualitative study of eight elite institutions including three CPGEs.

References

Albouy, V. and Wanecq, T. (2003). Les inégalités sociales d'accès aux grandes écoles. *Economie et Statistiques*, 361, 27–45.

Allouch, A. (2013). *L'ouverture sociale comme configuration. Pratiques et processus de sélection et de socialisation des milieux populaires dans les établissements d'élite. Une comparaison France-Angleterre*. Doctoral Dissertation, Sciences Po.

Baudelot, C. and Matonti, F. (1994). Les normaliens: origines sociales. Le recrutement social des normaliens 1914–1992. In J.-F. Sirinelli (Ed.), *École normale supérieure. Le livre du bicentenaire* (pp. 155–90). Paris: Presses Universitaires de France.

Belhoste, B. (2001). La preparation aux grandes écoles scientifiques au XIXe siècle: Établissements publics et institutions privées. *Histoire de l'éducation*, 90, 101–130.

Belhoste, B. (2002). L'anatomie d'un concours. L'organisation de l'examen d'admission à l'école polytechnique de la revolution à nos jours. *Histoire de l'éducation*, 94, 2–27.

Bourdieu, P. (1996). *The state nobility*. Cambridge: Polity Press.

Bourdieu, P. and Passeron J. C. (1977). *Reproduction in education, society and culture*. London: Sage.

Bourdieu, P. and Saint Martin (de), M. (1987). Agrégation et ségrégation. Le champ des grandes écoles et le champ du pouvoir. *Actes de la Recherche en Sciences Sociales*, 69(1), 2–50.

Cookson, P. W. and Persell, C. H. (1985). *Preparing for power. America's elite boarding schools*. New York: Basic Books.

Darmon, M. (2013). *Classes préparatoires. La fabrique d'une jeunesse dominante*. Paris: La Découverte.

Daverne, C. and Dutercq, Y. (2013). *Les bons elèves. Expériences et cadres de formation*. Paris: Presses Universitaires de France.

DiMaggio, P. J. and Powell, W. W. (1983). The iron cage revisited: Institutional isomorphism and collective rationality in organizational fields. *American Sociological Review*, 48(2), 147–160.

Euriat, M. and Thélot, C. (1995). Le recrutement social de l'élite scolaire en France. Évolution des inégalités de 1950 à 1990. *Revue Française de Sociologie*, 36(3), 403–438.

Gaztambide-Fernández, R. (2009). *The best of the best: Becoming elite at an American boarding school*. Cambridge, MA: Harvard University Press.

Green, A. (2013). *Education and state formation: Europe, East Asia and the USA*. Basingstoke: Palgrave.

Grodsky, E. (2007). Compensatory sponsorship in higher education. *American Journal of Sociology*, 112(6), 1662–1712.

Hill, L. D. (2008). School strategies and the college-linking process: Reconsidering the effects of high schools on college enrollment. *Sociology of Education*, 81, 53–76.

Karabel, J. (1984) Status-group struggle, organizational interests, and the limits of institutional autonomy: The transformation of Harvard, Yale and Princeton, 1918–1940. *Theory and Society*, 13(1), 1–40.

Karabel, J. (2005). *The chosen: The hidden history of admission and exclusion at Harvard, Yale and Princeton*. Boston: Houghton Mifflin.

Kerckhoff, A. C. (2001). Education and social stratification processes in comparative perspective. *Sociology of Education*, 74, 3–18.

Khan, S. R. (2011). *Privilege: The making of an adolescent elite at St. Paul's School*. Princeton, NJ: Princeton University Press.

Kingston, P. W. and Lewis, L. S. (1990). (Eds.). *The high-status track. studies of elite schools and stratification*. New York: State University of New York Press.

Lamont, M. (1992). *Money, morals and manners: The culture of the French and the American upper middle-class*. Chicago: University of Chicago Press.

LeTendre, G. K., Gonzalez, R. G. and Nomi, T. (2006). Feeding the elite: The evolution of elite pathways from star high schools to elite universities. *Higher Education Policy*, 19, 7–30.

Maxwell, C. (2015). Elites: Some questions for a new research agenda. In A. van Zanten, S. Ball and B. Darchy-Koechlin (Eds.), *Elites, privilege and excellence: The national and global redefinition of educational advantage* (pp. 15–28). London: Routledge.

Merle, P. (2000). Le concept de démocratisation de l'institution scolaire: Une typologie et sa mise à l'épreuve. *Population*, 1, 15–50.

MESR (Ministère de l'Enseignement Supérieur et de la Recherche). (2012). Les étudiants en classe préparatoire aux grandes écoles. *Note d'information*, 12(2).

Meyer, J. (1970). The charter: Conditions of diffuse socialization in schools. In R. Scott (Ed.), *Social processes and social structures: An introduction to sociology*. New York: Henry Holt Co.

Nakhili, N. (2005). Impact du choix du contexte scolaire dans l'élaboration des choix d'études supérieures des élèves de terminale. *Education et formations*, 72, 155–167.

Naudet, J. (2015). Paths to the elite in France and in the United States. In A. van Zanten, S. Ball and B. Darchy-Koechlin (Eds.), *Elites, privilege and excellence: The national and global redefinition of educational advantage* (pp. 185–200). London: Routledge.

Noël, E. W. (1962). Sponsored and contest mobility in America and England: A rejoinder to Ralph H. Turner, *Comparative Education Review*, 6(2), 148–151.

Power, S., Edwards, T., Whitty, G. and Wigfall, V. (2003). *Education and the middle class*. Buckingham: Open University Press.

Rauscher, J. B. (2010). *Les professeurs des classes préparatoires aux grandes écoles: Une élite au service des élites*. Doctoral Dissertation, Sciences Po.

Saint-Martin (de), M. (2008). Les recherches sociologiques sur les grandes écoles: De la reproduction à la recherche de justice. *Éducation et sociétés*, 21(1), 95–103.

Suleiman, E. (1978). *Elites in French society: The politics of survival*. Princeton, NJ: Princeton University Press.

Tenret, É. (2011). *L'école et la méritocratie. Représentations sociales et socialisation scolaire*. Paris: Presses Universitaires de France.

Tilly, C. (1998). *Durable inequality*. Berkeley: University of California Press.

Turner, R. H. (1960). Sponsored and contest mobility and the school system. *American Sociological Review*, 25(6), 855–867.

van Zanten, A. (2010). 'L'ouverture sociale des grandes écoles': Diversification des élites ou renouveau des politiques publiques d'éducation? *Sociétés Contemporaines*, 78, 69–96.

van Zanten, A. (2013). La competition entre fractions des classes moyennes supérieures et la mobilisation des capitaux autour des choix scolaires. In P. Coulangeon and J. Duval (Eds.), *Trente ans après la distinction* (pp. 278–89). Paris: La Découverte.

van Zanten, A. (2015a). A family affair: Reproducing elite positions and preserving the ideals of meritocratic competition and youth autonomy. In A. van Zanten, S. Ball and B. Darchy-Koechlin (Eds.), *Elites, privilege and excellence: The national and global redefinition of educational advantage* (pp. 29–42). London: Routledge.

van Zanten, A. (2015b). Les inégalités d'accès à l'enseignement supérieur. Quel rôle joue le lycée d'origine des futurs etudiants? *Regards Croisés sur l'Economie*, 16 (in press).

van Zanten, A. (forthcoming). *La formation des élites. Sélection et socialisation*. Paris: Presses Universitaires de France.

van Zanten, A. and Maxwell, C. (2015). Elite education and the State in France: Durable ties and new challenges. *British Journal of Sociology of Education*, 36(1), 71–94.

Veltz, P. (2007). *Faut-il sauver les grandes écoles?* Paris: Presses de Sciences Po.

Zimdars, A. (2010). Fairness and undergraduate admission: A qualitative exploration of admissions choices at the University of Oxford. *Oxford Review of Education*, 36(3), 207–323.

10
ELITE EDUCATION AND CLASS REPRODUCTION

Commentary

Magne Flemmen

In the *Communist Manifesto*, Karl Marx and Friedrich Engels famously described capitalism as simplifying the structures of inequality into two directly opposing classes. Much sociological study of stratification since then has centred on trying to account for why this turned out not to be the case. Accounts of class and stratification detail various attempts to account for the increasing differentiation of stratification structures, and whether these developments were compatible with what might be viewed as the basic tenets of class theory. In the adolescent years of modern sociology – the long post-war boom – it seemed as though class divisions were in fact buckling under the weight of increasing affluence, the growth of the welfare state and the institutionalisation of democratic class struggle (Korpi 1983), all of which were seen as factors promoting the development of more equal and harmonious societies. This led many sociologists to grant credence to the belief that capitalism and its supposedly endemic class divisions were perhaps nothing more than teething troubles of an industrial society (see the incisive review in Giddens 1976).

Much of this is now beginning to appear as anachronistic as the *Manifesto* itself. The success of Thomas Piketty's (2014) contribution has ushered in wide recognition of the U-curve in inequalities across a large number of national contexts. While decreasing in the post-war period, inequalities have been shown to have risen with a vengeance since the 1970s. The share of income and wealth now held by the richest 1 per cent is on a par with the gilded age of patrimonial capitalism. The British charity Oxfam has recently reported that the richest 1 per cent of the world's population will shortly own more than the remaining 99 per cent (Hardoon 2015). Remarkably, this bears an uncanny resemblance to the scenario envisaged by Marx and Engels – even if the prospects of proletarian uprising and a fair and humane post-capitalist social order seem further off. This has sparked new interest in the sociology of the elites, and to some extent the upper classes – as testified to by the present volume.

Adherents of the theory of liberal society thought that education would serve to undermine the reproduction of inequality and sound the death knell for so-called ascriptive inequality (see, for example, Treiman 1970, p. 218). However, decades of research detail a relationship that is far less neat. While the expansion of educational provision and opportunity has indeed been tied to an increasing significance of credentials in 'status attainment', the interpretation and significance of such a move appears to contradict liberal expectations. Rather than signalling the infamous move from 'ascription to achievement', scholars have demonstrated the various ways in which a new epoch of class reproduction has emerged – depicted by Bourdieu as a move from 'family mediated' to 'school mediated' forms of reproduction (Bourdieu 1996). Such theorisations argue that, while class positions are still largely inherited, this process is now more indirect and takes place through a system of complex mediations. The children of the bourgeoisie may still inherit the family's business but would now be much more likely to also have to acquire educational qualification so that they can compete with others for top positions in the business world. Bourdieu argues that this has the effect of stamping processes of class reproduction with a seal of normative approval, since it would appear in this way that the elite is constituted of the best and the brightest, testified to by the almost universally recognised sign of achievement – education. Hence, school-mediated reproduction would seem to help resolve what Parkin identified as a permanent tension within the dominant class, between the need to legitimate itself through relying on universal criteria of access and the desire to reproduce itself intergenerationally by closure on the basis of descent (Parkin 1979, p. 47).

It is important to emphasise, as others in this volume do, that the concept of elite education remains problematic – which is associated with the conceptual challenges found with the term 'elite'. Many sociological concepts double as lay concepts, which calls for some epistemological vigilance. Durkheim set the example of developing rigorous conceptualisations so as to avoid smuggling unscientific notions into the research process (Durkheim 1952). Scholars who belittle or even dismiss conceptual work inadvertently find themselves thinking '*with* these hidden concepts but not *about* them' (Sayer 1992, p. 52). This seems especially important given the inflammatory connotations the concept of elite engenders, and is a dilemma mentioned by Deppe and Krüger in their chapter focusing on the German context.

In fact, the polysemy of 'elite education' is problematic because, in its specification, we are introduced to phenomena of rather different sociological significance. The German contribution, for instance, draws largely on the notion of elite education in the sense of educational institutions which aim to be elitist in school terms, through their admission requirements, or a specified focus on identifying and educating 'gifted pupils'. Such ambitions sit well with widely shared, but frequently insufficiently problematised, ideals of meritocracy. In principle, gifted pupils from lower socio-economic classes can access an elite school based on their academic performance, which, in theory, means people have equality of opportunity. However, much research would suggest that these idealised processes of meritocracy are rarely unfurled unproblematically. There are well-documented class inequalities in school performance, connected to both the volume and composition of capital (Andersen and Hansen 2011) and also in the decision to continue into higher education (Goldthorpe 1996). As noted by van Zanten in the previous chapter, the supposedly meritocratic *concours* in France has not lessened the reproduction of privilege, which seems in fact to have grown stronger over the past 50 years. The study of elite education should, therefore, strive to conceptualise and examine the part that such education plays in the wider context of rising inequalities and their complex role in mediating and transforming such inequalities.

The four preceding chapters – in the section exploring the 'European' context – highlight various ways in which an elite education might support processes of social differentiation, distinction and closure. Among them, France clearly has the longest tradition of emphasising the eliteness of particular institutions, not only in terms of academic requirements, but also in setting them up explicitly as environments in which the elites of tomorrow are to be cultivated.

While the Scandinavian educational system does not have a strong history of distinct elite educational institutions, so familiar in France, the USA and England, a careful historical analysis such as that offered by the German and Swedish chapters, points to how certain institutions have always been understood as distinctive and particularly targeted at certain social groups. Even in Norway and Sweden, with their historically strong commitment to a state-funded, comprehensive schooling, the contributions highlight how processes of differentiation allow for the emergence of 'functionally' elite schools – which specialise in particular curriculum areas. This is forcefully brought out in the Swedish contribution, in which a detailed analysis of differentiation between schools is presented. Based on data gathered before the deregulation of the Swedish school system, which generated a massive expansion of so-called 'free schools', the analysis brings out the complex ways in which families of the higher classes flock to distinct schools and programmes. That is, even in the absence of the type of private and/or elite institutions typically associated with elite education, the educational strategies of different classes and fractions influence the composition of schools. This point is further emphasised by Aarseth when she discusses the Norwegian context, where the policy of admitting pupils solely on the basis of living in the school's district has led to processes of social exclusivity, as certain residential neighbourhoods are favoured by the most socially, economically and culturally elite families.

An important implication of this finding is that it shows how the potential elitist nature of certain schools need in no way be generated by particular traits of the institutions. Instead, the classed nature of the schools may well arise out of the mediation of class relations external to the school setting itself. When school places are allocated on the basis of place of residence, for instance, this mediation comes about through the housing market. In Norway, for example, it is now commonplace to use this information in advertising real-estate: if the property is in the catchment areas of highly reputed schools, this is highlighted in advertisements. However, when elite schools demand high academic performance from their applicants, the mediation comes about through the influence of class origin on grades. This is indicative of the complexity of the social processes involved in the working of closure strategies that rely on the education system.

The educational context set out in the chapters in this section, emphasises that the mobility strategies of contemporary classes are different to those pursued in earlier stages of capitalism, in which the ownership of the means of production could often be directly inherited, owing to the predominance of ownership by private persons, small groups or families. With the advent of so-called impersonal ownership, this became less salient, and the children of the higher social classes needed in some sense at least to *achieve* their privileged class positions. Given the centrality of credentials or formal qualifications to the process of achievement, privileged families resort to so-called strategies of reconversion, whereby economic resources are converted into cultural or educational ones, which the children in turn convert back into economic resources via the labour market (Bourdieu 1996).

That the privileged classes during this period of late capitalism can rely less on direct inheritance and must instead largely depend on processes of closure based on credentials, means that class reproduction becomes highly volatile, depending as it does on the outcome of a competition, albeit one taking place in some rather uneven playing fields. This is elegantly shown in the work of Fiona Devine, who draws out how middle class reproduction is accomplished – through the families' skilful mobilisation of economic, cultural and social resources. A significant point here is that, from the point of view of middle-class parents, these processes are riddled with anxiety. The parents know perfectly well there are no guarantees for their children's success (Devine 2004, see also Reay et al. 2011).

In the chapter on Norway, interviewees from the financial elite rely heavily on metaphors of competition as well as warfare to describe their work and careers. The parenting projects described were very explicitly conceived of as preparations for the race, organised specifically to produce a sound foundation to enable their children to accomplish as much as possible. Interestingly, for them, the school is seen as a 'safe haven' of sorts, at least in comparison to the fierce competition these parents know from the world of finance. Despite the imaginery of a safe haven, the education of their children is a worked-at strategy, carefully calculated to ensure they will be ready to take on the challenges ahead of them in the future worlds of work. That in no way means they have lax attitudes towards schooling and education – much effort goes into helping their children perform. Positions in the financial fractions of the Norwegian upper class are generally associated with higher education, implying that these positions are principally only attainable with some formal qualification (Flemmen 2012).

Much sociological work on inequalities and their potential reproduction focuses almost exclusively on the education system. That is, obviously, of huge importance to contemporary class relations, as I have indicated above. However, Aarseth forcefully shows the significance of the broader structures of privilege for processes of reproduction. In parental attempts to create a sound foundation for their children, this is largely achieved through mothers giving up full-time work to dedicate themselves to home-making (see also van Zanten (2015) on the situation in France). This somewhat luxurious option, a voluntary and temporary deviation from the predominant dual-earner household system that is such a feature of Norwegian society, is only open to this particular social group because of the significant economic resources accrued through work in the financial industries. On a similar note, the respondents emphasised their desire to live in a close, inclusive and supportive neighbourhood. Again, the possibility of freely choosing the neighbourhood you wish to live in is also highly dependent on economic means; the past 30 years have seen house prices in the Oslo region increase at more than twice the rate of wages.

Something very similar is suggested by van Zanten as taking place in France. However, other resources also appear to be essential in a discussion of the winners and losers within the French elite education system. A hallmark of this system is that many elite institutions are publicly owned, which should, in principle, lessen class inequalities insofar as attendance is more affordable. Indeed, these institutions prove to be dominated, not by the offspring of the economic elite, but by those most endowed with cultural capital. These parents are able to 'sponsor' their children through the elite education system by exploiting flexible working conditions so as to spend more time inculcating cultural capital in them. In addition, these parents have the networks or the know-how to help their children take the right paths through schooling – increasing their chances of success in the *concours*.

Taken together, the chapters in this section illustrate the different ways in which elites or privileged classes attempt to achieve intergenerational stability. While the tendency is for education to act as a key vehicle through which this ambition is realised, we can see how the particular manifestations of such processes are context-specific. van Zanten details how what she calls 'institutional sponsorship' involves parents mobilising economic, cultural and social capital to help realise the hope that their children will be most likely to succeed in a purportedly meritocratic system, thereby becoming seemingly a 'meritocratic' elite. It is crucial to recognise the distinctiveness of the workings of different forms of capital: whereas money can pay tuition fees, support attendance on language courses abroad and facilitate strategic moving (into desired catchment areas), cultural and social capital work through other routes (as mentioned above). In the more egalitarian societies of Scandinavia, still marked by a social-democratic institutional structure as well as ethos, the well-to-do seek to effect closure through the free public schools. In this context, a crucial 'mechanism' involves the mobilisation of economic and social capital to produce cultural capital: knowledge about 'good' schools and neighbourhoods are acquired through networks, although a family's ability to reside in the sought-after areas does critically depend on money. The German context is interesting because elite forms of education are now being promoted in a country, which until very recently was extremely apprehensive about any form of elitism. It will be interesting to follow the work of ZSB – the specialist research unit examining elite education in Germany – to understand how new strategies of reproduction and mobility are developed, and the role of economic and cultural capital in making these processes possible.

This section highlights the critical need for comparative work to understand more fully the ways in which multiple forms of capital are drawn on in different socio-historical and cultural contexts and the implications this has both for schooling systems and for processes of intergenerational reproduction.

References

Andersen, P. L. and Hansen, M. N. (2011). Class and cultural capital—The case of class inequality in educational performance. *European Sociological Review*, 28(5), 1–15.

Bourdieu, P. (1996). *The state nobility*. Cambridge: Polity Press.

Devine, F. (2004). *Class practices: How parents help their children get good jobs*. Cambridge: Cambridge University Press.

Durkheim, E. (1952). *Suicide*. London: Routledge & Kegan Paul.

Flemmen, M. (2012). The structure of the upper class: A social space approach. *Sociology*, 46(6), 1039–1058.

Giddens, A. (1976). Classical social theory and the origins of modern sociology. *American Journal of Sociology*, 81(4), 703–729.

Goldthorpe, J. H. (1996). Class analysis and the reorientation of class theory: The case of persisting differentials in educational attainment. *The British Journal of Sociology*, 47(3), 481–505.

Hardoon, D. (2015). *Wealth: Having it all and wanting more*. Oxfam International.

Korpi, W. (1983). *The democratic class struggle*. Boston: Routledge & Kegan Paul.

Parkin, F. (1979). *Marxism and class theory: A bourgeois critique*. New York: Columbia University Press.

Piketty, T. (2014). *Capital in the twenty-first century*. Cambridge, MA: Harvard University Press.

Reay, D., Crozier, G. and James, D. (2011). *White middle class identities and urban schooling*. Basingstoke: Palgrave Macmillan.

Sayer, R. A. (1992). *Method in social science: A realist approach*. London: Routledge.

Treiman, D. J. (1970). Industrialization and social stratification. In E. O. Laumann (Ed.), *Social stratification: Research and theory for the 1970s*. Indianapolis: Bobbs-Merrill.

van Zanten, A. 2015. A family affair: Reproducing elite positions and preserving the ideals of meritocratic competition and youth autonomy. In A. van Zanten, S. Ball and B. Darchy-Koechlin (Eds.), *Elites, privilege and excellence: The national and global redefinition of educational advantage* (pp. 29–42). London: Routledge.

PART III
Emerging financial powers in Latin America, Asia and Africa

11

'ELITENESS' IN CHINESE SCHOOLING

Towards an ethnographic approach

Peidong Yang

Introduction

The notion of *elite*, commonly taken to correspond with the Chinese term *jingying*, has complex connotations and a long trajectory unique to the Chinese socio-historical context. Arguably, the most well-known fact about pre-modern China with respect to education is that, since the Sui Dynasty (AD 581–618), an imperial examination system (known as the *keju* system) has existed for the purpose of selecting civil servants. For almost the entire second millennium, that is, until the system's demise in 1905, the *keju* examination in its mature form formed the backbone of the imperial governing structure in China, whereby a class of Confucian scholarly elites, more or less meritocratically selected through the examination, received the mandate to run the imperial bureaucratic machine and to wield sociocultural and political power. Notwithstanding the fact that the *keju* is now commonly seen as indoctrination, scholars have argued that the system provided social mobility on meritocratic principles (e.g. Ho 1964) and this meritocratic ideal continues to powerfully influence contemporary Chinese people's understandings of, and attitudes towards, issues around education, elitism and social mobility (Kipnis 2011).

Throughout the twentieth century, particularly during its latter half, elitism in education – both in meaning and in practice – faced fierce contestation and underwent tumultuous swings. With the founding of the People's Republic of China (PRC) in 1949, the country's Communist leaders launched the project of constructing a socialist modernity, in which the education system was charged with the important task of producing the technocratic and scientific elites. To this end, in the early years of the PRC and prior to the 1966 Cultural Revolution, the education system was characterised by an academically selective and elitist approach, using streaming, specialisation and hierarchisation to achieve the goal of producing talent as quickly as possible. To Mao and other radical left leaders, however, such elitist educational practices contravened the socialist ideal; and this was one of the reasons why they initiated the wide-ranging and devastating Cultural Revolution. The main implication of this change of policy for the education system was the enforcement of a radically egalitarian approach, dramatically expanding enrollment rates at the cost of academic quality and selectivity (Unger 1982). After the demise of Mao and radical socialism in the late 1970s, China entered an era of reform, and education policies were swiftly changed, reinstating many of the pre-Cultural Revolution institutions and practices (Pepper 1980, Thøgersen 1990).

More than three decades have now passed since China first embarked on its post-Socialist reform, and it is worth asking what 'eliteness' or 'elitism' have come to mean in the contemporary Chinese education system. This chapter offers a preliminary exploration of this question, drawing on findings from an ethnographic study. Although elite education in many countries is primarily associated with private/independent schooling, and researchers in this emerging field seem thus far to have focused mainly on this type of institution, in the Chinese context, the most relevant meanings and practices of educational elitism are to be found in relation to the institution of public/state schooling. Private elite education in some form no doubt exists in China, but this appears to be a recent development that still remains marginal in terms of scholarly research, and so is worthy of future study. The second caveat for this chapter is that, instead of providing a schematic overview, my approach offers a series of ethnographic vignettes as a somewhat fragmented lens through which to obtain some provisional glimpses into the meanings of eliteness in the Chinese education system today.

The chapter is organised as follows: first, I briefly describe the ethnographic fieldwork underpinning this chapter and the field site school; then I proceed to two ethnographic sections in which I elaborate on what I regard to be two of the most relevant meanings of eliteness in the Chinese state schooling system, which appear to be in tension with one another; finally, I close the chapter with some reflections on the notion of elite as it relates to my own personal biography and educational trajectory.

Ethnographic context

The fieldwork underpinning this chapter was carried out in China between April and June 2011, during which time I returned as a doctoral student of the anthropology of education to the very school ('School A') that I had graduated from ten years before. This three-month field trip formed the first stage of a 16-month period of dual-sited fieldwork, the second part of which I spent in Singapore (see Yang 2014a, 2014b, 2014c). Although it was a relatively brief stint, having been myself a 'product' of the Chinese school system and as an 'old boy' of School A, my intimate and 'sensuous' (Willis 2000) knowledge of the field site certainly expedited the 'finding-one's-way' stage of an ethnographer's typical entry into an unfamiliar territory, allowing me to plunge into the deep end of ethnographic data gathering much sooner than anticipated.

School A is located in Nanchang, the capital city of the southeastern inland province Jiangxi. With a per capita gross domestic product (GDP) that ranked twenty-seventh out of a total 34 administrative regions in China as of 2010, Jiangxi is one of the lesser developed and hence perhaps less heard-of Chinese places to an international audience. Nevertheless, the city of Nanchang itself, being the provincial seat of government, more or less exemplifies the typical, average Chinese urban milieu. School A is a public middle school affiliated to Jiangxi Province's Teachers College, and has long been regarded as one of the most academically successful schools in the entire province. As such, School A may be confidently viewed as representative of the 'normal' and normative conditions in which Chinese middle school education is delivered.

School A comprises a junior middle (*chuzhong*) section (grades 7–9, age 13–15 years) and a senior middle (*gaozhong*) section (grades 10–12, age 16–18 years). As of 2009, there were 71 home classes across these six grades, in which over 4,100 students were educated and supported by over 300 teaching and administrative staff members. As a school reputed for its academic excellence (measured in terms of its success in sending students to high-ranking, prestigious universities), School A usually manages to draw the most academically able students from Nanchang city, and a small number of top students from across Jiangxi Province. In the 2010 national university entrance exam (UEE), 22 students from the school gained admission to Tsinghua or Peking University – the two most prestigious and competitive universities in China that are often seen as belonging to a league of their own, much like Britain's Oxbridge. This number must be interpreted against the background fact that China's socialist planning legacies in the education system dictate that top national universities have only very limited admission quotas for the provinces. For example, in 2009, Peking and Tsinghua Universities had a combined admission quota of just 66 in Jiangxi; this quota being slightly higher at 84 in the year 2012. This means that the senior middle section of School A manages to turn out between one-quarter and one-third of all Peking/Tsinghua-admitted students in a province of 45 million people where 438 senior middle schools prepare some 251,060 students for higher education admission overall.[1]

I gained research access to School A thanks to the help of the school's Deputy Headmaster who had been my teacher when I was a tenth grader. During the three months I spent at School A, I was made an 'assistant teacher' to a grade 10 class, supporting the teachers in their work. In addition, I sat in and listened to lessons in all subjects as much as I could. After becoming acquainted with the students, I also had plenty of opportunity to interact with them in both formal and informal settings, such as over lunch or dinner in the canteen or occasionally helping them practise conversational English.

During my three-month stint in Nanchang, I also visited two other schools to gain comparative insights: 'School B' and 'School C'. School B is another top school in the city and the province, and has long been the arch-rival of School A. School C, on the other hand, usually ranks close to the bottom among middle schools in Nanchang based on exam benchmarking. My visits to these two schools gave me a better sense of perspective, but for ethnographic purposes, School A should be considered my sole fieldwork site.

Forging academic elites within the system: hierarchy and meritocracy

In this section, I elaborate using ethnographic material a possible first meaning of eliteness within the Chinese context, namely in the form of academic elitism, ruthless meritocratic selectivity, exclusivity and competitiveness geared towards forging the elites who are, in turn, supposed to champion the modernist nation-building project.

Systems and nomenclature

Consider first the following list of institutions and practices that characterise the Chinese middle school system (this is by no means an exhaustive list, most terms are generic and used widely throughout China, while a few others are part of a local 'lingo'):

- 'High exam' (*gaokao*): the university entrance exam (UEE) that takes place over the course of two or three days in June each year across the entire country for grade 12 graduates. In principle, provinces administer the high exam for the students under their jurisdiction, using different but comparable examination papers. Examinees are ranked within their province based on their scores and, in turn, this ranking determines whether they are to be admitted to the universities countrywide that they have chosen to apply to for entrance. As a legacy of the socialist command system, universities have pre-set quotas for each province, usually favouring the region in which the university is located. To most students and parents, the *gaokao* is considered very much the ultimate purpose of attending senior middle school.
- 'Key' versus 'ordinary' universities and 'first-/second-/third-tier universities': higher education institutions in China can be broadly divided into 'key universities' (*zhongdian gaoxiao*) and 'ordinary universities' (*putong gaoxiao*), whereby the key institutions receive more investment from the state. Another categorisation is the tiering system, which dictates the order in which institutions are to process student applications after the high exam takes place: 'first-tier' (*yiben*) universities admit students who have applied to them before the second-tier (*erben*) universities can do the same, and so on. This tiering system is supposed to ensure the rational outcome that the universities get the students they deserve and vice versa. Thus, the tiering is also an important indicator of the universities' perceived and real academic quality and prestige.
- 'Middle exam' (*zhongkao*) or the 'entrance exam for senior middle school': the city-/county-level examination that students take upon completing junior middle school (grade 7–9). It operates on a logic very similar to that of the high exam.

- 'Key school' (*zhongdian*), 'key school under construction' (*jiangshezhong zhongdian*) and 'ordinary school' (*putong*): three categories of senior middle schools at city/county level, determined by the provincial educational authority, that reflect in descending order their perceived or real quality, importance and prestige.
- 'Key class' (*zhongdian ban*): in any given senior middle school, a small number of classes in a grade cohort[2] – usually no more than two – are designated 'key classes', which gather together the 'best' students in the cohort, based on their termly or monthly exam score rankings. Students in key classes are given more attention by the school and by the teachers. Variations of the concept of 'key class' include, for example, the 'zero class' (*ling ban*), a term which offers a declaration of the class's superiority, because classes are normally numbered starting from One; the self-explanatory 'excellence-cultivation class' (*peiyou ban*); the 'experimental class' (*shiyan ban*), which experiments with more challenging content and faster teaching paces; and, interestingly, the 'golden-poster class' (*jinbang ban*), whose name takes its inspiration from the imperial mandarin examination in olden times whereby distinguished examinees' names were displayed on a yellow poster for public admiration.
- 'Ordinary class' (*putong ban*): the majority of classes in a grade cohort that are not designated 'key'. In recent years, there has been a tendency for this derogatory sounding term to be replaced by more palatable descriptors, such as 'parallel class' (*pingxing ban*).
- 'Monthly exam' (*yuekao*): in most Chinese senior middle schools, students sit monthly drill exams modelled on the high exam, testing all high exam-relevant subjects. After each monthly exam, students are ranked within the cohort based on their total scores. Normally, according to their new rankings, students may receive the honourable invitation to enter a 'key class' or face the dishonourable consequence of dropping out of the 'key classes' back to an 'ordinary class'.

Elitism through pyramidal stratification

Above, I have chosen to present some of the key (infra)structural elements of the Chinese middle school system in order to highlight its most salient feature, namely, its steep *hierarchisation* through a mechanism that is meant to sort out the academic elites from the mediocre. Ranking, tiering and differentiation *saturate* the system, constituting the key principle around which both institutional relationships and human subjectivities are configured in the life-worlds of Chinese middle school students, teachers and parents. This hierarchisation takes on a more or less pyramidal shape: thus, there will always be fewer key schools than non-key schools, fewer first-tier universities than second-tier universities, and so forth.

True to the principle of *exemplarity* which Bakken (2000) sees as a key cultural logic to Chinese politics and society, there is a tendency for institutional setups and practices at the higher levels to be replicated at lower levels of the hierarchy as well. For instance, in recent years in Jiangxi Province – as is very likely also to be the case elsewhere in China – the middle exam has become increasingly isomorphic with the high exam, whereby the three types of senior middle schools (key, key under construction and ordinary) correspond to the three tiers of universities (see also Wu 2014). The three types of exams, i.e. monthly, middle and high, resemble each other not just in format, but also in the effects these have of initiating processes of ranking, differentiation and hierarchisation. In fact, such replication can be seen further down the hierarchy, whereby junior middle school admission and even primary school admission in many places has now become competitive despite regulations explicitly prohibiting such practices.[3]

This steeply hierarchical system encourages circles of self-reinforcing stratification. As students who have done well in the middle exam flock to key senior middle schools such as School A, these key schools easily garner academically capable students who are likely to bring honour to their schools in three years' time in the high exam by scoring highly, which will further strengthen the schools' reputation. Hence, talents become pyramidally stratified within the system, with the most academically capable students in a city or across an entire province often concentrated in only a handful of schools.

During my fieldwork, a School A official proudly told me two facts: among their 2009 intake of freshers they had 88 of the top 100 students in that year's Nanchang middle exam; for their 2010 intake, the entirety of Nanchang's top 100 students came to School A. Yet, in spite of such success, School A was starting to spread its net out to the whole Jiangxi Province to recruit the best students from local districts. According to the students that I spoke to who had come up from the local districts to attend School A, teams of School A teachers would travel down to their local middle schools to administer tests and interviews, selecting the best 'crops' of new recruits. Technically, for School A to recruit students from outside Nanchang city constitutes a regulatory violation. However, the school has always enjoyed a good working relationship with the provincial educational authorities, and this regulatory inconvenience was elegantly dealt with by ensuring that School A became designated as a 'provincial level key school' (*shengji zhongdian xuexiao*).

Such stratification and the concentration of 'good' students in one or two key schools has the consequence of leaving many other less 'good' schools severely de-motivated. During my first visit to School C, a manager there revealed that in 2010 only ten students out of a graduating cohort of almost 300 at the school made it into some form of tertiary education, none of which were regarded as 'good' (all 'third-tier' institutions or technical colleges). Furthermore, upon learning that I was also doing fieldwork at School A, the School C manager lamented in metaphorical terms: 'In the past, we used to get small fish and shrimps, while key schools like School A got the big fish; now the key schools trawl away the big fish, the small fish and the good shrimps, so we are only left with the very small shrimps! However capable we are as teachers we can't help shrimps grow into fish – schools like ours are just hopeless!'

Students in Chinese middle schools are made painfully aware of their own place in this elitist hierarchy founded on the logic of academic distinction, which not only assigns symbolic privileges but also distributes real worldly rewards and punishments. For example, in Nanchang at the time of my fieldwork, the annual tuition fee for senior middle school was usually no more than 3,000 yuan (equivalent to about £300), but if a student failed to achieve the requirements and wished, nonetheless to enter the school, ten times as much in 'school choice fees' (*zexiao fei*) had to be paid to the school upfront in cash (see also Wu 2014). (Such a practice is not regarded as illegal or a form of bribery because a school normally can only admit a small number of such 'choice students', and the number is approved by the educational authorities; this practice is better understood as a measure of school autonomy under an otherwise highly regulated system, and the school sees 'choice students' as a source of extra funding.) At the same time, key schools in Nanchang and across China offer fee waivers to promising students who are spotted as possible 'seeds' for the high exam in three years' time. Although not practised by any Nanchang schools to my knowledge, commentators have noted that practices such as dishing out cash prizes worth as much as 200,000 yuan (approximately £20,000) to students who make it into Tsinghua/Peking Universities do occur in some parts of China.

Meritocracy and the legitimation of academic elitism

Although to some, the steeply hierarchical nature of the Chinese schooling system may seem to border on oppression, at School A, I often sensed among students an optimism and determination that spoke of their accommodation of, if not quite complete identification with, this ruthlessly elitist system.

During the many canteen lunches and dinners I shared with School A students, I often tried to work out their attitudes towards this gigantic schooling infrastructure that closes in on them and intimately shapes their subjectivities. It seemed many students did not want to dwell on such a serious topic, preferring to talk about more lighthearted matters with me; however, when they sensed my persistence in hearing their opinions, they opened up and offered some thoughts. Many seemed genuinely to believe in the meritocracy of the Chinese education system and approved of the academic elitism with which it is synonymous. 'Of course the system is not flawless – far from it – but can you tell me a fairer system that is possible in China's current situation?' one thoughtful grade 10 boy rhetorically questioned me. 'The Chinese educational system is such that as long as you put in hard effort, you can get results and succeed', echoed another. But the statement that left the deepest impression on me came from a grade 10 girl, who actually said: 'In our system, even a genius has to bow in front of the diligent (*tiancai zai qinfen mianqian ye yao ditou*)!'

The fact that the hierarchies in the school and the resultant distribution of superiority-/inferiority-markers, honour and shame, etc., are all based largely on students' exam performances means that there is an ethos of fairness and just desert in School A. Another fierce-sounding statement that came from a student informant captured this well – 'In school, one speaks with a volume proportional to one's exam results (*zai xuexiao yong chengji shuohua*)!' Discrimination or prejudice among students based on their families' socioeconomic backgrounds was absent so far as I could tell, and this was so notwithstanding the actual disparities between their backgrounds that I managed to gauge through interacting with them. In the school, students wear tracksuit-style uniforms at all times, follow the same daily routines, do the same thing – everything revolves around study. Those hailing from outside the provincial capital city even receive preferential treatment – negotiated with the local municipal authorities on their behalf by School A officials – to have their household registration[4] relocated to Nanchang for the duration of their studies so that they can eventually take their high exam there.

While limited space prevents a detailed discussion of this point, students' perception of meritocracy and relative fairness has to do with the systemic features of the Chinese middle school system. As anthropologist Andrew Kipnis (2001) has argued, the ways in which contemporary Chinese school pedagogy emphasises methodic, rote memorisation and other un-'creative' forms of learning (see also Woronov 2008) – reasons for which the education system is often severely criticised both within and outside China – actually ends up building some meritocracy into the system by reducing the disadvantages suffered by students from rural and/or lower socioeconomic backgrounds.

To sum up, I contend that the logic of meritocratic academic elitism in China's schooling system operates by affording symbolic as well as material privileges to that select stratum of students who, by virtue of their sheer brilliance and conscientiousness, reach the top, whereas the rest who are 'mediocre' are relegated to lesser symbolic positions and are confronted with extra costs in material terms. This system does not shy away from the act of selecting and grooming a minority of the academic elite who will in future enter top universities and assume important roles in society; indeed, these are the system's organising principles. Academic elitism thus comprises not only the ensemble of minute practices, 'tactics' (cf. Foucault 1977) and infrastructural layouts that are found in the system as I have described, it also becomes a mentality, a cultural practice and, in short, an ideology that to a greater or lesser extent shapes human subjectivities within the educational system. At the same time, this elitism is thought to be meritocratic, because access to that elite status is asserted to be open by the school and teachers, and is therefore believed to be so by many students and their parents as well.

This form of meritocratic academic elitism has been the dominant logic in the mainstream Chinese schooling system since the 1980s. However, it is starting to face a rather uncertain future, as post-reform Chinese society becomes increasingly affluent, more steeply stratified and more globally connected. Elite schooling in the sense that the term is commonly understood in the West (e.g. Howard 2008, Gaztambide-Fernández 2009, Maxwell and Aggleton 2010, 2013, Khan 2011) has not only made an appearance in China – although I do not look into the development of private elite schooling in China in this chapter – but seems to be infiltrating even the public schooling system in interesting ways that have been little explored so far. It is to this latter incursion of economically based elitism into the public middle school system in China that I now turn.

Re-routing the future socioeconomic elites: internationalisation and privilege

In 2011, when I returned to School A to carry out fieldwork, the Deputy Head of the school was an excited and busy man: he and his team were in the midst of juggling between negotiations with an American high school about setting up an International Programme at School A (a 'Sino-American Programme' or *zhongmei ban*) on the one hand, and dealing with the provincial educational authorities to obtain official approval for this programme on the other.

This, however, would not be the first international programme at senior middle school level in Jiangxi Province. Back in 2007, School B had started the first international collaborative programme – a 'Sino-Canadian' programme run jointly with the educational authorities of Nova Scotia, Canada. The programme charged at that time 30,000 yuan per year when the annual fees at a public senior middle school were less than 2,000 yuan. Enrolment in the programme grew from 18 in the inaugural cohort to over 20 students in the subsequent two cohorts, and over 60 students in the fourth cohort. According to information available from School B's official website, the programme involved Nova Scotia educational authorities sending teachers to School B to teach the Nova Scotia high school curriculum to the enrolled students, who must at the same time also complete the Chinese senior middle curriculum with School B teachers. The completion of the Nova Scotia curriculum enabled the students to apply directly to Canadian universities, which was the explicit *raison d'être* for this programme; thus, although students were still required to complete the Chinese curriculum, in fact they only needed to pass the senior middle school exit exam (*huikao*) and not the high exam. According to a student at the Sino-Canadian Programme I spoke to, as all those who enrolled had their minds set on going to universities in Canada, they were free from the pressure of studying as intensely as their high exam-taking peers in School B's normal senior middle section.

Importantly, this student also revealed that, although the entry criteria of the Sino-Canadian Programme put special emphasis on the applicants' English scores in the middle exam, it was true that the overall cut-off point for admission was some 20 to 30 points (out of a total possible point score of 610)[5] lower than School B's normal admission requirement. For some cynical observers, this was a programme that 'enabled rich but not very smart or hardworking kids to escape the high exam'; but the particular informant I spoke with praised the high quality and enjoyable Western style of learning it offered. School B's website shows that students of the first three cohorts who graduated between 2010 and 2012 went to destinations including University of British Columbia, University of Toronto, Dalhousie University, University of Ottawa and University of Prince Edward Island, among others.

School A's Deputy Head, however, was confident that the Sino-American Programme would be a greater success, and this was partly reflected in the fees School A was ready to charge: 80,000 yuan a year. 'Everybody wants to go to America', the Deputy Headmaster told me, articulating the new horizon of

Chinese educational desires: 'American college education is the best in the world'. The idea of the Sino-American Programme is similar: to give enrolled students direct access to American undergraduate admission. The partner American school would send five teachers to Nanchang to cover the American part of the programme, based on the Advanced Placement (AP) curriculum. Similarly, School A also stressed that Sino-American Programme students needed to complete their Chinese senior middle school curriculum, and thus, in one school official's words, the Programme 'should be seen as even more challenging in one sense'. Nevertheless, a glossy online brochure explaining the Programme shows that students are encouraged to take the Test of English as a Foreign Language (TOEFL), SAT and AP exams as early as at the end of their second year (i.e. Grade 11). Not dissimilar to what the School B informant told me: since students are only expected to take the exit exams, the Chinese curriculum is significantly reduced, enabling them to enjoy the much more lively, diverse and attractive 'American pedagogy'.

Although I left Nanchang just before the Sino-American Programme commenced, I was able to find out about the Programme's subsequent developments online. Between April and May 2013, the first cohort of 16 students one after another received multiple offers from US universities and colleges. Indeed, the Programme webpage was strewn with headlines screaming 'good news', announcing the admission triumphs of this inaugural cohort, which completed the course in just two years instead of the planned three. Among the 16 graduates, one received seven offers respectively from Syracuse University, SUNY Binghamton, Centre College, DePauw University, Agnes Scott College, Lawrence University and Augsburg College; even the student with the fewest offers received two, from Washington University and Indiana University Bloomington respectively.

Of course, international education is nothing new. At the pre-tertiary level, the 'American International Schools' that exist in many developing country metropolises, catering to expatriates and local elites, have long epitomised pockets of educational exclusivity and privilege. British elite school Harrow, for instance, now has international schools in several Asian cities, including Beijing. The type of collaborative programmes I describe above, however, is a more recent phenomenon. In China, the high exam used to be known as the 'single-log bridge' (*dumuqiao*) that millions of students squeeze through with sheer determination and hard work. This seems to be changing slowly but steadily. Currently, not only do over 70 per cent of all those who take the high exam end up in some form of tertiary education, but it was officially reported that in 2009 a staggering 840,000 eligible examinees across the country gave up taking the exam,[6] many probably thanks to the kind of developments I outlined in this section.

As urban Chinese residents become increasingly affluent, more and more parents entertain the option of letting their children receive less draconian and supposedly more enriching Western education by avoiding the local educational infrastructure. In this evolving Chinese public school set-up, which now includes 'escape routes' and 'flyover bridges', such as the Sino-Canadian/American programmes in Nanchang, a second meaning of elitism emerges, namely, as a kind of exclusivity of access and privilege of experiences that can be enjoyed if, and only if, the parents have the financial means. It is useful to remember that Nanchang parents who send their children to the Sino-American Programme not only have to pay two or three years of hefty programme fees in Jiangxi, they must also be wealthy enough to be able to afford their children's university education expenses once in the USA, because these students would no longer be able to pass the high exam with sufficiently good marks to compete for the top university places within China.

Under the same roof as School A, therefore, an old form of elitism is newly smuggled in through the back door: the Sino-American students' elegant grey knitted cardigan-style uniform contrasts interestingly with the sporty tracksuit-style uniform worn by the rest of School A students, making a less-than-subtle statement about the former's elite status. Trained by their US teachers, the level of fluency of their spoken English and even their social demeanour gradually show signs of divergence from that of their less elite peers – a divergence that will be radically widened when these privileged students actually head over to the USA to earn their college degrees, making them the 'bilingual global elite Chinese' that the Programme brochure promises.

In lieu of conclusion: some personal reflections

The notion of 'elite' or 'elitism' itself is not alien to the Chinese but, as I have tried to show, its semantics must be explored against a background of cultural historical traditions and socio-political contexts specific to China. For this exploratory chapter, which will hopefully be followed by more substantial research, a 'conclusion' would not be quite the right way to end. I close, therefore, with some reflections on educational elitism as it relates to my personal biography and educational trajectory.

Having been brought up in post-reform China and subsequently educated for a decade (1992–2002) under the Chinese school system, I had previously never perceived the word elite/elitism (*jingying*) in a negative light. As I grew up, for me and most people around me, 'elite' was a good word and a good idea – something one strived hard to become. In 2002, a year before I was due to take the high exam, I was awarded a scholarship by the Singapore government to pursue undergraduate studies in this city-state, which we knew as an advanced Asian country governed by modern 'Confucian elites'. The award of the scholarship, of course, was preceded by a selection process comprising written tests and interview, which in fact further vindicated for me and my fellow Chinese 'scholars' in Singapore the goodness of the term 'elitism', for, after all, where would we be if the Singapore system was not committed to an elitist educational philosophy and the value of meritocracy?

Subsequent exposure to Western academic discourses in the sociology of education made me realise that concepts of 'elite'/'elitism' are often viewed with suspicion, if not downright hostility, in at least the European context where the values of social democracy are still highly relevant. While I could understand this critical stance intellectually, I was never quite able to appreciate in a more experiential way the anti-elitism of implicitly leftist sociological discourses. Writing this chapter has made me more aware that the elitism I knew and grew up with in the Chinese context was somewhat different from the elitism that was commonly critiqued in Western sociological discourse.

The irony, however, is that on returning to my own alma mater School A to undertake fieldwork a decade after I had left, I learned that the relatively recent stratification of Chinese society had precipitated the inevitable development of the second kind of elitism, which threatens to undermine the first. With this new lesson from home, I was finally able to better appreciate the critical sociology on elite education that I first encountered abroad.

Notes

1 From the website of Jiangxi Education Bureau. Available at http://www.jxedu.gov.cn/jytj/2011jytj/2012/04/20120420032442400.html (accessed 9 June 2015, in Chinese).
2 Normally a senior middle school would have eight to 16 classes in each grade cohort; each class normally has 45–60 students.
3 *China Educational Daily*, 26 May 2011, page 1; 5 May 2011, page 6; and *China Youth Daily*, 19 May 2011, page 2.
4 In China, household registration (*hukou*) remains one significant tool for social regulation; people with rural household registration are denied many social welfares that apply to urban-registered citizens; similarly, people with household registration in a particular place may not be entitled to certain rights in other places; see Woronov (2004).
5 20–30 points out of 610 might seem moderate; however, given the number of candidates and the fierce competition, 20 points actually make a great difference in ranking.
6 See http://news.163.com/09/0603/02/5AROBFUU0001124J.html (accessed 9 June 2015, in Chinese).

References

Bakken, B. (2000). *The exemplary society: Human improvement, social control, and the dangers of modernity in China*. Oxford: Oxford University Press.
Foucault, M. (1977). *Discipline and punish*. London: Allen Lane.
Gaztambide-Fernández, R. (2009). *The best of the best: Becoming elite at American boarding school*. Cambridge, MA: Harvard University Press.
Ho, P.-T. (1964). *Ladder of success in Imperial China: Aspects of social mobility, 1368–1911*. New York: John Wiley.
Howard, A. (2008). *Learning privilege: Lessons of power and identity in affluent schooling*. London: Routledge.
Khan, S. R. (2011). *The making of an adolescent elite at St. Paul's School*. Princeton, NJ: Princeton University Press.
Kipnis, A. (2001). The disturbing educational discipline of 'peasants'. *The China Journal*, 46(1), 1–24.
Kipnis, A. (2011). *Governing educational desire: Culture, politics and schooling in China*. Chicago: Chicago University Press.
Maxwell, C. and Aggleton, P. (2010). The bubble of privilege. Young, privately educated women talk about social class. *British Journal of Sociology of Education*, 31(1), 3–15.
Maxwell, C. and Aggleton, P. (Eds.) (2013). *Privilege, agency and affect: Understanding the production and effects of action*. Basingstoke: Palgrave Macmillan.
Pepper, S. (1980). Chinese education after Mao: Two steps forward, two steps back and begin again? *The China Quarterly*, 81(1), 1–65.

Thøgersen, S. (1990). *Secondary education in China after Mao: Reform and social conflict*. Aarhus: Aarhus University Press.
Unger, J. (1982). *Education under Mao: Class and competition in Canton schools, 1960–1980*. New York: Columbia University Press.
Willis, P. (2000). *The ethnographic imagination*. Cambridge: Polity.
Woronov, T. (2004). In the eye of the chicken: Hierarchy and marginality among Beijing's migrant schoolchildren. *Ethnography*, 5(3), 289–313.
Woronov, T. (2008). Raising quality, fostering 'creativity': Ideologies and practices of education reform in Beijing. *Anthropology & Education Quarterly*, 39(4), 401–422.
Wu, X. (2014). *School choice in China: A different tale*. London: Routledge.
Yang, P. (2014a). *'Foreign talent': Desire and Singapore's China Scholars*. Unpublished DPhil, University of Oxford.
Yang, P. (2014b). A phenomenology of being 'very China': An ethnographic report on the self-formation experiences of mainland Chinese undergraduate 'foreign talents' in Singapore. *Asian Journal of Social Science*, 42(3–4), 233–261.
Yang, P. (2014c). Privilege, prejudice, predicament: 'PRC scholars' in Singapore – an overview. *Frontiers of Education in China*, 9(3), 350–376.

12

'ELITENESS' AND ELITE SCHOOLING IN CONTEMPORARY NIGERIA

Pere Ayling

The sociologist Pierre Bourdieu (1984, p. 244) postulates that 'social positions which present themselves to the observer as places juxtaposed in static order of discrete compartments [...] are also strategic emplacements, fortresses to be defended and captured in a field of struggles'. Accordingly, there has been a plethora of studies on the different strategies employed by the middle classes to 'defend', 'capture' and maintain their socially and economically advantageous position in society. In contrast, much less research has been conducted on how elite groups maintain their dominance. At a time of heightened neoliberalism, which in turn has intensified class struggle for positional advantage, it is not only imperative but also 'ethical' to subject elite groups to similar scrutiny in order to ascertain how they reproduce their position in society and, more importantly, legitimize their claim to social and moral superiority over other groups. This chapter will discuss how a group of Nigerian elite parents who were schooled in the early 1960s and 1970s, when education was for 'the very lucky few', are trying to ensure that their children enjoy similar status and therefore continue to retain and maximise their 'advantage under shifting global conditions' (Weis and Cipollone 2013, p. 704). Beyond this, the chapter will also discuss how British 'Whiteness'[1] is used to construct particular private schools in Nigeria as elite education establishments.

In seeking to understand how elite identity is formed and/or acquired in Nigeria today, the significance of the former British colonists needs to be acknowledged as having provided both the structure and the intrinsic properties – that is, the key social/cultural practices – for shaping the way that the African 'educated' elites and bourgeois classes are constituted (Fanon 2008, Ekeh 1975, Bassey 1999, West 2002, Simpson 2003). The African educated elites are different in composition, characteristics and practices to the traditional African elites, having no national upper class or 'aristocracy', over and above them, which they can situate themselves within and/or in relation to. More significantly, the African educated elites depended, and continue to depend, on 'colonialism for [their] legitimacy' (Ekeh 1975, p. 96).

It is worth mentioning that, while colonisation guaranteed the reproduction of the educated elites, independence, which led to the introduction of equalisation projects such as the move towards Universal Primary Education (UPE) (Aigbokhan *et al.* 2007) and Universal Basic Education (UBE) (Unagha, 2008), have weakened the reproductive capacity of education as a site of elite reproduction. Similarly, the massification of education has not only intensified the struggle for elite status, it has also changed the 'resources' and 'sites' of elite reproduction and maintenance in present-day Nigeria.

While the legacy of former colonists offers the main point of reference for African elites; colonisation, according to Fanon (2008), also led to a devaluation of African cultures and languages thereby constructing Blacks as the 'Other'. In other words, colonisation has made White the author of Black, meaning 'the archetype of the lowest values is represented by the negro [Black]' (ibid., p. 146). In his book *Black Skin, White Masks*, Fanon (2008) highlights the prestige and social status that was enjoyed by the colonised who had mastered the language of the colonisers. Speaking specifically about Martinicans, whose country had been colonised by the French, Fanon (1967/2008, p. 8 my emphasis) contended that a '[Black] of the Antilles will be proportionally Whiter – that is, he will come closer to being *a real human being* – in direct ratio to his mastery of the French language'. That is to say 'the Antilles [Black] who wants to be White [and thus gain the status of elite] will be Whiter as he gains greater mastery of the cultural tool that language is' (Fanon 2008, p. 25).

Nigeria was 'officially' colonised by Britain from 1901 until 1 October 1960, when she gained her independence, although British 'activity' in Nigeria goes as far back as the seventeenth century (Smythe and Smythe 1960). Colonisation not only led to a devaluation of Nigerian cultural practices and languages, but also heralded in a new type of high-status group in the form of the 'educated' elites. Colonisation weakened traditional modes of elite identity formation and reproduction, for example caste and blood lineage. Instead, Western forms of education became the singular 'determinant of ... economic, political and cultural elite status' in colonial and early post-colonial Nigeria (Bassey 1999, p. 45). Bassey has gone as far as to claim that:

> so high was the prestige of learning becoming that [...] it was *infra dig* [beneath one's dignity] for a man who knew how to *read* and *write* to carry any loads of any kind, including Bibles and hymn books which had to be carried by the Christians.
>
> *(ibid., p. 46 my emphasis)*

Stressing the transformative power of Western education in colonial and early post-colonial Nigeria, Bassey contends that the 'White man's clerk' (p. 46), a member of the indigenous population who had acquired basic primary education, became the embodiment of class, prestige and honour. Significantly, like the professional middle classes in Zimbabwe (West 2002) and India (Roy 1994, p. 97) where 'neither land nor wealth was their insignia', studies of Nigeria have also shown that Western education bonded and homogenised the country's elites while simultaneously setting them apart from other social groups (Smythe and Smythe 1960, West 2002).

While much has been written about elite identity formation in colonial Nigeria, there is very little sociological research on how elite status is acquired and/or maintained in Nigeria today. Significant changes in the educational landscape in Nigeria since independence have meant that education is no longer the exclusive enclave of the privileged few. Rather, the democratisation of education has led to a schooling boom and, as a result, families that were previously unable to access the education system, can do so now. The popularisation of education has also devalued it to the extent that being educated, regardless of the level one attains, is no longer a key marker of contemporary elite status in Nigeria. Rather, like most contemporary societies, the *place* where one is educated (Cookson and Persell 1985, West and Noden 2003), and by whom one is taught, whether or not they are 'experts', now takes precedence over how educated one is. Furthermore, if as Bourdieu (1996, p. 112) claims, 'manners and style are among the surest signs of nobility', this raises important questions about elite identity formation in present-day Nigeria. For example, what types of *distinctive* and *distinguishable* manners and style are Nigerian elite parents seeking to acquire for their children in order to ensure that these confer upon them the elite status their parents already enjoy?

To date, Smythe and Smythe's (1960) research into the new Nigerian elites remains the only study that has attempted to provide a comprehensive definition and description of Nigerian elites. However, even these authors allude to the difficulty in defining Nigerian elites, stating that the huge variations among Nigerian elites make it 'difficult to define clearly a framework in which the elites can be placed' (p. 74). Nonetheless, they note that education and occupation are two of the main factors involved. Of course, Nigerian elites have undergone significant changes since 1960. For example, the substantial growth in the Nigerian movie and music industries has led to the creation of new elite groups, while the democratisation of education has meant that this alone is no longer perceived to be a core characteristic of elite status. Both changes suggest at the very least a growth in the number and composition of Nigerian elites.

Against this background, the chapter focuses on one particular group of Nigerians – parents who have chosen to send their children abroad for their education, primarily to the UK – and examines in greater depth the role British boarding schools play in shaping Nigerian elites today. The analysis will be further extended by reflections on how schools in the Nigerian private education market are drawing on similar markers of distinction to construct themselves as elite education institutions at home. Although Bourdieu's theorisation of elites and elite formation provides an initial theoretical framework for this work, the chapter will conclude by extending these ideas to make them relevant to an African, or more specifically, a Nigerian (post-colonial) context.

In my own work I draw on Boyd's (1973, p. 16) characteristics of 'elites in modern democratic society', which sets out nine key features and values that define these groups. These defining features include holding high occupational positions, a distinctive lifestyle, group consciousness, a sense of exclusiveness, being seen to hold a functional capability and positioning of moral responsibility within society (p. 16). Some of Boyd's characterises of elites have been supported by other writing which emphasises minority status and the exclusivity of holding such a positioning (Keller 1991, Ellersgaard *et al.* 2012). I used Boyd's framework to develop a sampling frame for recruiting parents in a recently completed study of Nigerian elite parents' education choices for their children, especially focusing on those who buy an overseas schooling experience; at UK-based private boarding schools to be more precise. At the time of carrying out the research, it was estimated that there were only 802 Nigerian children in private boarding schools in the UK (Brooks 2011). This indicated, among other things, that the parents recruited for this study were both a minority and an exclusive group.

This chapter is organised into four main parts. The first part briefly discusses the design of the study that informs this chapter. The second part explains Bourdieu's theorisation of elite and elite identity formation. The third and fourth parts present and analyse the data. The third section more specifically examines the 'distinction strategies' (Bourdieu 1993, p. 115) adopted by Nigerian elite parents in their attempt to confer elite status upon their children while the fourth section examines private (elite) schools in Nigeria and strategies for distinction within this sector. The chapter concludes with a discussion that considers how Bourdieu's theorisation of elite identity formation needs to be extended to adequately capture key features of the situation in modern-day Nigeria.

In all, 39 participants took part in the study, which was conducted between 2012 and 2014. The participants consisted of 26 parents (11 fathers and 15 mothers) and 13 gatekeepers (defined as education agents and consultants, head teachers, heads of department in various elite schools in Nigeria and the Head of visa section, British High Commission, Lagos). All the head teachers and head of departments were White British. The study used a broadly qualitative approach, employing semi-structured interviews with parents and gatekeepers. Twenty-one of the 26 parents had sent their children to be educated in the UK. The fathers tended to be directors or CEOs of major organisations or owned their own companies while two of the mothers held political appointments at federal and state government levels – one was the commissioner of education in one of the southern states in Nigeria and the other was the chair of a special advisers' committee to the President. A further four were fathers who held managerial positions in the Shell Petroleum Development Company, Nigeria, and who sent their children to be educated in Canada. The last parent in the sample – a mother – was schooling her daughter in Ghana. Pseudonyms are used throughout the chapter to protect the parents' identity.

Theorising elite identity formation

> If a distinctive element is necessary to gain status, a distinctive manner is necessary to maintain it.
>
> *(Boyd 1973, p. 21)*

Bourdieu (1984) argued that distinction is an integral part of class struggle over legitimate taste and social prestige. To 'win' the struggle, he contended that individuals and groups must consciously and unconsciously distinguish themselves from other groups viewed as beneath them, while simultaneously aligning themselves with those perceived as equals. Crucially, Bourdieu argued that symbolic goods, especially those regarded as the 'attributes of excellence' (p. 66) constitute one of the key markers of class and also 'the *ideal weapon in strategies of distinction*' (p. 66, my emphasis). These attributes of excellence are usually associated with aristocratic aesthetics and are manifested in comportment and dress, having a 'refined' accent (Entwistle 1978, Bourdieu 1996, 1984), and the display of appropriate etiquette and habit (Scott 1991, Berghoff 1990, Kendall 2002). According to Bourdieu (1996, p. 315 my emphasis):

> No noble title suffices in and of itself [...]. So, for example, the highest academic titles are necessary but *insufficient*, possible but not inevitable, conditions for access to the *establishment*. And wealth, when it is not accompanied by the *appropriate 'manners'* is even less sufficient.

In other word, 'elites [...] must have distinguishing features of style which set them apart from other groups and/or individuals not only from other societies but also within their own society' (Boyd 1973, p. 21). Bourdieu (1984) also posits that having a socially distinctive lifestyle and set of practices and manners, which are manifested in ways of walking, manner of speech and delivery, provide the 'foundation for an exclusive and "elite" group identity' (Waters 2007, p. 478). Status, on the other hand, is the 'esteem which a person attracts' as a result of acquiring and possessing distinction (Ball 2003, p. 33). In other words, distinction begets status, which in turn qualifies a person to join the 'circle of eligibles' (Parkin 1979, p. 44).

These distinctive lifestyles and practices also create symbolic boundaries that not only regulate membership into elite groups but also provide the legitimation that enables elites to claim and maintain economic, moral and social superiority over other groups (Lamont and Molnar 2002). In their attempt to legitimate their newly gained elite status and also claim social and moral superiority over the rest of the masses, Bassey (1999, p. 51) claimed that, during the colonial period, Nigerian educated elites not only adopted European lifestyles by 'maintain[ing] nuclear families', rather than the 'traditional' practice of polygamy, but also followed European styles of dress. West (2002) has made a similar observation in Zimbabwe asserting that due to 'their vociferous claims to Western civilisation and Christianity' (p. 107), the African bourgeois class adopted the Western 'ideology of domesticity', Christian values and practices and preferred living in Western-style living quarters which were perceived as more 'respectable'.

A refined accent is not only considered a highly profitable and valuable cultural and symbolic capital, as argued by Bourdieu (1996) among others, but also as an essential requirement for elite membership. Berghoff (1990, p. 152), indicates this when he posits that a refined accent 'is one of the most important indicators of status' in contemporary societies. Extending the argument further, Bourdieu (1996, p. 316) asserts that 'entrance into "society" [elite membership] assumes that one refines one's upbringing and loses one's local accent'. In his analysis of the symbolic value of a refined accent, Bourdieu (1993, p. 63) claims:

> words are not uttered solely to be understood; the relation of communication is never just a relation of communication, it is also an economic relation in which the *speaker's value* is at stake: did he speak well or poorly? Is he brilliant or not?

To retain their distinctiveness, access to the cultural and symbolic capitals, such as linguistic competency, must be scarce and only accessible to a privileged few in any given society. Furthermore, these capitals should be exclusive both in terms of who can acquire them and where and how they can be acquired. Economic capital plays a crucial role here because it enables individuals to access exclusivity through the consumption of scarce goods and services, such as elite schooling. Indeed, the role of economic capital cannot be over-emphasised in the acquisition and/or maintenance of elite identity, particularly in non-Western countries like Nigeria where Western lifestyles and products are 'the criterion for the indigenous elite class formation' (Woolman 2001, p. 37). That said, it is important to note that having a large volume of economic capital does not automatically makes one a member of an elite (Bourdieu, 1984). Rather, economic capital needs to be converted into other forms of capital (e.g. cultural and social capitals). To put this differently, economic capital enables individuals or groups to acquire the appropriate traits and practices — that is, high cultural capital — essential for elite identity formation.

Yet, as Waquant (2000 cited in Skeggs 2004, p. 141, my emphasis) warns, 'cultural practice takes its social meaning and its ability to signify social difference and distance, not from some *intrinsic property*, but from location of cultural practice in a system of objects and practices'. In other words, while the practices, accent and manners of elites are misrecognised as 'natural distinction' (Bourdieu 1984, p. 250), such dispositions are socially constructed and are acquired through early socialisation.

Elite identity formation in contemporary Nigeria — the role of British boarding school

One of the aims of my recent work has been to understand why Nigerian elite parents who have the financial capacity to buy any type of education they might want in Nigeria or other parts of Africa choose instead to send their children to the West for schooling. All the parents I spoke with explained that their search for what they perceived to be a good quality education had taken them out of Nigeria. Underlying the intent to provide their children with good quality education was the desire for distinction. Such a focus was part of parents' strategy to differentiate themselves and their children from 'Money Miss Road' Nigerians (a colloquial term used to describe the *nouveaux riche*) or, as one of the parents described them, 'those with money but no class' (Mrs Gbenga). Another parent emphasised this point:

> Not everybody that can afford to send their children to these private schools in Nigeria can send their children to private schools in the UK. I will say [sending your children to] the private schools in the UK separates people. It shows what class you are.
>
> *(Ms Ambrose)*

So, for parents such as these, the decision to buy a private British schooling was a symbolic expression of their class position (Bourdieu 1984).

The desire to express social distinction and acquire what they perceived as valuable symbolic capital for their children can also be seen in parents' choice of school in the UK. All the parents chose schools that were predominantly White spaces, wishing specifically to avoid schools where other Nigerian children were studying. Mr Okon (parent) explained:

> I found out he will be one of the few Nigerians in that school and one of the very few Nigerians that have been to Holyhouse and that is why I chose Holyhouse because I like to think my son is one of *the very few Nigerians* to have been to that school.

Bourdieu (1993) posits that the 'simplest strategy' for defending a group's distinction is by 'shunning works [or places/spaces] that have become popularised, devalued and disqualified' (p. 115). Thus, choosing schools where their children will be 'one of the very few Nigerians' (Mrs Bridge) ensures there will be few imitators that 'may pose a threat to the integrity of the [...] symbolic body of the community' (Lupton 1999, p. 3) or the social group that these parents belong or perceive themselves as belonging to. However, the parents interviewed elaborated that it was not simply the fact of being educated abroad that was critical to strategies for distinction – it was the particular deportment and accent acquired through a good quality 'British' education that were the critical resources to be gained.

Learning 'the proper British way' – English deportment and accent

> We wanted our children to learn *the British way*. I mean the 'proper' British way. The British aristocrats' way of life, like the royal families and top respectable families like that.
>
> *(Mrs Gbenga)*

Mrs Gbenga's earlier reference to 'those with money but no class' offers an indication that parents are aware that 'having access to economic resources alone does not give a person elite status' (Gaztambide-Fernández 2009, p. 11). Rather, to secure their children's future position as members of the 'authentic' Nigerian elites, parents know that a 'scholastic investment strategy' (Ball 2003, p. 71) — that is, the 'delicate inculcation' (p. 71) of the *correct* dispositions, deportments, knowledge and accent into their children — was essential.

For parents in the study, White British upper class deportment and lifestyle were conceived of in terms of 'attributes of excellence' and thus could be used as a signifier of distinction and status. The data indicate that one of the ways by which parents hoped to transform their children into 'respectable' gentlemen and ladies of class was to polish away their children's perceived 'ruggedness' and 'brashness' — traits that are seen as signifying the backwardness of Black Africans — and replace these with a Western gentility.

> This school [UK based British private boarding school] has polished him, which is what I expected, as opposed to the ruggedness he got from Lagos [Nigeria] some of the brashness is gone. He is more of a gentleman and has some more values.
>
> (Mrs Adu)

As well as equipping their children with the skill and taste for the 'White man's sports and activities' (Nigerian education agent 1 — Lagos), such as 'golf, sailing, kayaking and skiing' (Mrs Gbenga), which according to Bourdieu (1984, p. 283) 'characterise the [Western] bourgeoisie', parents also believed that a UK-based boarding school would teach their children how to 'dress like proper ladies and gentlemen' (Mrs Gbenga) and instil in them appropriate 'etiquette' such as 'how to sit down, how to eat properly, how to use fork and knives' (Mrs Ola). Arguably, parents' attempts to refine their children's otherwise wild bodies indicate their awareness that the body is a marker of class, and that status and distinction must be embodied (Bourdieu 1986).

In examining the formation of the 'New Nigerian elites', Smythe and Smythe (1960, p. 65) noted that the ability to 'speak grammatically' and adopt 'accents, intonation and diction' which were markedly different from 'their less well-educated countrymen' became one of the insignias of the Nigerian educated elites. Data from the current study also support the importance of the English language in the construction of elite identities. More precisely, it is a 'posh British accent' that was seen as one of the main hallmarks of distinction and status by parent participants. Consequently, words and phrases, such as 'intonation' and 'diction', and phrases like having a 'real' and 'proper' 'accent' were prevalent in the interview transcripts. Specifically, because it is 'different from the way most people speak in England' and therefore 'rare' and 'exclusive', it is the British 'aristocrat' accent that parents wanted their children to acquire.

> My children now have the correct proper British accent. The accent of the British aristocrats and that is *one of my goals*. I love the way the British top class speak, very proper. This is different from the way most people speak in

England. You hear many 'Have been to' [a colloquial term used to describe Nigerians who have travelled to Europe or America but who are not necessarily elites] speaking badly. They don't speak the correct, proper English, they say 'init' instead of 'isn't it'. Things like that. This is gutter English. It is not how the British elites speak.

(Mrs Kuti)

The suggestion that the British elite's accent is 'the correct proper British accent' effectively constructs it as authentic and original. The acquisition of a distinctive, exclusive and authentic British accent enables parents to construct their children as the genuine elite, distinguishing them from lower social groups. Fanon (2008, p. 25) argues that as well as giving Blacks 'honorary citizenship' in the 'Whiteworld', the mastery of the coloniser's language, manifested in the form of refined accent and diction, is one of the ways by which the colonised can prove that he has 'measured up' to the coloniser's culture that he/she has appropriated.

Constructing elite (private) schools in Nigeria

While motivations for sending their children abroad to boarding school were clearly articulated by parents in this study, we need to place these particular practices of distinction in context. In particular, how do private schools construct themselves as elite education institutions in contemporary Nigeria? All the parents interviewed had used the private education sector in Nigeria at some point. Prior to sending their children to the UK, all had sent their children to so-called 'British' private schools at home. Importantly, they consistently described these schools as 'elite' or 'top' private schools. However, with over 60 per cent of the schools in Nigeria being privately owned (Theobald et al. 2007), we need to understand how these so-called 'elite private schools' may be differentiated from other fee-paying educational institutions. The elite schools examined for this study were located in Abuja (the capital of Nigeria) and Lagos.

Although there is a dearth of literature on the composition of the private education sector in Nigeria, it could be said to comprise three main categories. The first group, which consists of the most expensive private schools in Nigeria, are institutions that can best be described as replicas of foreign schools (e.g. the British public schools), emulating their ethos, practices, curriculum content and pedagogical approaches. The majority of the schools in this group also belong to the Association of International School Educators of Nigeria (AISEN) and Council of International Schools (CIS).

The second category of private schools comprises those that combine an international curriculum, such as the International Primary Curriculum (IPC), with the Nigerian curriculum, but whose ethos, practices and pedagogical approach might be described as *Nigerian*. Unlike those in the first group, which only offer their pupils the opportunity to take international exams, usually run by foreign examination boards, private schools in the second category also offer their pupils the option of taking the national examinations organised by Nigerian or African examination boards, such as the West African Examinations Council (WAEC). The third category of private schools consists of private schools for poorer fractions of Nigerian society (Tooley *et al.* 2005), who use only the Nigerian curriculum and linked pedagogical approaches.

Whiteness: a salient characteristic of elite schools in Nigeria

So how might we define the private schools that are elite schools in Nigeria? Like elite groups themselves, elite schools must have unique features that set them apart from other private schools. A common characteristic of elite private schools in Nigeria derives from the fact that most of them appear to favour the recruitment of White teachers. This may be because, as Molande (2008, p. 182) perceptively notes, Whiteness has 'the highest possible concentration of values'. While some of these schools have 'a few White teachers' (White British head teacher 1 – Nigeria – Abuja), others claim that '40% of ... [its] teaching staff are White British' (White British head teacher 3 – Nigeria – Lagos). Since only a few private schools in Nigeria have the financial capacity to recruit White head teachers and teaching staff, having even a few White teachers enables such schools to create the impression of a 'well-heeled establishment' while 'alluding to a range of understated meanings' at the same time (Symes 1998, p. 143). Considering the historic construction of Whites and Whiteness as being symbolic of elite status, the employment of White head teacher and teachers, who are often strategically positioned as heads of department, could be described as a type of strategy of distinction which enables private schools in the first category to highlight their *international status* and *distinctiveness* while constructing the type of education they provide as *authentic*. I will look at each of these three distinguishing features in a little more detail below.

International status

Intense competition within the private sector has resulted in the over-use of the word 'international' by the majority of private schools. Yet in Nigeria, an affiliation with, and use of, Western curricula is a key marker for being an elite school. Having a White head teacher and a few White teachers is an effective way of communicating and projecting a school's international status, since Whiteness acts as a visual representation of their 'internationalness'. In other words, Whiteness enables elite schools to create a symbolic distance between themselves and their competitors that might also draw on the term 'international'.

Distinctiveness

As alluded to earlier, schools with White Western teachers and/or head teachers, are the exceptions rather than the rule in Nigeria. The scarcity of White teachers in Nigerian private schools is what gives these private schools their distinctiveness. Being distinct and rare means that these schools can portray themselves as 'the educational establishments reserved for the "elites" (Bourdieu 1993, p. 119). Having White teachers is their way of 'projecting the class identity of the school to the wider community' (Lynch and Moran 2006, p. 227). Indeed, parents' willingness to pay what even they described as 'exorbitant prices' (Mrs Ayo) can only be understood in light of the perceived exclusivity that such schools provide. With fees up to $12,800 (US dollars) per year, these schools can function as cocoons that limit the degree of social mixing.

Authenticity

Since Western education was largely introduced to Nigeria by British missionaries and colonists (Bassey 1999), Nigerians have come to perceive Westerners in general, and the British in particular, as the 'experts' in education. The comment below typifies such a perspective:

> I also believe that because [...] it is their curriculum, their education, they [the British] developed education so it makes them the expert in education.
> *(Mr Akpan)*

The recruitment of British White teachers therefore allows Nigerian private schools seeking elite status to communicate their expertise in, and link to, the supposed birthplace of world-class education. This benefits the schools in three significant ways. First, it allows them to communicate to prospective Nigerian parents that while they may be based in Nigeria, they are essentially Western rather than Nigerian schools. Second, maintaining close proximity with a real British education is the schools' way of suggesting that they provide an authentic rather than counterfeit education. Third, these schools can lay claim to a particular 'history' and tradition of high quality education.

The above analysis reinforces what I have argued earlier, which is that deportment, language and accent, and ultimately Whiteness (in particular, British Whiteness) is what is seen to constitute eliteness in Nigeria today. As a valuable and profitable capital, Whiteness/Britishness not only endows Nigerians who can successfully embody these qualities with elite status, but also enables private schools in Nigeria to construct themselves as elite institutions.

Concluding remarks

This chapter has shown that Whiteness – and British upper-class Whiteness more specifically – is a highly valued source of cultural and symbolic capital that is used to construct as well as legitimise the status of being elite in contemporary Nigeria. British upper-class lifestyles, forms of deportment and accent are considered 'attributes of excellence' by Nigerian parents who aspire to class. Now that being educated is, in and of itself, no longer a sufficient mark of elite status in contemporary Nigeria, elite families have had to find new ways of maintaining their social position. Nigerian elite parents see their children's embodiment of Britishness as a sure way of transforming their children's 'rugged' and 'uncivilised' bodies into more refined and civilised ones. The acquisition of a suitably 'posh British accent' allows 'genuine' Nigerian elites to be differentiated from imposters – such as their 'money miss road' peers. This would suggest that national independence has not weakened the high value that Nigerian elites attach to British culture, lifestyles and education. Instead, driven by the democratisation of education, these particular attributes are in fact now considered to be essential rather than desirable elements for those wishing to enter elite circles in contemporary Nigeria.

Such an emphasis on Britishness and the valorisation of Whiteness, for the singular purpose of acquiring and/or maintaining distinction and elite status (by both parents and schools), simultaneously highlights both the usefulness and also some limitations of Bourdieu's theorisation of elite identity formation. Bourdieu's work provides a useful way of not only understanding the difference between elite and social class identity formation, but also of specifying 'distinction' as a central element in the construction of eliteness. His assertion that distinction is a crucial aspect of elite identity formation allows us to pay close attention to the ways and means by which elites or those seeking the status of elite acquire and, more importantly, legitimise their claim to social and moral superiority. Thus, the parents interviewed here were keen for their children to attend predominantly White schools in the UK, while the head teachers of elite private schools in Nigeria interviewed were eager to stress that, although some of their teachers may be Black, they were not Black Nigerian but Black British.

Implicit in Bourdieu's theory, however, is the idea that these so-called aesthetic tastes, lifestyles, accents and distinguished deportments have their roots in, and therefore originate, within a particular nation-state. More specifically, Bourdieu's (1996) analysis does not recognise the role that foreign deportment and accent play in the formation and maintenance of local elites, especially in southern contexts. The literature on colonisation has shown that imperialism simultaneously rendered Blacks and Black culture worthless while making the West, and by extension Whiteness, one of the key markers of 'class', prestige and status in non-Western countries (Fanon 2008, Molande 2008). This suggests we may need to challenge what Johnson (2013) has described as Bourdieu's 'methodological nationalism' (p. 178), and highlight how Whiteness may be a highly profitable strategy of distinction that in the case of Nigeria is used by schools (and parents) in their struggle for dominance in the 'space of production' (Bourdieu 1993, p. 111).

In this chapter, I have argued that the acquisition of elite identity in contemporary Nigeria is dependent on the invisibility or effacement of one's Nigerianness or Blackness. Nigerian elites not only appear to accept the supposed superiority of Whiteness over Blackness, but also, through their practices, perpetuate this hegemonic discourse, albeit for instrumental and personal gain. Thus, as during the colonial era, a person of 'value' and 'status' in contemporary Nigeria remains one who although 'Black in blood and colour', is White 'in taste, in opinions, in morals, and in intellect' (Macauley, 1995, p. 430 cited in Molande, 2008, p. 186).

Note

1 Parents' narratives are permeated by the concepts of Whiteness and Britishness. Interestingly, the data indicate that the parents in this study perceived British and Britishness to be synonymous with English/Englishness. Consequently, they use the term Britishness when in actual fact they mean to imply a degree of Englishness. The fact that all the parents had placed their children in English boarding schools, and made constant reference to the Royal Family as a role model in terms of the type of dispositions and traits they wanted their children to acquire, and were keen for their children to be accent-free, indicate this.

References

Aigbokhan, B., Imahe, O. J. and Ailemen, M. I. (2007). Education expenditure and human capital development in Nigeria: Any correlation so far? *Ambrose Ali University Working Paper*, Ekpoma, Nigeria.
Ball, S. (2003). *Class strategies and the education market: The middle classes and social advantage.* London: RoutledgeFalmer.
Bassey, M. O. (1999). *Western education and political domination in Africa: A study in critical and dialogical pedagogy.* London: Bergin & Garvey.
Berghoff, H. (1990). Public schools and the decline of the British economy 1870–1914. *Past & Present*, 129, 148–167.
Bourdieu, P. (1984). *Distinction*. Cambridge, MA: Harvard University Press.
Bourdieu, P. (1993). *Sociology in question*. London: Sage.
Bourdieu, P. (1996). *The state nobility*. Stanford, CA: Stanford University Press.
Boyd, D. (1973). *Elites and their education*. Windsor: NFER.
Brooks, M. (2011). *Nigeria: An analysis of the market in Nigeria for school-age education in the UK.* London: British Council's Education UK Partnership.
Cookson, P. and Persell, C. (1985). *Preparing for power*. New York: Basic Books.
Ekeh, P. (1975). Colonialism and the two publics in Africa: A theoretical statement. *Comparative Studies in Society and History*, 17(1), 91–112.
Ellersgaard, C. H., Larsen, A. G. and Munk, M. D. (2012). A very economic elite: The case of the Danish top CEOs. *Sociology*, 47(6), 1051–1071.
Entwistle, H. (1978). *Class, culture and education*. London: Methuen.
Fanon, F. (2008 [1952 in French, 1967 in English]). *Black skin, White masks.* London: Pluto Press.
Gaztambide-Fernández, R. A. (2009). *The best of the best: Becoming elite at an American boarding school.* London: Harvard University Press.
Johnson, M. (2013). The aesthetics of diaspora in colonial fields of power: Elite nationalism, art and the love to die for. *Journal of Anthropology*, 78(2), 175–199.
Keller, S. (1991 [1963]). *Beyond the ruling class: Strategic elites in modern society.* London: Transaction Publishers.
Kendall, D. (2002). *The power of good deeds: Privileged women and the social reproduction of the upper class.* Oxford: Rowman & Littlefield.
Lamont, M. and Molnar, V. (2002). The study of boundaries in the social sciences. *Annual Review of Sociology*, 28, 167–195.
Lupton, D. (Ed.). (1999). *Risk and sociocultural theory: New directions and perspectives.* Cambridge: Cambridge University Press.
Lynch, K. and Moran, M. (2006). Markets, schools and the convertibility of economic capital: The complex dynamics of class choice. *British Journal of Sociology of Education*, 27(2), 221–235.
Molande, B. (2008). Rewriting memory: Ideology of difference in the desire and demand for Whiteness. *European Journal of American Culture*, 27(3), 173–190.
Parkin, F. (1979). *Marxism and class theory: A bourgeois critique*. London: Tavistock.
Puwar, N. (2004). *Space invaders: Race, gender and bodies out of place.* Oxford: Berg.

Rollock, N., Gillborn, D., Vincent, C. and Ball, S. (2011). The public identities of the Black middle classes: Managing race in public spaces. *Sociology*, 45(6), 1078–1093.

Roy, M. (1994). 'Englishing' India: Reinstituting class and social privilege. *Social Text*, 39(1), 83–109.

Scott, J. (1991). *Who rules Britain?* Oxford: Polity Press.

Simpson, A. (2003). *'Half London' in Zambia*. Edinburgh: Edinburgh University Press.

Skeggs, B. (2004). *Class, self, culture*. London: Routledge.

Smythe, H. H. and Smythe, M. M. (1960). *The new Nigerian elite*. Stanford: Stanford University Press.

Symes, C. (1998). Education for sale: A semiotic analysis of school prospectuses and other forms of educational marketing. *Australian Journal of Education*, 42(2), 133–152.

Theobald, D., Umar, A., Ochekpe, S. and Sanni, K. (2007). *Nigeria: Country case study*. Available at http://unesdoc.unesco.org/images/0015/001555/155589e.pdf (accessed 10 June 2015).

Tooley, J., Dixon, P. and Olaniyan, O. (2005). Private and public schooling in low-income areas of Lagos State, Nigeria: A census and comparative survey. *International Journal of Educational Research*, 43(3), 125–146.

Unagha, A. O. (2008). Implementing universal basic education (UBE) through the strategic provision of school library services. *Library Philosophy and Practice* (E-journal) Paper 161. Available at http://digitalcommons.unl.edu/libphilprac/161 (accessed 10 June 2015).

Waters, J. L. (2007). Roundabout routes and sanctuary schools: The role of situated educational practices and habitus in the creation of transnational professionals. *Journal of Global Networks*, 7(4), 477–497.

Weis, L. and Cipollone, K. (2013). 'Class work': Producing privilege and social mobility in elite US secondary schools. *British Journal of Sociology of Education*, 34(5–6), 701–722.

West, A. and Noden, P. (2003). Parental choice and involvement: Private and state schools. In G. Walford (Ed.), *British private schools: Research on policy and practice*. London: Routledge.

West, M. (2002). *The rise of an African middle class*. Bloomington: Indiana University Press.

Woolman, D. (2001). Educational reconstruction and post-colonial curriculum development: A comparative study of four African countries. *International Education Journal*, 2(1), 27–46.

13

THE EDUCATION OF BRAZILIAN ELITES IN THE TWENTY-FIRST CENTURY

New opportunities or new forms of distinction?

Maria Alice Nogueira and Maria Teresa G. Alves

In March 2014, Nizan Guanaes, a successful and acclaimed Brazilian advertising executive, opinion maker and writer, wrote a piece for the magazine *Vogue* entitled: 'Looking for a new upper class'. Nizan argued that Brazilian elites should aim to combine 'books and money'. To create such an elite, he argued that instead of giving him [his own child] a Ferrari, he had 'enrolled him in the best school in São Paulo – , Graded (The American School of São Paulo)'. Afterwards, his son had asked to go to one of the best prep schools in the USA – Philips Exeter Academy – which was founded in 1781. 'Mark Zuckerberg studied there ... that is an inheritance'. Nizan Guanaes' article highlights two themes that capture important developments in Brazilian elite education today: namely, the intensification in the use of private education; and, linked to this, the growing internationalisation of schooling trajectories.

What do we know about elite education in Brazil?

In Brazil, as in other Latin American countries, there exists a paucity of sociological research on the lifestyles of elites and their strategies of social reproduction, especially when compared to the much larger literature on the experiences of lower social classes (Medeiros 2005, Heredia 2012). The little knowledge that exists on elites focuses largely on their economic and political role, with little or no focus on their private lives (Musse 2004). Regarding sociological studies of upper class education strategies, most work has been of a qualitative nature and highly influenced by Pierre Bourdieu's work (Almeida and Nogueira 2002). As Heredia (2012) argues, what is required is 'an update of the theoretical frameworks and assumptions we now hold' (p. 277), so as to be able to deal with the specificities of capitalism in the context of Latin America today.

Following the 1930 Revolution in Brazil, there was a reconfiguration and diversification of national elites. Initially, members of the elites had mainly been land- and slave-owners from the colonial period. This remained so until around the 1980s, when processes of denationalisation and capital concentration led to the creation of a new 'super-elite', which included senior executives in industry, commerce, transport, finance and communication together with the professionals serving these sectors. By the 2000s, Brazil was among the top ten countries with the highest number of 'super-rich' people according to *Forbes Magazine* (Pochmann et al. 2009, p. 78). Bourdieu's conceptual framework is therefore useful in thinking further about the Brazilian dominant classes, where it is possible to distinguish between those with economic capital and groups with cultural capital. Social hierarchies within Brazil today are largely driven by economic wealth, and yet these groups are very concerned to accrue a variety of cultural capitals, which in part drive their education strategies.

Two important studies have been undertaken on elite families in Brazil to date, both by Nogueira (2000, 2004). Conducted in the city of Belo Horizonte (the capital city of the Brazilian state of Minas Gerais), the first study looked at the cultural elite, focusing on families ($N = 37$) whose parents (both fathers and mothers) were university teachers and researchers. The second study shifted the focus to economic elites, more specifically families ($N = 50$) in which the primary breadwinner (usually the father) was a business owner in industry, commerce or the service sector. The findings from this research showed striking differences, but also some similarities, between how these families viewed the role of education.

Within cultural elite families, the schooling trajectories of their children could be categorised as following a 'scholastically elite' pathway, while economically elite families were less likely to focus on 'academic excellence' when making their choices. Thus, while three-quarters of the children of university academics had begun university at or before the usual starting age of 18 years, less than half of those from economically elite families had done so, often because they had been held back a year during their primary or secondary schooling, or because they had failed their university entrance examinations. However, both groups of families were inclined to send their children to private schools, although culturally elite parents tended to choose private schools (usually religious ones) known for a focus on academic rigour, while the economic elite opted for less academically demanding private schools, characterised by social selectivity.

Obviously, such investments in their children's education are possible only because families have privileged access to economic resources, when compared to the rest of the Brazilian population. Income inequality in Brazil is among the highest in the world, where the richest 10 per cent earn 50 times more than the poorest 10 per cent of the population.[1] However, the richest stratum has an enormous range of per capita income. This makes it hard to ascertain the income levels of families belonging to cultural and economic elites, as they rarely declare their total income for the purposes of official statistics. Nevertheless, demographic data indicates that only 2 per cent of Brazilian families have an income higher than US$6,160 a month (the equivalent of 20 times the monthly minimum wage). This figure corresponds to the average income of a family in which both parents are university academics at the beginning of their careers. Thus, part of this 2 per cent of the Brazilian population – one possible definition of being elite – includes families working in relatively different sectors – both public and private. For the cultural elite in particular, such income levels have made the buying of a private and academically elite education feasible, which increases the chances of their children being admitted to the most selective and prestigious higher education programmes, all of which are to be found in the large public universities of Brazil. However, in recent years, due mainly to the new education policies implemented by the ruling Worker's Party, the educational landscape has been changing. This has led to an intensification and refinement of the strategies employed by elite parents to maintain access to the best schooling opportunities for their children.

A new educational landscape for Brazilian elites?

Since the 2000s, education policy has focused on increasing the access of all Brazilian young people to higher education. Different models of affirmative action and social inclusion have been developed and implemented, some of which include:

- the *Universidade para Todos* (ProUni or University for All) programme, established in 2005 by the federal government, offers scholarships to lower income students and Brazilian nationals of African descent to study in for-profit private higher education institutions
- the *Ciência sem Fronteiras* (Science without Borders) programme implemented in 2011 by the federal government, grants scholarships to Brazilian university students wishing to spend one year in prestigious universities in the North, as a way of fostering technological innovation within Brazil
- the *Lei das Cotas Sociais e Raciais* (Law of Social and Racial Quotas), established in 2012 by federal government, which introduced affirmative action policies and requires that by 2016, 50 per cent of first year places in each major study programme at federal universities should be reserved for those who have completed their secondary education in a public high school (now officially used as a quasi social class criterion). Within this 50 per cent, a proportion should be students of African or native Brazilian descent (an ethnic/racial criterion), calculated in proportion to the population in each state.

Among these initiatives, it is the third which has most directly influenced the educational strategies of the Brazilian elites, as it significantly reduces the chances of socially and economically privileged young people (who will have been more likely to have studied in a private secondary school) securing a place at the most prestigious universities. Given the relatively recent implementation of this policy change, it is still very difficult to predict precisely the effect it will have on elite groups' educational strategies. However, it is likely that these significant changes will further strengthen the 'parentocracy' of these consumers of education (Brown 1990). Hence, Brazil is likely to witness, as in other countries that have already undergone more extensive transformations under neoliberal market reforms, such as Chile, a transition from a 'meritocracy' (a system which rewards the capacity and effort of students in education), to a 'parentocracy' in which 'a child's education is increasingly dependent upon the wealth and wishes of parents' (Brown 1990, p. 66). Two significant features of this transition in Brazil are the intensification in the take-up of private education and an increase in the internationalisation strategies employed by parents.

Intensification in the use of private schools and the refinement of school choice

One of the motivations behind the 2012 introduction of the Law of Social and Racial Quotas by the federal government was to strengthen the public school system and motivate its teachers and students to improve the quality of the education received and the academic outcomes secured. In the words of Aloízio Mercadante, the Education Minister: 'what we intend is to give an opportunity for these youngsters [from public schools], so that they can study even more, and that we improve high school quality' (Agência Brasil 2012).

A second motivation for the law has been to encourage middle-class families to transfer their children from the private sector into the public sector, in an attempt to increase their chances of gaining a place at an elite university. Although it is still too early to identify trends, there is little evidence that middle-class and elite families are moving their children into the state system. On the contrary, the annual School Census (carried out by the Education Ministry) from 2003 to 2013 shows an increase from 12 per cent to 17 per cent in private school enrolments (for primary, elementary and high school students). Furthermore, in the two states (Rio de Janeiro and the Distrito Federal) where there are two public universities that are considered to be pioneers in supporting affirmative action, there is still an enrolment rate of 30 per cent for students who have been privately educated (a far higher percentage than the total proportion of the Brazilian population who attend a private school). Another trend suggesting that the private sector is still growing, despite a potentially more hostile policy context, is the fact that the number of private schools increased by 9 per cent between 2002 and 2013, while local government (state and municipal) schools decreased by 13 per cent throughout Brazil over this same time period.

The only exception to the growth of the private education sector take-up, can be found in a very small part of the public education system – the network of military and vocational high schools run by the federal government, whose enrolment rates have almost doubled (from 0.9 per cent in 2002 to 1.7 per cent in 2013). These schools tend to have better infrastructure and educational resources, more qualified teachers, and better salary and work conditions when compared to public schools run by the states and cities. However, access to these schools is highly restricted. Besides the low number of places, the selection process includes an examination similar to those of prestigious public universities, which requires a lot of preparation, thereby privileging children from families with cultural and educational capital, or who have previously been privately educated. Many parents pay for their children to attend specially designed preparatory classes, run by for-profit organisations, to increase their chances of success in this highly demanding selection process.

In summary, over the past 11 years, despite the introduction of affirmative action policies both locally and nationally, privileged families have intensified their take-up of private education. Such a strategy is understandable in the context of persistently identified concerns about the quality of the teaching and learning in public schools, where strikes, violence and discipline problems characterise this form of education in national discourses as well as parental accounts of their experiences (Nogueira 2013). The only public schools that the middle class and elite groups of Brazilian society are willing to contemplate are the federally funded military or vocational schools that are linked to the big public universities.

Such a segmentation of the secondary school sector – between state/municipal, private and the small number of federal schools – highlights important trends in different socio-economic groups 'choosing' these schools and the academic outcomes secured. We can use data from *Exame Nacional do Ensino Médio* (ENEM – the National High School Examination) to consider the implications of these developments further. ENEM was created in 1998. Although it has been voluntary since 2004, the number of candidates taking the exam has risen exponentially as it is a key qualification used in admission processes for federal universities, as well as the scholarship programmes in for-profit universities (ProUni) and the *Ciência sem Fronteiras* (CsF) programme.

ENEM analysis highlights a number of interesting findings. Table 13.1, for example, shows the association between average socioeconomic status (SES) of ENEM 2012 candidates and the type of school attended. This analysis reveals that state and municipal schools have the highest proportion of low- and middle-income students. Meanwhile, federal schools are predominantly for medium SES students, though one-third come from high SES families. Within the private school sector, the vast majority of pupils come from high SES groups.

TABLE 13.1 Proportion of students from different SES groups by type of high school attended (ENEM 2012)

Average high school SES	Federal public school (%)	State or municipal public school (%)	Private school (%)	Total (%)
Low	6.9	21.9	0.7	17.7
Medium	60.1	75.2	27.5	66.0
High	33.0	2.9	71.8	16.2
Number of schools	215	19,901	6,240	26,356

Source: Alves et al. (2014).

TABLE 13.2 Average grade by type of high school (ENEM 2012)

Type of high school	Mean essay writing test	Mean natural sciences	Mean human sciences	Mean languages	Mean mathematics
State/municipal	479.1	448.5	496.6	472.5	476.1
Private	602.2	540.6	583.2	544.1	614.3
Federal	623.6	554.9	597.6	552.3	639.0

Source: Authors' analysis based on ENEM 2012 data.

TABLE 13.3 Average in ENEM 2012 by high school SES

High school SES	Mean composition	Mean natural sciences	Mean human sciences	Mean languages	Mean mathematics
Low	449.6	431.0	473.1	446.7	437.1
Medium	492.8	456.6	506.2	481.8	491.3
High	615.2	553.4	594.7	554.6	635.2

Source: Authors' analysis based on ENEM 2012 data.

Table 13.2 looks at students' average scores across the five component exams in the ENEM. Final marks received by federal and private school students are almost always 100 points above those from state/municipal school students, with the exception of languages (Portuguese and foreign language tests). The largest differences can be seen in the essay writing test and mathematics, which are crucial in determining access to the most highly competitive study programmes in elite universities.

The association between SES background and results obtained in the ENEM is further emphasised by data shown in Table 13.3. Here, the group with high SES is seen as securing marks which are 200 points above their lower SES peers in mathematics, for instance.

Research by Curi and Menezes-Filho (2013), who analysed ENEM 2006 data from the state of São Paulo, points to a strong correlation between ENEM performance and school tuition fees, suggesting that there is a hierarchy within the private school sector itself. They found that a 10 per cent increase in the monthly tuition fees charged by a school, increased a student's ENEM grade by 1.1 per cent, after controlling for students' background. Thus, if a family opts for a school that charges a monthly tuition of US$990, instead of another that charges US$490, the child's ENEM grade should increase by 25 per cent. Furthermore, the same authors found that peer effects could explain around 24 per cent of ENEM grade variation across the schools.

The increasing internationalisation of schooling trajectories

Recently, the principal of one of the best-known private schools in São Paulo said in an interview in the *Folha de São Paulo*, one of the most widely read Brazilian newspapers: 'Since the public universities have become drivers for inclusion in Brazil, I have noticed that many good students talk more and more about studying in the USA' (23 November 2013). In fact, more than 20 private schools located in large urban areas of Brazil are currently authorised to run the SAT (Scholastic Aptitude Test) or the ACT (American College Testing) exams, used by US universities as part of the admission process for undergraduate students. An article in the newspaper *Folha de São Paulo*, on 10 March 2014, discussed at length the changes in the 2016 edition of the SAT and what implications this might have for Brazilian students.

There has also emerged a new type of for-profit organisation, which offers the services of a Personal Prep consultant[2] whose job it is to 'prepare high school graduates planning to do their undergraduate studies abroad'. This service provides clients with advice and support during all phases of 'the process of undergraduate admission in other countries, mainly the USA'. The website continues by explaining that these professionals will also advise on the choice of a foreign university, ensuring a 'perfect match'. The cost of the service depends on the length of time for which it is needed. For example, a charge of approximately US$5,000 is made for the provision of coaching services for a year (normally during the last year of secondary school). The website boasts success in admitting students in 'various universities of excellence, such as Harvard, Yale, MIT, Columbia, and Stanford among others'.

Such desires for internationalisation are not restricted to higher education choices. Recent research in Belo Horizonte illustrates how private primary and secondary schools are implementing pedagogical strategies to meet parental demands for securing international capital, which parents consider critical to their children's future success (Aguiar and Nogueira 2012). Our research focused on private schools ($N = 65$) with students aged 4–18 years, located in upper-class neighbourhoods in Belo Horizonte. Based on interviews with school staff and an analysis of their websites and other printed materials, we found that more than half of the sample had developed new internationalisation initiatives, including those detailed below.

Special programmes for foreign language learning

Foreign language provision in private schools begins at an early age. They tend to offer at least one foreign language (usually English) from the first years of primary school (some even starting in kindergarten/nursery), in contrast to public schools (where most working-class children can be found) in which the teaching of foreign languages starts only when the students are 11 years old. More than one-third of the surveyed private schools ran two English classes a week. The focus of teaching was usually on oral expression and English fluency.

Bilingual pedagogical projects

A more novel and emerging trend in the internationalisation strategies developed by schools is the provision of bilingual education. Three types of bilingual programmes were found in the research: (i) preschools run by international educational chains aiming to foster language learning through total immersion (children only speak English inside the school); (ii) agreements with US institutions to offer an optional high school programme that can be undertaken simultaneously with the Brazilian curriculum (the diploma is recognised by the US government and valid for university entrance there); (iii) bilingual programmes throughout the school (from kindergarten/nursery to the end of secondary schooling) where, during the first part of the school day students follow the Brazilian national curriculum, which is then followed, during the second part of the school day, by a summary of what has been learned, where the medium of instruction is English.

Promotion of international travel

Since the 1990s, a small number of schools have started to offer students aged between 14 and 18, trips to foreign countries during their holidays so they can attend additional language courses. The most frequent destinations are Spain, Canada, the USA, Australia, Ireland, Argentina and Chile. These visits are often organised through agreements with foreign schools, which, in some cases, share the same religious affiliation as the Brazilian partner school. Teachers too are encouraged to spend time abroad, seeking to 'internationalise' them and better prepare them to meet the needs of the families whose children they are employed to teach.

Overall, schools are using a variety of strategies in the struggle to place themselves at the forefront in the race to satisfy parental demands for internationalisation, whether by the early introduction and increased pedagogical sophistication of foreign language acquisition, or by contributing to the production of cosmopolitan identities through international travel and an international curriculum.

It could be argued that the increasing demand by socially and economically privileged groups for the internationalisation of their children's schooling is a response to the current context of massification and expansion of educational opportunities for all in Brazil. This behaviour constitutes a critical strategy employed by elite parents to effectively maintain inequalities (Lucas 2001), by creating qualitative differences between their children and others (Lopes 2014).

Concluding comments

It has been argued that in many Northern countries political reforms accompanied by deregulation and the rollback of the state are fundamental in the transition from a 'meritocratic' model of education to a 'parentocratic' one (Brown 1990). In Brazil, there has been a concurrent strengthening of state regulation of the educational system, through positive discrimination, that has propelled an intensification and diversification of elite groups' strategies for securing educational advantage and the reproduction of elite status. In the context of a country whose economic growth has been closely tied to becoming an international player in terms of technology, finance and the service industry sectors, schooling that equips Brazilian children with the knowledge, skills and cosmopolitan orientations to lead these domains in the future appears to be what is demanded by those families with the expertise and financial resources to secure such provision.

The findings presented in this chapter show that students from private schools, or from the very small number of federal vocational high schools, gain the highest educational results, when compared to their peers educated in state or municipal schools. There is also a direct association between family income and parents' educational level and the likelihood of attending these two more successful types of secondary schools. Despite increasing competition for places at the most prestigious federal universities (still the elite providers of higher education), students from families with greater levels of cultural capital and income are still more likely to secure admission to these tertiary institutions. Furthermore, given the cultural and economic capital to which Brazilian elite families have access, even in an environment of increasingly intense competition for elite higher education places, their resources make available to them alternative, potentially more advantageous options – such as studying abroad at elite universities in the USA or elsewhere.

It is still not possible to assess the effects of affirmative action policies on the social composition of the student body in large and prestigious public universities. The Law of Social and Racial Quotas is still being implemented and universities have until 2016 to reach the targets they have been set. However, two years after the law's implementation, there is some evidence to challenge the Education Ministry's expectations for these policies – namely, that they will encourage middle-class and elite families to move their children back into the public education sector, which in turn will improve teaching and learning experiences in these contexts.

The same time period has also witnessed a rapid growth in the private education sector (for instance, enrolment in private higher education institutions has increased from 69.8 per cent to 83.4 per cent over the past ten years, while public sector enrolment has decreased from 30.2 per cent to 16.3 per cent). This growth is partly driven by a diversified expansion strategy, which has included the development of private higher education satellite units in both metropolitan and more rural settings, while public universities have focused only on expanding their main campuses. Furthermore, the private sector has benefitted from the receipt of public funding via the Universidade para Todos programme, whereby the Education Ministry offers scholarships to allow students from public schools to attend private institutions.

Despite the intentions behind current government policies to widen participation in higher education, the quotas have favoured those from selected public schools – specifically federal and vocational ones. These students largely come from families with higher cultural capital (even if they do not necessarily have higher incomes) and are now favoured in the competitive process for entering the most prestigious federal universities. Meanwhile the families at the top of the social hierarchy will probably continue to pursue educational trajectories for their children through the private sector.

The Law of Social and Racial Quotas will most likely be reviewed in 2020, ten years after its introduction. Until then, it is important to continue observing the changes taking place in different social groups' access to the more prestigious parts of the educational system. However, such research will only be possible if researchers focus more closely on the educational practices of the dominant groups, track developments within and across the private education sector and begin to collect more comprehensive forms of quantitative data on elite groups, their educational trajectories and longer term academic and employment outcomes.

Notes

1 The Brazilian Gini index is 51.9, placing the country among the 20 most unequal in the world. CIA – Central Intelligence Agency. (2013). *The World Factbook* 2013–14. Washington, DC. Information retrieved from https://www.cia.gov/library/publications/the-world-factbook/index.html (accessed 19 June 2015).
2 Available at http://www.estudarfora.org.br/personalprep/ (accessed 19 June 2015).

References

Agência Brasil. (2012). *O que nós pretendemos é dar oportunidade para esses jovens, dar estímulo para que eles estudem cada vez mais, é que a gente melhore a qualidade do ensino médio.* 15 October. Available at http://www.ebc.com.br/2012/10/lei-das-cotas-e-estimulo-para-alunos-estudarem-mais-diz-mercadante (accessed 19 June 2015, in Portuguese).

Aguiar, A. and Nogueira, M. A. (2012). Internationalisation strategies of Brazilian private schools. *International Studies in Sociology of Education*, 22(4), 353–368.

Almeida, A. M. F. and Nogueira, M. A. (Eds.). (2002). *A escolarização das elites – um panorama internacional da pesquisa.* Petrópolis: Vozes.

Alves, M. T. G., Soares, J. F. and Xavier, F. P. (2014). Índice Socioeconômico das Escolas de Educação Básica Brasileiras. *Ensaio: Avaliação e Políticas Públicas em Educação*, 22(84), 671–703.

Brown, P. (1990). The third wave: Education and the ideology of parentocracy. *British Journal of Sociology of Education*, 11(1), 65–85.

Heredia, M. (2012). La formación de quién? Reflexiones sobre la teoría de Bourdieu y el estudio de las elites en la Argentina actual. In S. Ziegler and V. Gessaghi, V. (Eds.), *Formación de las elites. Investigaciones y debates en Argentina, Brasil y Francia.* Buenos Aires: Manantial-FLACSO.

Lopes, A. D. (2014). Ciência sem Fronteira: como as classes média e alta mantêm vantagens educacionais no Brasil. Paper presented at *IV Colóquio Luso-Brasileiro de Sociologia da Educação.* Universidade do Porto, Porto, Portugal, 19–21 June 2014.

Lucas, S. R. (2001). Effectively maintained inequality: Education transitions, track mobility, and social background effects. *American Journal of Sociology*, 106(6), 1642–1690.

MEC – Ministério da Educação (2014). *Programa Universidade para Todos (ProUni).* Available at http://prouniportal.mec.gov.br (accessed 11 June 2015).

Medeiros, M. (2005). O estudo dos ricos no Brasil. *Econômica*, 7(1), 128–199.

Musse, R. (2004). Lacunas brasileiras: A elite invisível. *Folha de S. Paulo: Caderno Mais!* 28 November, p. 4.

Nogueira, M. A. (2000). A construção da excelência escolar – um estudo de trajetórias feito com estudantes universitários provenientes das camadas médias intelectualizadas. In M. A. Nogueira, G. Romanelli and N. Zago (Eds.), *Família & Escola – trajetórias de escolarização em camadas médias e populares.* Petrópolis: Vozes.

Nogueira, M. A. (2004). Favorecimento econômico e excelência escolar: Um mito em questão. *Revista Brasileira de Educação*, 26, 144–133.
Nogueira, M. A. (2013). No fio da navalha. A (nova) classe média brasileira e sua opção pela escola particular. In G. Romanelli, M. A. Nogueira and N. Zago (Eds.), *Família & Escola – Novas perspectivas de análise*. Petrópolis: Vozes.
Pochmann, M. *et al.* (2009). *Proprietários concentração e continuidade*. São Paulo: Cortez.
Vogue RG (2014) Procura-se uma nova classe alta. http://siterg.terra.com.br/news/2014/03/18/procura-se-uma-novaclasse-alta-por-nizan-guanaes/accessed (accessed 18 March 2014).

14
SERVICING ELITE INTERESTS

Elite education in post-neoliberal Argentina

Howard Prosser

The educational standards of Argentina's prestigious schools are highly regarded in Latin America and beyond. Both public and private elite institutions produce students who go on to study at esteemed universities in the USA and Europe as well as becoming leaders in governance and industry in Argentina itself. Despite this, there has not been great deal of research carried out in, or with, these schools. In keeping with this volume's purpose, this chapter provides something of an overview of private and elite schooling in Buenos Aires as it has developed over the past decade or so. It also indicates how local scholars are beginning to discuss the schooling of elites in Argentina. The analysis it provides is not exhaustive, but rather plots the educational landscape with specific attention to elite education and one school in particular.

In Argentinian elite education there is a specific private-school domain that caters to the entrepreneurial or other economic elites. This sphere is distinct from the public space of elite education filled by select-entry schools. Private elite schools are geared more towards global notions of eliteness that offer attributes and trajectories, via private universities, that are useful in transnational contexts. This is especially the case in what are locally called 'English schools'. My focus here is on one of the most well-known of these schools – the Caledonian School – in which I spent six months carrying out ethnographic fieldwork in 2011. After first positioning the school in a broader educational and scholarly context, I will examine how the school has responded to the post-neoliberal milieu into which Argentina entered at the turn of the twenty-first century.

What I found from my time at the school were a number of tensions or paradoxes. The past decade has seen the Caledonian School became more socially engaged. And yet such social engagement, via community service, also serves the interests of the school. Social engagement keeps the school up to date with trends in elite education around the world and it also mollifies the widely perceived aloofness of the school culture. This paradox serves the school well because it is able to respond to social issues as well as its clientele's demands for a world-class education. Elite schools like the Caledonian School survive by adjusting themselves to the current sociopolitical climate. Ultimately, however, such adaptation shows that elite schools, in spite of sincere attempts to soften elitism, are always geared to favour the interests of the elite groups they serve.

Argentina's schooling complex

Education plays a central role in the history of Argentina's national project. Like many new nations forged in the revolutions of the early nineteenth century, the need to 'make' citizens was well understood by its founders. This process became especially important when the relatively new nation found itself inundated with hopeful migrants from around Southern and Central Europe who were often unskilled and illiterate (Shumway 1991). The major figures of Argentine liberalism promoted education using various constitutional framings. The two presidents most usually linked to this work are Domingo Faustino Sarmiento and Carlos Pellegrini: the former promoted the idea of universal primary education and his legacy is still manifest in the white coats worn by schoolchildren; the latter saw the need for expertise beyond that which primary education could provide and so promoted state-funded elite secondary schooling based on his personal admiration of the British Public Schools (Finocchio 2009). During the first half of the twentieth century, Argentina developed a proud public education system. To this day, public education remains an important driver of social programmes, especially those associated with social equality and economic redistribution, and it has remained a bulwark against pro-market reforms (Beech and Barrenechea 2011).

But private education is not included within this narrative. The importance of the state education system within the Argentine foundational story means that any private arrangements are often hidden from discussion. However, private education has been on the rise in Argentina since the 1960s (Narodowski 2008). Moreover, there has been a clear trend towards the socioeconomic differentiation of education systems in Argentina (Narodowski 2002). One peculiarity of Argentina is that the majority of its population lives in the City of Buenos Aires and its surrounding Province of Buenos Aires. This makes the federal education system under which state-provided schooling is governed heavily focused on this particular area's inhabitants. When it comes to education, the Greater Buenos Aires area sees students fairly evenly divided between private and public schools, whereas in the whole of Argentina the number of students attending private schools is around 25 per cent (Morduchowicz 2005).

The range of schools that fall under this rubric complicates understandings of the form and purpose of private schooling. The situation is worth considering further in order to fully understand the context in which the elite schools sit. State schools are completely government-run, whereas private schools range from those that receive a heavy subsidy for teachers' wages to those that are completely independent, not-for-profit institutions. Another division along this spectrum can be drawn between Catholic and non-Catholic schools. The majority of 'private' schools in Argentina are low-fee Catholic primary schools. Such schools account for the heightened numbers of private school children in the capital and its surrounds. And yet, for all intents and purposes, these are quasi-state schools because of their reliance on government finance. These schools stand in contrast to Catholic schools that cater to the more wealthy, which are better resourced and are thus more on a par with their non-Catholic private counterparts (Morduchowicz 2005).

This non-Catholic sector is made up of schools that are independent of government subsidy and associated with particular cultural groups, especially those affiliated to various religions or migrant groupings. So, there are a significant number of Jewish, Protestant or bilingual schools that fall into this category. However, since the 1990s, a significant number of private schools, with little specific cultural identification, have also opened their doors to meet a growing demand (Banfi and Day 2004). All of these schools, like the more affluent Catholic ones, exist in a hierarchy of their own based on hearsay and reputation. But often the primary indicator of school status, in this sector at least, is fees.

Elite education in Argentina

Economic factors such as the fees charged to parents tend to define elite private schools in contrast to the selective entry characteristic of the elite public institutions. The situation is no different in Argentina. The Argentine elite public school system begins in secondary school. Students have to compete for places by taking rigorous courses and entry exams. The handful of schools to which they aspire – including the *Colegio Nacional Buenos Aires* and one named after Pellegrini – are affiliated to the University of Buenos Aires (UBA) and the education received there is highly regarded. The tutelage they provide has long been associated with nation building and thus the production of future leaders, intellectuals and professionals. Like most select-entry elite schools, the system favours children from educated families, especially those who attended such schools themselves. Apart from their high educational standards, the schools are well known as political nurseries. As such, they are often sites of political apprenticeship and protest, usually with the staff's collusion. These schools therefore serve to produce and reproduce networks that are closely linked to public governance through party- or union-based politics.

The high-fee (private) elite schools cater to quite different groups in different parts of the city. While elite public schools are bastions of government power, their high-fee equivalents are the mainstay of economic influence. These schools usually offer both local and international curricula, usually in two languages. There is some diversity between them, but an obvious group within this suite comprises the 'English' or 'British' schools. The focus below is on one of these schools, but first I will make a few general remarks about how these schools fit into the Argentine education landscape.

First, these schools share a history of catering to Britons during the high point of their 'informal' imperialism within the region between the 1830s and the 1940s. This informality assisted in the fledgling Argentine Republic's unification during the mid-nineteenth century (Barton 2014) and then largely took the shape of major infrastructural investment, especially in the railways (Rock 2008). The schools sought to offer 'British' educational standards and were, until the 1960s, largely independent of state scrutiny (Morduchowicz 2005). Second, despite aspirations to grandeur, many of the schools remained quite humble. A few stood out and went on to become the elite schools they are today. This rise was largely due to the post-war success of Anglo-Argentine businesses or businessmen working for international firms as well as to the attractiveness of such schools to the new rich emerging during the neo-liberal boom of the 1990s. Third, there is a spatial aspect to these schools that reveals much about their position in Argentina society. While elite public schools are usually located close to the university and government, the 'English' schools are situated in areas to the north of Buenos Aires to which the affluent have retreated. Often the schools themselves have migrated or have opened second campuses in the new northern suburbs or satellite towns that are characterised by high-security living. And, if the schools in these areas are not from these traditional 'British' backgrounds, they often mimic their appearance – with a saint in their name and some tartan in their uniforms.

This situation amounts to a divide within the elite education system of Argentina between publically oriented elites and privately oriented elites. This scenario is not unique in global education. However, there is also a relatively new situation arising at the tertiary level which means that these groups are likely to remain segregated. In the past, students from these different schools tended to come into contact with each other at UBA. Until the 1980s, UBA was the main option for tertiary study in Argentina. It was also a solid choice as one of Latin America's largest and most prestigious universities. However, during the late 1980s and into the 1990s a number of private universities were permitted to open as a result of government deregulation of the tertiary sector (Zelaya 2012). Since then these newer universities have consolidated themselves within the educational marketplace and now attract students from the private school system, especially from the elite schools. Some graduates from these schools choose to attend UBA alongside their elite public school peers; but the university's reputation has declined as the private institutions' standing has improved. As a result, there is now an entrenched division between the provision of private (and elite) education and public (and elite) education that stretches throughout the primary, secondary and tertiary levels.

Scholarship on Argentine elites

Much more work is needed to properly theorise the issues raised by the schools discussed above: worthy of particular attention are the specific gradations of the various private schools, their gender characteristics and a better understanding of the new aspirational private schools that have emerged in the last decade or so.

Previous scholarly attention tended to fall solely on poverty-stricken schools with little consideration of the middle classes or those above (Meo 2008). But things have changed more recently. Given the global groundswell of scholarly interest in elites, it comes as no surprise that Argentina's sociologists have turned their attention to them as well. There are at least two reasons for this new focus.

First, Argentina's experience as a setting for neo-liberalism's early collapse drew specific attention to capitalist hubris long before the 2008 financial meltdowns of North America and Europe. With the government's subscription to the Washington Consensus of the 1990s, massive privatisation and wealth concentration led to accentuated social divisions and set in motion Argentina's 'Latinamericanisation' on the one hand (Ko 2013), and Buenos Aires' 'Losangelisation' on the other (Guano 2006, p. 185). Previous national egalitarianism, however mythological, was displaced by pronounced inequalities that made poverty and insecurity an obvious presence on the streets of Buenos Aires and beyond (Adamovsky 2010), while a more North American culture of shopping malls and country clubs became the lifestyle of the affluent. Maristella Svampa's work in this area remains instructive in the way that she points to the 'winners and losers' under this neo-liberal compact (Svampa 2004, Svampa 2005).

Such class divisions were accentuated during and after the late-2001 crisis. The crisis stemmed from a number of factors – from IMF demands and government mismanagement to middle- and working-class discontent (Blustein 2005). Once the government defaulted on its debts in December 2001 it collapsed and widespread civic unrest ensued. A major rupture was experienced throughout Argentine society: more than 55 per cent of the population slid below the poverty line in 2002 (Cohen 2012, p. 95). This collapse led to even more pronounced class differences in the nation. The wealthy were certainly affected, but those who managed to ride out the tsunami were in a very strong position once the economy rallied in 2004. Indeed, the rapid recovery that began just two years after the collapse, significantly improved the status of the very wealthy relative to the rest of the population.

Second, Argentine scholarly analyses are as closely linked to global trends in scholarship as elsewhere. There are specific links to French scholarship, à la Bourdieu, which makes an interest in the sociology of elites a neat fit. The one text that has examined elite schooling in Argentina, Guillermina Tiramonti and Sandra Ziegler's *La educación de las elites* [The Education of Elites] (2008), brought together a couple of local studies and compared them with the situation in France. This work, produced by a team of scholars from the Latin American Faculty of Social Sciences (FLACSO), arguably preceded North Atlantic attention to elites and their education. Tiramonti and Ziegler's work examined a number of schools that catered to high-status groups – from upper-middle and upper-class backgrounds – and focuses on the issue of school choice among parents as well as how culture and pedagogies within middle- and upper-class schools create particular individuals, especially in relation to social 'others'. The different schools under examination may make the work appear somewhat unspecific and disjointed.

Mariana Heredia's work on elites is not specifically focused on schools, but on the nature of new elite habitus. Heredia (2012) explores the concentration of power and wealth within specific historical and new elites. This is distinct from Tiramonti and Ziegler, who chose to see Argentine elites as a more nebulous group made up of those who look to survive in fickle social and economic circumstances by adopting 'strategies of individuation' that may provide some future advantage (Tiramonti and Ziegler 2008, p. 43). Heredia (2012), by contrast, associates elites more with ruling-class power. She identifies how elites are linked to cultural processes of class formation by describing different signifiers of their status. Elsewhere, she has researched the 'new rich' [*nuevos ricos*] and their role in re-adjusting upper-class composition in Argentina since the 1990s. Attendance at a private school, the best that can be afforded, is part of the performance of 'eliteness' for these groups (Heredia 2011).

The existing work on elites in Argentina fits within a larger continental examination of elites. To some extent, elite formations differ from nation to nation. In many nations, like Peru or Brazil, there are particular families that have long held positions of power. Membership in Argentina's elites, by contrast, has been more fluid than in other parts of Latin America and has relied on resourcefulness rather than genealogy (Losada 2009). Indeed, current changes in the elites of Argentina, thanks largely to the 1990s boom, can be read as a part of this history.

The Caledonian School

Some work has been carried out on the 'English' schools, but they still remain part of a remote culture of eliteness for the majority of Argentines. There are strong historical grounds for this separation and isolation. From the late-nineteenth century, the Anglo-Argentines held status and the admiration of their bourgeois compatriots, but they largely remained ghettoized within their own businesses and institutions. They held little sway within the nation itself and were wary of becoming pariahs when anti-British sentiments peaked during the interwar and postwar periods (Graham-Yooll 1999). Today, however, their cultural traits – business acumen, the use of the English language and civic politesse – have become desirable as the Esperanto of transnational capitalism. For this reason, the Caledonian School appeals to Argentina's current elites irrespective of their background.

The Caledonian School caters for around 2,000 students from kindergarten to year 12. It is considered one of Argentina's best schools. My six months of fieldwork was carried out during the middle of 2011 when the school graciously allowed me to conduct participant observation with semi-structured interviews as well as archival research. The examples I offer here in this more general discussion of elite schooling are limited in their scope; but they do offer some insight into the way in which students, staff and alumni think about the position of the school within Argentine society and its educational context.

The school's importance resides in its position as a trendsetter within a specific group of elite independent schools. This group includes other 'English' schools in Buenos Aires and beyond, as well as some that cater to a similar demographic – namely an economic elite of entrepreneurs or highly paid professionals. The Caledonian School's leadership stems from its administration's commitment to educational innovation over the past two decades. In 1997, for example, the school was one of the first to introduce the International Baccalaureate (IB) at the upper levels and carries out innovative curriculum programmes at the primary school level that make connections with other schools around the world. More recently, as will be discussed below, the school has turned its attention to social engagement via a whole school service-learning curriculum.

Such engagement represents a significant shift in the school culture. The school has a long history that harks back to its initial position as a school for Scottish Presbyterian migrants during the nineteenth century. The influence of these origins persists today, albeit in a latent fashion. During the twentieth century, the school aligned itself with other British schools that emerged to cater to the migrant workers associated with British-owned railway companies. These schools were highly regarded, but remained quite parochial (Rock 2008). Such schools' commitment to the Argentine project often came under suspicion during periods of intense nationalism. In the interest of self-preservation, these schools therefore kept a low profile in times of political and economic unrest.

With the nationalisation of the railways, the influence of the British community in Buenos Aires started to wane. The Caledonian School, however, continued to cater to the remnants of this, now Anglo-Argentine, community during the postwar period. The business acumen of the school's clientele ensured its survival during periods of instability and authoritarianism. And this same astuteness was passed on to the students of the school who overwhelmingly went on to study and work in the commercial sector. During this time, the Caledonian School taught two curricula in English and Spanish – one based on preparing students for the Cambridge exams and another on the national and provincial Argentine systems. This situation continues to this day; however, the IB has now displaced the Cambridge system as the capstone of a 'Caledonian' education.

Since the introduction of the IB, the school has changed in a number of ways, thanks to both external and internal shifts. Such changes have seen the school's reputation rise. That is, the school's eliteness, which is not a way that it describes itself, has emerged in tandem with the increased elite status of its clientele. Externally, the school's clientele did very well from the neoliberal revolution undertaken by Carlos Menem's Peronist government between 1989 and 1999 (Cooney 2007). This meant that the student body was made up of some vestiges of the Anglo-Argentine community alongside well-heeled *parvenus*. When the 2001 crisis hit, some of this clientele could no longer afford the fees; but, for the most part, their relative wealth increased as the majority of the population slid into poverty. This meant that the school was now not only a well-regarded institution of the Anglo-Argentine community, but one that catered to both the 'winners' of the 1990s and the survivors of the *fin de siècle* depression.

Internally, the school responded to these external situations by both heightening and mollifying its eliteness. Increased connection between schools during the twenty-first century, thanks largely to digital communication strengthening existing networks, meant that the school continued to innovate in line with its peers around the world. Often this meant engaging with topics that focused more on global issues than those with a direct bearing on Argentina or Latin America. The international curriculum meant that, for example, students often found themselves studying the geography of Australia and Southeast Asia rather than that of Argentina. After the 2001 crisis, however, the school began to reconsider its position, returning some focus to its regional and local environment. While the school continued to remain global in its general ambitions – in its curriculum and desired student trajectories – there was a strong concern within the senior leadership team that their students, whose wealth survived the collapse, were out of touch with their fellow citizens. The larger post-neoliberal discourse was most likely the main influence over this decision. But a number of issues influenced this way of thinking – from nostalgia for social egalitarianism to concerns about amoralism among the student body as well as the combination of globally oriented imaginations and sybaritic lifestyles among the clientele.

One major change which ensued was the introduction of a community-service programme that was covered in all subject areas. The school already had some small projects under way as well as those associated with the IB requirements. A few years after the economic collapse, however, the heads of departments agreed that incorporating a service-learning aspect in their curriculum would be pedagogically and socially beneficial. Students found themselves spending class time on community service projects either at school or during excursions to homes for the elderly, orphaned or mentally disabled. This programme, one of the first within schools of this type in Argentina, reflected not only a commitment by the school's administration and staff to social engagement, but also a keen appreciation of pedagogical trends within elite and private schools around the globe. The introduction of this kind of service learning has been one of the hallmarks of such schools over the past decade (Gaztambide-Fernández and Howard 2010).

The tension within this situation is whether such internal shifts are predominantly self-serving. In the past two decades, the school has gone from being a producer of business-oriented students who play rugby or hockey to one in which the students are given all manner of options to follow. And yet they still feel a pressure to excel at everything they undertake. The community-service component is designed in part to reduce such pressure; however, students and teachers alike often regard it as a less serious programme than other subjects although it is a necessary requirement for the IB's 'creativity, action, service' component.

Post-neoliberal paradoxes

The move to service learning within the Caledonian School must be read within a post-neoliberal context. The recent shift within Latin American societies away from a neoliberal model of economics and governance has caused a great deal of concern in parts of the globe that have not followed suit. As part of this 'pink tide' or 'new left' movement, each nation on the continent has approached this restructuring differently, just as each has applied neoliberal policies in their own way (Sader 2011, Wylde 2012). Since 2003, Argentina has rejected a previous enthusiasm for neoliberalism in favour of new industrial development under the protectionist and redistributive policies of the successive governments of Nestór Kirchner and Cristina Fernández de Kirchner. *Kirchnerismo* also advocates for improving human rights and embracing diversity as part of its social policy; while foreign affairs concentrate on limiting US involvement and strengthening ties with neighbours in the Mercosur regional trade arrangement (see Castorina 2012).

The post-neoliberal turn in Argentina, as elsewhere, is thus an ideological shift that manifests itself in different policies and practices. As Julian Yates and Karen Bakker suggest in their review of the issue, this form of post-neoliberalism is characterised by '(1) redirecting a market economy towards social concerns; and (2) reviving citizenship via a new politics of participation and alliances across sociocultural sectors and groups' (2014, p. 64). The move to incorporate service learning within the school, as well as a desire to improve the students' political awareness (Prosser 2014), is a sign of social elites engaging with the discourse of post-neoliberalism. The climate in Argentina is such that remaining aloof from this social discussion is no longer possible.

There is an obvious irony within such engagement since the economic elite were advocates and beneficiaries of neoliberal largesse under the 1990s presidency of Carlos Menem. Moreover, the eliteness of the school was increased as a result of such largesse and the collapse that followed it. Consequently, two caveats are important here. One is that the impetus for social engagement largely comes from the school staff rather than the parents. As a result, the idea behind the social engagement derived not from the economic elites themselves. That said, the relationship between the two groups (parents and staff) is difficult to unpack since they often overlap – a significant number of teachers, for example, are alumni of this or other 'English' schools. Suffice it to say that the push for more social engagement comes from those already working in a civically minded, helping profession.

The second caveat is that the clientele of the Caledonian School are overwhelmingly against the Kirchnerist government. That is, they do not see the government as sound in either its political or economic policies. Students often expressed dismay at the various 'stunts' that the 'corrupt' government pulls to show their animosity toward elites and oligarchs whom they believe to have been undermining the national reconstruction since 2003. The school's involvement in social projects such as service learning and community service was largely developed outside of the framework provided by the government – one obvious exception being the school's involvement in a national housing construction programme. In this sense, social engagement is therefore on the school community's terms rather than those of the government, which it largely opposes. The cultural shift within the Caledonian School is thus an elite contribution to civil society in Argentina, which has undergone major rejuvenation in the last decade (Centner 2012).

Such caveats point to paradoxes within the school's current social turn. The social programmes offered have to be seen as part of the educational provision of an elite school. For this reason, despite the rhetoric of subject integration, service-learning takes second place within many classes. The level of integration is dependent on the teacher's personal commitment to the idea as well as being contingent on the amount of class time available in a very demanding schedule. If community service was genuinely pushed to the fore it would be likely to undermine the school's culture of educational ambition. This ambition, often exhibited more by the staff and parents than the students, is the school's chief offering, to which community service is supplementary.

Moreover, a more rigorous service-learning programme could shake the very economic and cultural foundations of a school like Caledonian. Addressing current social problems demands consideration of more structural issues. For now the programmes target relatively innocuous issues – the elderly or disabled – rather than having a more pronounced activist bent. Were the reasons for Argentinian social inequalities more explicitly engaged with, the culpability of the economic elites would be likely to emerge. When some teachers in history and politics classes raise such issues, students tend to characterise the poor as 'lazy' and 'uneducated' rather than recognise a relationship between their own position of privilege and their compatriots' contrasting fates. As one teacher put it to me, Caledonian students are often told how their privilege brings with it responsibilities towards the rest of society – to be met either in their educational pathways or by the giving of time or money. But the message is so constant that it tends to be just white noise to most.

Consequently, while the Caledonian School's attention to social responsibility certainly has important local determinants, the main driver can be seen as a global discourse in elite schooling – via the IB – about service-learning. Actions amounting to social justice are very fashionable among elite schools and the Caledonian School is attuned to these trends. By having a wholesale service-learning curriculum, the Caledonian School offers a means through which it can attest its position as an educational leader, up to speed with the latest pedagogical trends. While the work being done within the school is sincere, the school community seems not to acknowledge the larger social processes of class formation of which they are a part and which community service does little to address.

Serving elites

Despite a post-neoliberal context existing within Argentina at the government and popular level, there remains a culture within elite groups that continues to subscribe to a reconstructed version of neoliberal culture. In education, these groups have different motivators to those who seek to send their children to the select-entry elite public schools. Sticking to the private sphere of primary, secondary and tertiary education, means eschewing the pubic nature of education in favour of individual success, albeit with a degree of acknowledgement of the importance of the public through community service or *noblesse oblige*. A preference for the private sector is linked to larger processes of globalisation with which these groups engage – not just through their means of income but also the global culture they inhabit – as well as providing a survival mechanism in the face of Argentina's long history of social and economic instability. However understandable this orientation may be, the arrangement reinforces ongoing social divisions. Disagreement with the public sector – or the current Kirchnerist version of Peronism – distances the private sector from civic involvement. Economic elites are able to do this through the wealth they have accumulated; a wealth that is invested in separation from the larger populace, inside closed neighbourhoods, private vehicles and shopping malls.

Such withdrawal is deleterious to the students in both systems. To be sure, there are concerns within Argentine society, and not just among the wealthy, that aggression and fear have replaced civility on the streets of Buenos Aires. Personal security is often its citizens' chief concern. But to remain completely removed from public spaces, except through economic exchange, does not allow a sense of collective citizenship to develop. Ongoing socioeconomic division does not bode well for Argentine society. There is already a strong precedent for social and economic collapse followed by reactionary governance. Class resentment can metastasize into class violence, as in the 2001 protests and riots (Auyero 2006), which is a likely outcome of the subtle brutalities of everyday capitalism (Auyero 2007). Any future paroxysm of social unrest would erase the social gains made in the last decade – not only in terms of grassroots social movements and governmental redistribution programmes, but also the trend towards civic mindedness among the very wealthy.

In educational terms, the Caledonian School's socially minded turn in its curriculum is a response to this prognosis. Rather than standing aloof from the rest of society, the school wants to be engaged and, in turn, for its alumni to remain engaged in the provision of social good. Just what the latter looks like remains to be seen, although philanthropy may trump direct politicking. There are already signs among recent alumni who have chosen less orthodox pathways as social entrepreneurs, journalists or even politicians. Indeed, a previous complacency within the school's political culture could be shifting in a way that would further promote the interests of the school's clientele within the public sphere. That is, by teaching students to become active, if not activists, there is a strong likelihood that they will do so with their own class interests at heart.

This leads to a more troubling reading of the Caledonian School's social mindedness – that it is mainly self-serving. Being able to include service learning in the school's brand shows the school as more up to date with pedagogic trends than the schools with which the Caledonian School competes. As a school that introduces global trends to Argentina, there is a chance that other schools will imitate its example with similar programmes, designed more as résumé boosters than elements that have lasting social benefits. These two alternatives are not mutually exclusive, of course. The Caledonian School's administration is certainly genuine in its social concerns and engagement, just as they recognise how this type of curriculum distinguishes it from other competing schools locally and aligns them with similar schools globally.

This tension indicates something of the paradox being faced by elite schools around the world. The rhetoric of democracy, equality and inclusiveness is all-pervasive and runs counter to any socially elevated and exclusive institution; and yet the schools must negotiate this rhetoric in a way that does not allow them to seem prejudicial. Such a move illustrates the savvy of class interests. A continued commitment to private and elite education shows a lack of faith in public education among Argentina's upper classes. There is a growing concern, that has arisen in the past decade, largely stemming from the teaching staff, that such schools should not be seen as callous. But such anxieties are addressed internally, often as curricular tokenism, rather than through the structural adjustments that would be necessary to overhaul the school's contribution to ongoing social reform. Argentina's post-neoliberal moment may have arrived much earlier than elsewhere; but the elite, private schools have adjusted their own position, just as their clients did, to ensure future liquidity.

References

Adamovsky, E. (2010). *Historia de la clase media argentina: Apogeo y decadecia de una ilusión* [History of the Argentine middle class: The rise and fall of an illusion]. Buenos Aires: Planeta.

Auyero, J. (2006). The political makings of the 2001 lootings in Argentina. *Journal of Latin American Studies*, 38(2), 241–265.

Auyero, J. (2007). *Routine politics and state violence in Argentina: The gray zone of state power*. New York: Cambridge University Press.

Banfi, C. and Day, R. (2004). The Evolution of Bilingual Schools in Argentina. *International Journal of Bilingual Education and Bilingualism*, 7(5), 398–411.

Barton, G. A. (2014). *Informal empire and the rise of one world culture*. London: Palgrave Macmillan.

Beech, J. and Barrenechea, I. (2011). Pro-market educational governance: Is Argentina a black swan? *Critical Studies in Education*, 52(3), 1–15.

Blustein, P. (2005). *And the money kept rolling in (and out): Wall Street, the IMF, and the bankrupting of Argentina*. New York: Public Affairs Press.

Castorina, E. (2012). Crisis and recomposition in Argentina. In J. R. Webber and B. Carr (Eds.), *The new Latin American left: Cracks in the empire* (pp. 233–254). Lanham, MD: Rowman & Littlefield.

Centner, R. (2012). Microcitizenships: Fractious forms of urban belonging after Argentine neoliberalism. *International Journal of Urban and Regional Research*, 36(2), 336–362.

Cohen, M. (2012). *Argentina's economic growth and recovery: The economy in a time of default*. Abingdon: Routledge.

Cooney, P. (2007). Argentina's quarter century experiment with neoliberalism: From dictatorship to depression. *Revista de Economia Contemporânea*, 11(1), 7–37.

Finocchio, S. (2009). *La escuela en la historia argentina* [The school in Argentina's history]. Buenos Aires: Edhasa.

Gaztambide-Fernández, R. and Howard, A. (2010). Conclusion: Outlining a research agenda on elite education. In R. Gaztambide-Fernández and A. Howard (Eds.), *Educating elites: Class privilege and educational advantage*. Lanham, MD: Rowman & Littlefield.

Graham-Yooll, A. (1999). *The forgotten colony: A history of English-speaking communities in Argentina*. Buenos Aires: LOLA.

Guano, E. (2006). Spectacles of modernity: Transnational imagination and local hegemonies in Buenos Aires. *Cultural Anthropology*, 72, 185–186.

Heredia, M. (2011). Ricos estructurales y nuevos ricos en Buenos Aires: Primeras pistas sobre la reproducción y la recomposición de las clases altas [Wealth structures and new rich in Buenos Aires: First clues on the reproduction and recomposition of the upper class]. *Estudios Sociológicos*, 85, 61–97.

Heredia, M. (2012). ¿La formación de quién? Reflexiones sobre la teoría de Bourdieu y el estudio de las elites en la Argentina actual [The formation of who? Reflections on Bourdieu's theory and the study of elite in today's Argentina]. In S. Ziegler and V. Gessaghi (Eds.), *Formación de las elites: Investigaciones y debates en Argentina, Brasil y Francia* [Formation of elites: Investigations and debates in Argentina, Brazil and France]. Buenos Aires: FLACSO.

Ko, C. T. (2013). From whiteness to diversity: Crossing the racial threshold in bicentennial Argentina. *Ethnic and Racial Studies*, 37(14), 2529–2546.

Losada, L. (2009). *Historia de las elites en la Argentina: Desde la conquista a hasta el surgimiento del Peronismo* [History of elites in Argentina: From conquest to the rise of Peronism]. Buenos Aires: Editorial Sudamericana.

Meo, A. (2008). Mapping the field of studies on social class and educational inequalities in Argentina. *Revista Enfoques Educacionales*, 10(1), 199–220.

Morduchowicz, A. (2005). Private education: Funding and (de)regulation in Argentina. In L. Wolff, J. C. Navarro and P. González (Eds.), *Private education and public policy in Latin America*. Washington: PREAL.

Narodowski, M. (2002). Socio-economic segregation in the Argentine education system: School choice without vouchers. *Compare*, 32(2), 181–191.

Narodowski, M. (2008). School choice and quasi-state monopoly in education systems in Latin America: The case of Argentina. In M. Forsey, S. Davies and G. Walford (Eds.), *The globalisation of school choice*. Oxford: Symposium Books.

Prosser, H. (2014). Reach for the stars: A constellational approach to the ethnographies of elite schools. *Globalisation, Societies and Education*, 12(2), 275–289.

Rock, D. (2008). The British in Argentina: From informal empire to postcolonialism. In M. Brown (Ed.), *Informal empire in Latin America: Culture, commerce and capital* (pp. 49–77). Oxford: Blackwell.

Sader, E. (2011). *The new mole: Paths of the Latin American left*. London: Verso.

Shumway, N. (1991). *The invention of Argentina*. Berkeley: University of California Press.

Svampa, M. (2004). *La brecha urbana: Countries y barrio privados* [The urban gap: Country clubs and private neighbourhoods]. Buenos Aires: Capital Intellectual.

Svampa, M. (2005). *La sociedad excluyente: La Argentina bajo el signo del neoliberalismo* [The exclusionary society: Argentina under the sign of neoliberalism]. Buenos Aires: Taurus.

Tiramonti, G. and Ziegler S. (2008). *La educación de las elites: Aspiraciones, estrategias y oportunidades* [The education of elites: Aspirations, strategies and opportunities]. Buenos Aires: Paidós.

Wylde, C. (2012). *Latin America after neoliberalism: Development regimes in post crisis states*. New York: Palgrave Macmillan.

Yates, J S and Bakker, K. (2014). Debating the 'post-neoliberal' turn in Latin America. *Progress in Human Geography*, 38(1), 62–90.

Zelaya, M. (2012). La expansión de universidades privadas en el caso argentino [The expansion of private universities. The Argentinian case]. *Pro Posições*, 23(2), 179–194.

15
ELITE EDUCATION SYSTEMS IN THE EMERGING FINANCIAL POWERS

Commentary

Julia Resnik

The four cases presented in this section have specific socio-historic contexts that explain the particular evolution of their elite education systems. Nevertheless, it is important to stress the similarities between them, similarities that stem from global economic and cultural processes.

First, the neoliberal global economy has facilitated the emergence of new, non-traditional elites in Argentina, Brazil, Nigeria and China. Second, efforts to improve the economic development of nations previously considered to be second- or third-world countries has entailed the adoption of world education cultural mandates which have pushed for the democratisation of secondary and higher education (Meyer 1999, Resnik 2006). This has led to the devaluation of high school diplomas as a marker of class distinction and the institution of a fierce competition for places in highly reputed high schools and universities. Third, the promotion of new public management and market logics into the education field by international organisations has encouraged an increasing privatisation of education (Mundy and Menashy 2014), even in the poorest parts of the world (Oppenheim and Stambach 2014). Fourth, the emergence of standardised comparisons (PISA or Shanghai rankings) has contributed to the development of an 'education industry' with headquarters in the global north (mainly in the UK, the USA, Canada, Australia and Germany) (Steiner-Khamsi forthcoming). Among the main business aims of the global education industry is the recruitment of foreign students to leading universities, and the export of education products and packages, such as curriculum standards (e.g. the International Baccalaureate), examination systems and teacher training around the world.

Although these processes influence education systems in a wide range of contexts, their impact is amplified in countries of the global south. Here, I highlight a few of these. First, in many of these countries the private education sector has become an important profit-making space for education corporations, usually located in the global north. Although such edu-businesses have an increasing track record of providing private education for the poor (Ball 2012, Juneman *et al.* 2016), they are also investing in the provision of international programmes of study, which will appeal to economically and culturally advantaged sections of these societies. Thus, as the global economy has given rise to new economic elites in countries such as Argentina, Brazil, Nigeria and China, the education industry is providing 'international education products' that are proving particularly appealing to these emerging elites – who are already very internationally oriented due to their business interests. All four chapters in this section highlight how new elites in these countries engage in internationalisation strategies in their attempts to mark themselves out as elite.

The analyses of the situation in Brazil and China emphasise how the chances of securing a place at the most prestigious national high schools and universities for children from elite families have been reduced because of the democratisation of education. Thus, in China, for instance, economic elite families are now able to avoid the rigid meritocratic academic elitism in the schooling system, by paying to attend the newly developed international programmes found in high-status public high schools. The Sino-American/Canadian programmes therefore enable wealthy families in China to avoid the local educational infrastructure.

In Brazil, the massification and expansion of educational opportunities for all has led to elites developing a range of internationalisation strategies that seek to protect their status and 'effectively maintain inequalities' (Lucas 2001 in Nogueira and Alves, Chapter 13 of this volume), among them: foreign language learning beginning at the kindergarten level, bilingual pedagogical projects and the promotion of international travel for students and staff. The separatist pattern – namely, being educated in private instead of public schools – appears to be undermining the Brazilian government's efforts to promote affirmative action at the university level.

Furthermore, as shown in Argentina, a more traditional, 'escape route' used by elite families has been enrolment in private US and English schools – both those schools located within countries of the global south, as well as private institutions in the USA, Canada and the UK (Brooks and Waters 2011, Kenway *et al.* 2013). The establishment of such schools in southern countries, serving expatriates and local elites, has grown in recent years at a tremendous speed. We now find private schooling, the preferred choice for many of the culturally and economically more advantaged members of society, stretching from kindergarten provision to the tertiary education level.

A second significant similarity found across the chapters in this section is the importance of having an 'English' education – whether within-country or by securing a place at a school abroad. Thus, Ayling's analysis of the situation in Nigeria argues that sending their children to boarding schools in England is the preferred strategy of the elites in Nigeria. This choice appears to be driven by a desire to enable their children to learn the proper manners and English accent that will, in the particular context of Nigeria, provide them with status, the 'esteem which a person attracts' as a result of acquiring and possessing these markers of distinction (Ball 2003 in Ayling, Chapter 12 of this volume). 'Whiteness', as a symbol of distinction can be embodied through particular dispositions acquired by being sent abroad, or, by attending private schools in Nigeria that have a white head teacher or white members of staff. Ayling emphasises that the British colonial past of the country is significant in explaining the centrality of 'Englishness' to elite education in Nigeria, while to a lesser degree, colonialism can also explain the internationalisation of elite education in Argentina. The 'informal' British imperialism in Argentina (from the 1830s to the 1940s) (Rock, 2008 in Prosser, Chapter 14 of this volume) led to the establishment of English schools in the province of Buenos Aires. These schools, founded originally to cater to those British people who settled in Argentina in the nineteenth century, now cater for a growing number of students belonging to new economic elites.

Together, these four chapters offer insights into the varied purposes, nature and pedagogical approaches to international education desired by elite and economically and culturally advantaged sections of these societies. Although, the number of international programmes has multiplied since the 1980s all over the world, such an international orientation is not always synonymous with an elite education. In the global north, and particularly in Anglophone countries, elite education is often defined according to different criteria. These include schools with a small number of students and high fees, schools with specific pedagogies, schools with highly selective entrance criteria, as well as institutions offering international programmes. In contrast, the large majority of elite schools in the global south provide some kind of international education, organised around the study of a foreign language, mainly English, and often involving the taking of examinations set by UK, US and other international examination boards.

Given that the literature points to various understandings of what constitutes an international education – cosmopolitanism, global studies, multiculturalism, international mindedness and so on – it is important to consider how a commitment to international education affects curricula content and the pedagogical approach implemented. Daverne and Dutercq (2013) found, for instance, that teachers in the new preparatory courses for the *grandes écoles* in France did not see their role simply as to transmit knowledge, but also to establish open, respectful relationships between themselves and their students. In the case of the international programmes in elite public schools in China, Yang argues that these seek to offer a 'high quality and enjoyable Western style of learning' instead of the contemporary Chinese school pedagogy that promotes methodical, rote memorisation and other un-'creative' forms of learning (Kipnis 2001 in Yang, Chapter 11 in this volume).

A second, important implication of the growing desire for international curricula within particular elite schools in these southern contexts, is a consideration of how these international curricula affect the development of national and local curricula (Doherty and Shield 2012). Elsewhere, I have argued that the expansion of International Baccalaureate (IB) schools in a country contributes to the denationalisation of its education system, with implications for social justice efforts (Resnik 2012a). In the specific case of the Argentinian Caledonian School, Prosser analyses the effect of Community Activity Service (CAS) and how it led to a socially minded turn in its curriculum in a school that used to stand aloof from the rest of society. Democracy, equality, inclusiveness and multiculturalism are often viewed as integral elements of international curricula. However, as Prosser found through his daily observations, the way in which CAS is implemented in an elite school does not encourage structural adjustments or social reforms but a more philanthropically informed kind of activism that in fact serves to secure students' social class position. At the Caledonian School, Argentina, implementing the CAS enabled the school to add service learning to its school brand, thereby positioning it as working within progressive pedagogic principles, while also promoting the participation of its students in the current Argentinean post-neoliberal turn, which emphasises concerns for equality and active citizenship. Such arguments are in line with previous findings that suggest the IB curriculum in general, and CAS more specifically, does not incite students to demand structural, social reforms, but rather encourages them to develop an orientation which calls for assisting the poor and needy, but without questioning or disrupting the current social order (Resnik 2009).

A further observation that can be made based on the four chapters in this section is the relevance and prominence of Bourdieu's work in writings on elite education (Zweigenhaft 1993, Bauchat and Saint-Martin 2010) and international education (Doherty 2009, Weenink, 2008). Both Nogueira and Alves, and Ayling draw on the concepts of cultural capital and strategies of distinction. Yet, Ayling points to the important limitations of Bourdieu's cultural capital theory: 'Bourdieu's (1996) analysis does not recognise the role foreign deportment and accent play in the formation and maintenance of local elites, especially in southern contexts' (Ayling, Chapter 12 in this volume). In the case of Nigeria, the integration of theories of postcolonialism, espoused by Fanon for instance, has been productive in understanding more fully how socio-historical contexts shape strategies for distinction today.

The methodological nationalism (Robertson and Dale 2008) of Bourdieu's work has also been argued to limit scholars' analysis of processes of international education (Resnik 2012b). As Larsen and Beech argue, education research should shift 'our attention to the relational conceptions of space, through the analysis of networks, connections, and flows' (2014, p. 92). For instance, using actor-network theory (ANT) it is possible to analyse local and global actors in the same conceptual framework. Thus, using such an approach, Resnik (forthcoming) analyses the expansion of the International Baccalaureate programme in private and public schools, in different countries. More generally, the study of international education through a network approach may open up new avenues for research on elite education and include questions that transcend locality: flows of education business (Stromquist 2002) and international teachers (Reid et al. 2014) through the world, global networks of elite schools or connections between flows of immigrants and flows of international programmes.

In the global south, elite education has become largely synonymous with international education. Neoliberal policies and severe cuts to education budgets have had disastrous consequences for public schooling in many of these countries (Arnove et al. 1996), pushing not only the upper classes but also the middle classes and new elites into the private education sector. The education industry originating in the global north now provides private schools with a large array of international products, from foreign teachers to opportunities to travel abroad. This development contributes to a growing gap between public and private schools – not just a gap in the quality of learning and teaching conditions between the two sectors as in the past, but also a significant differentiation in terms of curricula (national curriculum for public schools and international curriculum for private institutions). The internationalisation and privatisation of elite education reinforces the separation within the education system between social classes, as found in countries such as Brazil, Argentina and Nigeria, but that has also begun to impact on countries like China, which have hitherto boasted a long tradition of meritocratic public education.

References

Arnove, R. F., Torres, A., Franz, S. and Morse, K. (1996). A political sociology of education and development in Latin America: The conditioned state, neoliberalism, and educational policy. *International Journal of Comparative Sociology*, 37(1–2), 140–158.

Ball, S. J. (2012). *Global Education Inc: New policy networks and the neo-liberal social imaginary*. Abingdon: Routledge.

Bauchat, B. and de Saint-Martin M. (2010). Les bourgeoisies à Strasbourg. La préservation de l'entre-soi ou l'ouverture? In M. de Saint Martin and M. D. Gheorghiu (Eds.), *Éducation et frontières sociales. Un grand bricolage* (pp. 173–200). Paris: Ed. Michalon.

Brooks, R. and Waters, J. (2011). *Student mobilities, migration and the internationalization of higher education*. Basingstoke: Palgrave.

Daverne, C. and Dutercq, Y. (2013). *Les bons élèves. Expériences et cadres de formation*. Paris: PUF, coll. Education et Société.

Doherty, C. (2009). The appeal of the International Baccalaureate in Australia's educational market: A curriculum of choice for mobile futures. *Discourse: Studies in the Cultural Politics of Education*, 30(1), 73–89.

Doherty, C. and Shield, P. (2012). Teachers' work in curricular markets: Conditions of design and relations between the International Baccalaureate Diploma and the local curriculum. *Curriculum Inquiry*, 42(3), 414–441.

Junemann, C., Ball, S. J. and Santori, D. (2016). Joined-up policy: Network connectivity and global education policy. In K. Mundy, A. Green, R. Lingard and T. Verger (Eds.), *Handbook of global policy and policy-making in education* (Handbook of Global Policy Series). Oxford: Wiley-Blackwell.

Kenway, J., Fahey, J. and Koh, A. (2013). The libidinal economy of the globalising elite school market. In C. Maxwell and P. Aggleton (Eds.), *Agency, affect and privilege* (pp. 15–31). Basingstoke: Palgrave Macmillan.

Larsen, M. A. and Beech, J. (2014). Spatial theorizing in comparative and international education research. *Comparative Education Review*, 58(2), 191–214.

Meyer, J. W. (1999). The changing cultural content of the nation-state: A world society perspective. In G. Steinmetz (Ed.), *State/culture: State-formation after the cultural turn* (pp. 123–143). New York: Cornell University Press.

Mundy, K. and Menashy, F. (2014). The World Bank and private provision of schooling: A look through the lens of sociological theories of organizational hypocrisy. *Comparative Education Review*, 58(3), 401–427.

Oppenheim, W. and Stambach, A. (2014). Global norm making as lens and mirror: Comparative education and gender mainstreaming in northern Pakistan. *Comparative Education Review*, 58(3), 377–400.

Reid, C., Collins, J. and Singh, M. (2014). *Global teachers, Australian perspectives: Goodbye Mr Chips, Hello Ms Banerjee*. London: Springer.

Resnik, J. (2006). International organizations, the 'education-economic growth' black box, and the development of world education culture. *Comparative Education Review*, 50(2), 173–195.

Resnik, J. (2009). Multicultural education – good for business but not for the state? IB curriculum and the global capitalism. *British Journal of Educational Studies*, 57(3), 217–244.

Resnik, J. (2012a). De-nationalization of education and the expansion of the International Baccalaureate. *Comparative Education Review*, 56(2), 248–269.

Resnik, J. (2012b). Sociology of international education – an emerging field of research. *International Studies in Sociology of Education*, special issue – International Education, 22(4), 291–310.

Resnik, J. (Forthcoming). Global comparative approach and the development of the International Baccalaureate in Spanish speaking countries. Special Issue: The power of numbers and networks: understanding the mechanisms of diffusion of educational models. J. Resnik (Ed.), *Globalisation, societies and education*.

Robertson, S. and Dale, R. (2008). Researching education in a globalising era. In J. Resnik (Ed.), *The production of educational knowledge in the global era*. Rotterdam: Sense Publishers, pp. 19–32.

Steiner-Khamsi, G. (Forthcoming). Standards are good (for) business: Standardized comparison and the private sector in education. *Globalisation, Societies and Education*. Special issue: The power of numbers and transnational networks: understanding the mechanisms of diffusion of education models. J. Resnik (Ed.), *Globalisation, societies and education*. http://dx.doi.org/10.1080/14767724.2015.1014883

Stromquist, N. P. (2002). *Education in a globalized world: The connectivity of economic power*. Oxford: Rowman & Littlefield.

Weenink, D. (2008). Cosmopolitanism as a form of capital: Parents preparing their children for a globalizing world. *Sociology*, 42(6), 1089–1106.

Zweigenhaft, R. L. (1993). Prep school and public school graduates of Harvard: a longitudinal study of the accumulation of social and cultural capital. *The Journal of Higher Education*, 64(2), 211–225.

SOME FINAL REFLECTIONS

Claire Maxwell and Peter Aggleton

Both individually and together, the chapters in this book explore the nature of elite education in different national contexts. Each author looks back to understand how forms of elite education became established, before tracing changes in their function over time, and the impact of neoliberal, marketised, globally oriented forces on current configurations.

As the chapters from France, Sweden and China so powerfully demonstrate, even elite education configurations that ostensibly were once committed to meritocratically selecting the 'best of the best' in terms of academic achievement, have developed so that the end effect seems to be such that they privilege the interests of the more financially and culturally advantaged social groups. At the same time, however, what many chapters in this book point to is that those most able to access elite forms of education have become more diverse, in line with a progressive fractionalisation of elite groups in society (Savage and Williams 2008, Dogan 2003, Savage 2014). As a result, institutions nowadays more actively position themselves within an education marketplace, with concomitant effects for the shaping of the elite education experiences they offer (Windle and Nogueira 2015, Ye and Nylander 2015).

The contributions included here remind us of the value of understanding 'elite education' in a number of different ways. First, elite education is something that individuals actively participate in, functioning to guide children, young people and young adults through the education system via Nespor's (2014) 'institutional wormholes', linking family origin to future socioeconomic position. Such a perspective directs attention towards the ways in which an elite education is understood both by those who experience it directly (as students and pupils), and by the parents and other family members who purchase it.

Beyond this, however, it is important to understand how particular schools or universities become consecrated as 'elite' and how stable such a status is. Critically examining what takes place within these institutions, and how these processes contribute to the socialisation of future elite group members, sheds light on both the specificities of elite education and the status it confers. Reinforcing 'concerned' and 'concerted' cultivation within the family, elite educational institutions promote a sense of 'entitlement and belonging' that, as Gaztambide-Fernández and colleagues (2013), Howard and colleagues (2014), Khan (2015), Forbes and Lingard (2015) and we ourselves (Maxwell and Aggleton 2013a, 2014a and 2014b) have argued, is so critical to legitimising the elite positions that pupils and students go on to occupy.

But we also need to understand elite education as a set of culturally and socially connected systems and practices, more or less loosely configured and with a history of their own, that stretch out their tendrils across a diversity of social spaces. Mapping how elite educational institutions and tracks are developing and growing to perform their socially reproductive 'duties' while responding to new challenges, tells us much about structural and discursive continuity within and across societies.

This kind of analysis encourages us to think about a fourth dimension that a focus on elite education may illuminate: namely, the broader structure of local, regional and national educational systems. As most of the chapters highlight, elite and non-elite sectors within an educational system are intimately linked: relationally and symbolically, but also because the consumers of private education make a choice about which part of the system to buy into, metaphorically and/or financially. Actions in one part of the education system have ripple effects on other parts – as Resnik (Chapter 15) forcefully demonstrates in her commentary on the effects of 'international' elite programmes on broader schooling systems; and as Gaztambide-Fernández and Maudlin (Chapter 4) show in their exploration of how the creation of elite programmes in parts of the North American public school sector draws some well-resourced families away from private education.

The overwhelming sense that most chapters leave us with, is that the reproduction of privilege is more or less guaranteed, even in systems that claim to reward academic ability, or in circumstances where national governments make concerted efforts to increase the opportunities for less well-resourced groups to access elite education tracks (see the chapters on France and Brazil, for instance). Such a conclusion troubles us. While Piketty's (2014) work strongly suggests that inequality is rising in Europe and the USA, with elite groups becoming increasingly separated from the rest of society (see also Rothkopf 2009), and while it is beyond dispute that elite education systems most benefit those dominant groups in society, social reproduction is never a given, but rather must always be achieved – triggering often unintended effects in the process.

Indeed, there is a serious 'messiness' to the ways in which economic, social and cultural capitals are activated and converted (to employ a Bourdieusian term) so as to benefit a few. For instance, the reproduction of social class inequality through education may create a dissidence, interrupting the reproduction of other forms of inequality and allowing some young women, for example, opportunities for advancement of a kind unimaginable to their forebears (Maxwell and Aggleton 2013b, Maxwell and Aggleton 2014a). Moreover, the history of girls' elite education in England enunciated in Chapter 1 highlights how, through such processes, possibilities for more radical projects may come to be conceived of and linked to broader emancipatory struggles.

Against this background, what might a future research agenda look like? One key question to be answered in this respect concerns how best to define *elite education*, *elite educational institutions*, and *elite education systems*. These three concepts are distinct, yet they shape one another. Fundamentally, 'elite' is a relational term, and to understand it we must historicise and contextualise what we understand an elite to be. Likewise, in order to fully understand elite forms of education, we must first examine processes of elite group formation at a local, regional, national and international context. This macro-level analysis is critical in our view, and requires both a quantitative approach (to map structures, forms of organisation and their effects) alongside more qualitative and interpretative enquiry to shed light on the everyday practices of elite groups (such as articulateness, entitlement and social confidence) – that help set their members apart.

A second and rather different set of research questions link to the roles played by internationalisation, globalisation and cosmopolitanism in determining, and yet perhaps to a degree also undermining the socially reproductive potential of elite education within a country. Increasingly, it is international elite recruitment and reproduction that matters most, although as Chapters 3, 5 and 12 show, the desirability of a distinctively 'English' education remains strong. Such issues are engaged with here, but are also the focus of strongly innovative work by Kenway and colleagues (see McCarthy and Kenway 2014, for instance), who have sought to map the international mobility of students and educational programmes, as well as the formation of the social networks that connect key elite institutions around the world. Similarly, in our own writing we have examined the subtle ways in which cosmopolitanism as both an ideology and a linked set of practices, may or may not be taken up by elite schools as part of the curriculum offer (Maxwell and Aggleton 2015).

Third, we should emphasise the necessity of continuing to examine ways in which elite education tracks and institutions offer opportunities for interrupting the reproduction of privilege, broadening the pool of those eligible to compete for future position within the elites. Such a focus encourages us to look closely at the ways in which social justice work is performed within elite spaces (see Chapter 14) but requires us to consider how these practices may be built upon subsequently to achieve less socially reproductive effects. This work also encourages a longitudinal perspective, following different individuals and groups to map whether and how they move into and out of elite tracks, and how trajectories into professional lives are mirrored in or different from the social positions that students from elite education institutions go on to occupy.

Our fourth and final suggestion for future research is to extend the kinds of theoretical concepts and tools that are drawn upon when researching elite education. Bourdieu's work continues to dominate much of the field, although his ideas are being extended and re-interpreted. Writers such as Kenway and colleagues (Kenway *et al.* 2013, Fahey 2014, Kenway and Fahey 2015), Resnik (this volume), Ball (this volume) and others have engaged with a wide range of social theorists to examine, among other concerns: processes of internationalisation and globalisation; historicising processes in elite production; the structural, affective and aesthetic architectures of elite spaces; and the social networks between particular elite groups, institutions and tracks. What was once a somewhat rejected field within the sociology of education now shows vibrancy, determination and growth.

We hope you have found your engagement with the writings in this collection both thought-provoking and generative. We see this book as marking a particular moment in the development of the field of elite education – one in which there is a coming-together of a critical mass of scholarship from across many continents. Research networks are strengthening, innovative ideas are being developed, and progress is being made as light is shed on what have hitherto been the 'darker sides' of cultural and social reproduction that elite forms of education bring about and achieve.

References

Dogan, M. (2003). Introduction: Diversity of elite configurations and clusters of power. *Comparative Sociology*, 2(1), 1–15.

Fahey, J. (2014). Privileged girls: The place of femininity and femininity in place. *Globalisation, Societies and Education*, 12(2), 228–243.

Forbes, J. and Lingard, B. (2015). Assured optimism in a Scottish girls' school: Habitus and the (re)production of global privilege. *British Journal of Sociology of Education*, 36(1), 116–136.

Gaztambide-Fernández, R., Cairns, K. and Desai, C. (2013). The sense of entitlement. In C. Maxwell and P. Aggleton (Eds.), *Privilege, agency and affect* (pp. 32–49). Basingstoke: Palgrave Macmillan.

Howard, A., Polimeno, A. and Wheeler, B. (2014). *Negotiating privilege and identity in educational contexts*. New York: Routledge.

Kenway, J. and Fahey, J. (2015). The gift economy of elite schooling: The changing contours and contradictions of privileged benefaction. *British Journal of Sociology of Education*, 36(1), 95–115.

Kenway, J., Fahey, J. and Koh, A. (2013). The libidinal economy of the globalising elite school market. In C. Maxwell and P. Aggleton (Eds.), *Privilege, agency and affect* (pp. 15–31). Basingstoke: Palgrave Macmillan.

Khan, S. R. (2015). Changes in elite education in the United States. In A. van Zanten, S. Ball and B. Darchy-Koechlin (Eds.), *Elites, privilege and excellence: The national and global redefinition of educational advantage* (pp. 59–70). London: Routledge.

Maxwell, C. and Aggleton, P. (2013a). Becoming accomplished: Concerted cultivation among privately educated young women. *Pedagogy, Culture and Society*, 21(1), 75–93.

Maxwell, C. and Aggleton, P. (2013b). Middle class young women: Agentic sexual subjects? *International Journal of Qualitative Studies in Education*, 26(7), 848–865.

Maxwell, C. and Aggleton, P. (2014a). Agentic practice and privileging orientations among privately educated young women. *The Sociological Review*, 64(2), 800–820.

Maxwell, C. and Aggleton, P. (2014b). The reproduction of privilege: Young women, the family and private education. *International Studies in Sociology of Education*, 24(2), 189–209.

Maxwell, C. and Aggleton, P. (2015). Creating cosmopolitan subjects – the role of families and private schools in England. *Sociology*.

McCarthy, C. and Kenway, J. (2014). Introduction: Understanding the rearticulations of privilege over time and space. *Globalisation, Societies and Education*, 12(2), 165–176.

Nespor, J. (2014). Schooling for the long-term: Elite education and temporal accumulation. *Zeitschrift für Erziehungswissenschaft*, 17(3 Supplement), 27–42.

Piketty, T. (2014). *Capital in the twenty-first century*. Cambridge, MA: Harvard University Press.

Rothkopf, D. (2009). *Superclass: The global power elite and the world they are making*. London: Abacus.

Savage, M. (2014). Piketty's challenge for sociology. *The British Journal of Sociology*, 65(4), 591–606.
Savage, M. and Williams, K. (Eds.). (2008). *Remembering elites*. Oxford: Blackwell.
Windle, J. and Nogueira, M. A. (2015). The role of internationalisation in the schooling of Brazilian elites: Distinctions between two class fractions. *British Journal of Sociology of Education*, 36(1), 174–192.
Ye, R. and Nylander, E. (2015). The transnational track: State sponsorship and Singapore's Oxbridge elite. *British Journal of Sociology of Education*, 36(1), 11–33.

INDEX

Abitur 105
academic attainment 24–5
'academic capitalism' 93
academic education 23, 25, 26, 35, 105
academic elite 34, 89, 141–2, 187; *see also* parents
academic excellence 137, 163
academic performance, effect of class 80, 128–9
academic qualifications 22, 30, 105, 119; *see also* International Baccalaureate (IB)
academic segregation 105
academic selection 31, 34, 43, 135–6
Academies 23, 25
accent 152–3, 154, 155–6, 158, 159, 187
achievement 24–5, 44, 79, 80, 81, 82, 93, 107, 127, 129; *see also* examinations
actor-network theory (ANT) 189
admissions process 63, 64, 127, 143, 168
Advanced Placement (AP) courses 64, 144
advantage 35, 42, 69, 73
affirmative action 164, 166, 170
Africa 2, 148–59, 187–8, 189, 190
America 2, 3, 55–66, 143, 162–71, 173–84, 187
American International Schools 144
Ancient Nine 18, 23
'Anglo-Scottish' schools 32, 36, 37
anxieties and success 81–2
Argentina 2, 3, 173–84, 187, 188–9, 190
aristocracy 18–19
Arnold, Thomas 17, 19
arts programmes/schools 59, 60, 62–3, 64, 65

Assisted Places Scheme 22
assuredness 73
Australia 2, 42–51, 71–2
authenticity 157, 158

baccalauréat 119
Ball, S. 23, 42, 81, 82–3, 152, 155
banking elite 57, 80–1, 82–9
Bauman, Z. 71
BBC's *Great British Class Survey* 15
belonging 71, 86–7, 88, 193
bilingual education 168–9
bilingual Gymnasiums 108
Black Skin, White Masks (Fanon) 149
Blackness 159
boarding schools 71, 72; England 19, 20–1, 23, 24, 25, 151, 154–6, 187; Scotland 32, 33, 35; Sweden 95, 101; USA and Canada 43, 56, 64
Bourdieu, Pierre 38, 47, 50, 51, 59, 83, 97, 98, 148, 155, 162, 189, 194; and capital 36, 60, 94, 163; and class reproduction 127; and distinction 151, 152, 154, 158, 159; and elites 150; and habitus 74; on refined accent 153
boys' schools 19, 21, 51
British schools 175–6, 178–80, 181–2, 183, 187, 188
Britishness 154–6, 158, 159
bursaries 32, 33, 34, 36; *see also* scholarships

capital 36, 38, 50, 60, 94, 98, 100, 193; access to 153; Australia 47; Brazil 163,

166; France 122, 130; Germany 108, 109; Scotland 39; Sweden 99, 100; *see also* cultural capital; symbolic capital
capitalism 126
catchment areas 80–1, 86, 122, 128
Catholic schools 42, 43, 44, 45, 46, 175
charitable educational institutions 32, 33
charitable status 34
charter schools 55, 56, 58, 60, 63–4
chartered academies 56–7
China 2, 3, 135–46, 187, 188, 190, 192
choice *see* school choice
the Church 16, 107
chuzhong 137
civic elite 34
civil servants, China 135
Clarendon Commission 16, 18, 24
class 18, 19, 21–2, 23, 38, 190; and academic performance 128–9; Argentina 177, 178, 182, 183, 184; Australia 47–8; and Bourdieu 60, 152; differences 63; France 116, 118, 121, 122; inequality 49, 128, 193; mobility 74; Nigeria 154, 158; origin 93; Scotland 31, 32; and stratification detail 126; survey 15; Sweden 99, 100, 101, 102
'class meritocracy' 122
class reproduction 127, 129, 130
classes préparatoires aux grandes écoles (CPGE) 95, 118–22, 123
closure 122, 129, 130
co-educational schools 22, 23, 24, 36, 37
Colegio Nacional Buenos Aires 175
collectivism 30, 32, 39
colonisation 149–50, 152, 159
community-service programme 180, 181, 183, 188–9
'compensatory sponsorship' 123
competition 93, 102, 129, 186; open 115, 116, 119, 121, 122, 123
competitive examinations 115–18; *see also* examinations
competitiveness 81–2, 88, 89
comprehensive schools 21–2, 31, 34, 79–81, 85, 88, 89
concours 115–18, 122–3, 128, 130
continuity 81, 82
Cookson, P. 47, 97
cosmopolitanism 194
cultural capital 47, 50, 60, 94, 130, 152, 153, 189, 193; Brazil 163, 166, 170; France 122; Nigeria 158; Scotland 39; Sweden 98, 99, 100
'cultural cloning' 32

cultural elite 163, 164
Cultural Revolution 136
curriculum 143, 188–9, 190; Argentina 179, 180; Brazil 169; China 143; England 18, 19, 21, 23, 24, 25, 26; France 121; girls' schools 20; Nigeria 156, 157; USA and Canada 57, 64

day schools 16, 18, 23, 56, 71, 72; girls 20, 21; Scotland 32, 33, 35
Delamont. Sara 20, 25, 31
democratisation 92, 93, 97, 150, 186, 187
deportment 154, 155, 158, 159
diasporic identity 71
differentiation 139, 140
direct-grant grammar schools 34
disadvantaged students 61, 63, 64, 66
disidentification 71
distinction 151, 152, 154, 155, 159, 189
distinctiveness 157–8
diversity 60–1
'double conformity' 20, 25
Durkheim, E. 127

l'École normale supérieure (ENS) 115, 117
l'École polytechnique 115, 117
economic capital 94, 130, 193; Brazil 163, 170; France 122; Germany 108; Nigeria 153; Norway 80–1; Sweden 100
economic power 100, 102
economically disadvantaged students 61, 63, 64, 66
economically elite families 163
educated elites, African 148–9, 152, 155
Education Act, 1902 (England) 21
education industry, global 186–7
Education Reform Act 1988 (England) 31
educational capital 98, 99, 100, 166
egalitarianism 80
elite formation mechanisms 107
elite groups 94, 150–2, 162–3, 194
elite identity 153–6
elite sport 72
elite status 61–6, 72, 159
enchanted perceptions 83–4, 88
engagement 62, 64, 173–4, 179, 180, 181
England 2, 15–26, 48, 72, 97, 151, 154–6, 187
'English' schools 173, 175–6, 178–80, 181–2, 183, 187, 188
Englishness 49, 188
enrichment activities 81; *see also* extra-curricular activities
enrolment rates 165

entitlement, sense of 48–9, 60, 62, 65, 73, 82, 193
equality: of citizenship 30; of opportunity 1, 127
equity 49, 93
ethnic background and academic qualifications 21–2
ethos 48
Eton College 16, 72
examinations 119, 179; Argentina 175; Brazil 166; China 135, 137, 138, 140, 143, 144; France 115–17; Nigeria 156–7; Scotland 30, 36, 37; USA 168; *see also concours*
excellence 62, 64–5, 106, 107, 137
excellence-cultivation class 139
Excellence Initiative 106, 109, 110
exclusion 61, 62, 63, 66
exclusivity 48, 128, 144, 145, 153, 158
extra-curricular activities 23, 81, 96

failure, fear of 84
fairness 142
family sponsorship 121–2
Fanon, F. 149, 156
fee-paying schools 19, 22, 23, 25, 26, 44; Scotland 31–5, 38, 39; *see also* private schools
fees 33, 36, 72, 92, 101, 110, 141, 158, 167
Fettes College, Edinburgh 32
financial elite 57, 80–1, 82–9
foreign language learning 168–9, 187
Foucault, M. 36, 142
France 2, 89, 97, 114–23, 128, 130, 188, 192; French School in Sweden 95
functional education 94, 101
funding 21, 45, 47, 110

gaokao 138
gaozhong 137
Gaztambide-Fernández, R. 43, 47, 57, 60, 62, 64, 154
Gemeinschaft 86
gender 37, 38
gentry 18–19; *see also* upper classes
George Heriot's School, Edinburgh 32
Germany 104–10, 128
Giddens, A. 126
gifted children 105–6, 107, 108, 110, 127
Girls' Public Day School Company 21
Girls' School Association (GSA) 36
girls' schools 19–21, 31, 36, 37, 50, 72, 73, 193–4; boarding schools 24, 25; local day 25

global academic rankings 105
'global cities' 70, 71
global education industry 186
government: Australia 45; England 21, 22, 23, 31; Germany 105–6; Scotland 32, 34; Sweden 93, 102
grades 98, 100, 102
grammar schools 16, 17, 21, 22, 95
grandes écoles 95, 97, 115, 116–17, 121, 188
grandes lycées 95
grant aid 34
grant-aided/maintained schools 23, 34
Great British Class Survey (BBC) 15
Great Schools 16–17, 18, 19, 21, 23, 26
gymnasieskolan 92
Gymnasiums 104, 105, 107–8, 110

Harrow School 144
Headmasters' and Headmistresses' Conference (HMC) 36
hierarchisation 139, 140
high exam 138, 140, 143, 144
high schools 20, 43, 63–4; *see also* secondary schools
higher education 186; Brazil 170; France 115–17, 123; Germany 104–5, 106, 107, 109–10; Sweden 93, 96–7, 101; *see also* universities
högskolan 92, 101
högskolor 96
hospital schools 32–3, 34
huikao 143, 144
Humanistic Gymnasiums 105, 107

identity 71, 153–6, 159
imperialism 159, 188
income inequality 163–4, 170
independent schools 22, 29–40, 42, 43, 44–6, 100; *see also* private schools
individualism 61
industrial elite 57
inequalities 47, 50, 60, 61, 66, 69, 127, 193; Argentina 177; Australia 49; Canada 63; class 128; France 123; income 163–4, 170; Scotland 31; U-curve 126
influence: people of 32, 39; spheres of 47
informal networks 109
institutional sponsorship 119–21, 130
'institutional wormholes' 1
International Baccalaureate (IB) 25, 97, 108, 188, 189; Argentina 179, 180, 182; Scotland 30; Sweden 95–6, 99, 101
international education 188–9
international elite recruitment 194

200 Index

international mobility 194
international programmes 143–4, 187
international schools 106, 108, 110, 144
internationalisation 110, 168–9, 188

jiangshezhong zhongdian 139, 140

Karolinska Institutet 96
keju system 135
Kenway, J. 45, 47, 50, 51, 194
key classes 139
key schools 139, 140
key universities 138
Khan, S. R. 2, 23, 73

Landesschulen 104
lärovek 92, 95, 100, 101, 102
Latin America 2, 3, 162–71, 173–84, 187, 188–9, 190
Law of Social and Racial Quotas (*Lei das Cotas Sociais e Raciais*) 164, 165, 170, 171
leaders, preparing 46–7
lottery admission 63, 64, 65, 66
lycées 95, 118, 119, 120–1

magnet programmes/schools 56, 58, 62
manners 95, 150, 152, 153, 187
market pressures 23
marketisation 2, 22, 93
Mechanisms of Elite Formation in the German Education System 106–7
meritocracy 2–3, 187; Brazil 165, 169; China 135, 141–2; France 123; Germany 127–8; Sweden 93, 98, 100, 101, 102
meritocratic competitive examinations 115–17
middle classes 69, 70, 129, 189–90; Argentina 177; Australia 44, 45, 50, 51; Brazil 165; England 18–19, 20, 21, 22, 25–6; France 121, 122; Scotland 33; Sweden 93, 95
military high schools 165–6
mobility 71, 74, 130; *see also* social mobility
moral character, development of 96

national elites 70
neighbourhood differences 21–2
neoliberal global economy 186
neoliberalism 61, 189
networks 36, 38, 81, 109, 130, 194, 195; *see also* social networks
'new rich' 178
Newcastle Commission 18
nobility 94, 95, 102

non-government sectors 45; *see also* private schools
non-selective, state comprehensive school system 79–81, 89; *see also* public schools
norms, shared 36
North America 2, 3, 55–66, 71–2, 143, 187
Norway 79–89, 128, 129–30

'the old school tie' 35
'open competition' 115, 116, 119, 121, 122, 123
opportunity 1, 30
'origin–education–destination pathways' 15

parentocracy 164, 165, 169
parents 48, 82–9, 122, 129–30, 153–6, 158, 159
Parkin, F. 127, 152
Peking University 137
perceptions, enchanted 83–4, 88
Persell, C. 47, 97
Piketty, Thomas 126, 193
PISA (Programme for International Student Assessment) 80, 105, 108
poor scholars 16
'positional advantage' 42
post-neoliberalism 180–2
postcolonialism 189
power 32, 36, 37, 38, 46, 47, 48, 88, 178; economic 100, 102
preparatory schools 18, 35, 97; *see also* private schools
prépas 95, 118–22, 123
private public schools 60–1
private schools 44–7, 59–60, 72, 186–7, 190; Argentina 173–6, 178–80, 181–4; Australia 42, 43, 49; Brazil 163, 165–7, 168, 170; England 22, 23, 25, 72; France 118, 119, 120; Germany 106, 108; Nigeria 156–8, 187–8; Scotland 31; Sweden 93, 95, 101, 102; USA and Canada 55, 56–7, 64
private tertiary institutions 106
private universities 109–10
privatisation 22–3, 93, 186
privilege 46, 63, 108, 116, 128, 144, 145, 193, 194
ProUni (for-profit universities) 164, 166, 170
public examinations 36, 37; *see also* examinations
public schools: Argentina 174, 175, 176; Australia 42, 43, 44, 45, 47; Brazil 165, 166, 167, 168, 170; China 137; England

16, 17, 19, 21, 22, 23, 24, 72; English influence 32, 37, 46, 48; France 120–1; global south 189–90; modelled on English 95; Sweden 100, 101; USA and Canada 55–6, 57, 58–9, 60–6
Public Schools Commission 18
publification 61, 65

qualifications, internationally recognised 25; *see also* International Baccalaureate (IB)

racial quotas 164, 165, 170, 171
rankings 105, 139, 140
Realschule 105
refined accent 152–3
Remembering elites (Savage and Williams) 72–3
reproduction, class 72, 127, 129, 130, 149, 194
Roedean School 20
royal family, Swedish 94, 102
Rugby School 17
ruling class 46, 47, 49, 178
Russell Group universities 95

safety 87, 88, 89, 129
SAT (Scholastic Aptitude Test) 168
Savage, M. 15, 69, 72–3, 81
scholarships 22, 32, 33, 34, 36, 108, 110; Brazil 164, 166, 170
'scholastically elite' pathway 163
school catchment areas 80–1, 86, 122, 128
school choice 22, 23, 47, 48, 55–6, 57–9, 61–6, 177
school ethos 48
'schooling process' 35
schools: Argentina 173–80, 181–4; Australia 42–6, 47, 48, 49; Brazil 165–70; China 137, 138–45; England 16, 18, 19, 20–6; France 118, 120–1; Germany 104, 105–6, 110; influence of class on composition of 128; Nigeria 153–8; Norway 80–1, 85, 86; Scotland 29–35; Sweden 92, 95–6, 97–8, 99–100, 101; USA and Canada 55–7, 58–66
Scotland 2, 29–40, 70
Scottish Council of Independent Schools (SCIS) 36
secondary schools 186; Argentina 174, 175–6; Australia 46; Brazil 165–6, 168, 170; England 18, 19–22, 24–5; France 118, 123; Germany 105, 106, 107–8, 110; Norway 80; Sweden 92, 94, 95, 96, 98, 99–100, 101–2

segregation 60, 105
select-entry schools 173
selection processes 108, 109, 123, 165–6
selective recruitment 95
selective schools 43, 44, 45, 46, 47
selfhood 50
Simon, B. 18, 19
single-sex public schools 22
single-sex selective schools 45
Sino-American Programme 143–4, 145, 187
Sino-Canadian programme 143, 187
SISP (Scottish Independent Schools Project) 29, 35–8
social capital 36, 37, 47, 50, 60, 108, 109, 130, 193
social class *see* class
social closure 123
social disadvantage 69
social education 94, 100, 101, 102
social engagement 62, 64, 173–4, 179, 180, 181
social exclusivity 128; *see also* exclusivity
social groups, effect on curriculum 24
social inequality 47; *see also* inequalities
social justice 194
social mobility 1, 19, 22, 26, 72, 122, 135
social networks 25, 26, 36, 81, 96–7, 194, 195
social power 48; *see also* power
social privilege 46; *see also* privilege
social programmes 180, 181, 183
social quotas 164, 165, 170, 171
social selection 123; *see also* selection processes
social solidarity 30
socially inclusive education 25–6
socioeconomic diversity 60–1
Sociology of Education and Culture (SEC) research unit 98
South America 2, 3, 162–71, 173–84, 187, 188–9, 190
spatial mobility 71
specialisation, curricular 121
specialised arts programmes/schools 59, 60, 62–3, 64, 65
sponsorship 115, 116, 117–23, 130
sports 72, 86
'star classes' 121
state schools: Argentina 174; England 22, 25; Norway 79–81; Scotland 30, 33, 34; Sweden 93, 95, 102; *see also* public schools
state sponsorship 117–19
status 60, 72, 73, 187; Australia 49; China 145; definition 152; Nigeria 150, 155, 157, 159; USA and Canada 61–6

Stockholm School of Economics 96
stratification 140
'studying up' 48
style 150
success, striving for 83–4, 88
'super-elite' 163
'super-rich' people 163
surety 73, 81, 82
Sweden 2, 3, 92–102, 128, 192
symbolic capital 152, 153, 154, 158

Taunton Commission 18, 19, 20
tertiary education 96–7, 104–5, 106, 109–10, 176; *see also* universities
tiering system 138, 139
travel, international 169, 187
tuition fees 33, 36, 92, 101, 110, 141, 158, 167
Turner, Ralph 115, 117

U-curve 126
UEE (university entrance exam)/China 137, 138
UK 31, 70, 95, 151, 154–6, 187; *see also* England; Scotland
understatedness 24, 30, 37, 39
uniform 145
Universidade para Todos (ProUni or University for All) programme 164, 166, 170
universities: Argentina 176; Brazil 165, 170; China 137, 138, 140; Germany 104–5, 106, 109–10; for profit 166; Sweden 93, 95, 96–7; USA 168
university entrance 25
upper classes 189–90; Argentina 177, 178, 184; Brazil 162; England 18, 20, 21, 24, 25, 154–6, 158; France 116, 118, 121, 122; Scotland 32; Sweden 94, 95, 100, 102
upper middle classes 32, 95, 100, 101
upper secondary schools 92, 94, 95, 96, 98, 99–100, 101–2
Uppsala University 96, 98
USA 3, 43, 55–66, 95, 97, 122; Brazilian programmes 169; Sino-American Programme 143, 144, 145, 187; universities 168

vocational high schools 165–6, 170
Volksschule 105
voluntary aided schools 22

Walford, G. 19, 22, 30, 31, 32
wealth 38, 66, 69–70, 72, 145, 178
welfare sociology 97
well-being 81, 82, 86, 88
Westminster School 16, 72
White teachers 157, 158
Whiteness 44, 46, 49, 157, 158, 159, 187–8
Why we can't afford the rich (Sayer) 69–70
women 19–21
working classes 118